THE PSYCHOLOGY
OF SPIRIT

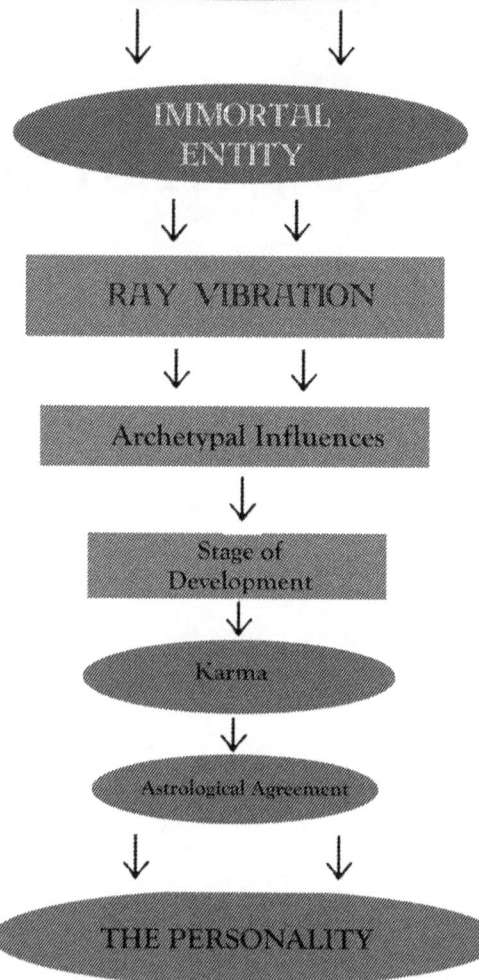

THE INFINITE

IMMORTAL ENTITY

RAY VIBRATION

Archetypal Influences

Stage of Development

Karma

Astrological Agreement

THE PERSONALITY

INFLUENCES ON THE PERSONALITY
AS DISCERNED BY THE PSYCHOLOGY
OF SPIRIT

THE PSYCHOLOGY
OF SPIRIT

MARY DEVLIN

Graphics by Edward Sparks

Writers Club Press
San Jose New York Lincoln Shanghai

The Psychology of Spirit

Writers Club Press
an imprint of iUniverse.com, Inc.

For information address:
iUniverse.com, Inc.
5220 S 16th, Ste. 200
Lincoln, NE 68512
www.iuniverse.com

ISBN: 0-595-16139-1

Printed in the United States of America

Dedication

To Allan
my son in many lifetimes;

to Carol
my friend and helpmate for thousands of years;

and to Don
You may not remember it, but it was a chance
remark by you that set my mind thinking
along the lines that led to this book.

Contents

List of Illustrations

Preface and Acknowledgments

This book begins with past lives, but strictly speaking it is not a book on past lives, past-life regression, or regression therapy. There are many fine books on the market on that subject by a number of accomplished people, to whose work I have nothing to add. Nor is it about psychology per se—at least not the psychology of the personality as is commonly practiced today. Though I have studied the subject extensively and have incorporated it into my work as a regression therapist and psychic and astrological counselor, I hold no degrees in the subject, nor do I consider myself an expert. I have been certified by the American Federation of Astrologers as a qualified professional since 1975, and in 1976 was certified by my mentor, Marcia Moore, as having been trained by her in the field of past life regression.

This book concerns the study of the soul itself—how individuality develops in the immortal soul-entity, the Higher Self if you will, from the point of separation from the Absolute to the end of the cycle of earthly incarnations, and how events during each person's path back to God both helps and hinders that process. It traces the effects of the individual entity's experiences as it makes its way through life after life, and outlines how knowledge of those effects can be used to clear blocks towards progress on all levels. This information is based on my own work as well as the work of several other regression therapists dating back to the early 1970's, and is drawn from thousands of case histories. The idea for this book was born when I began studying the subject of transpersonal psychology, based on the works of Carl Jung, Alice Bailey,

Ken Wilber, Kenneth Pelletier, and the channeled entity Michael—among others too numerous to mention. I was amazed at how the theories of these gifted individuals seemed to parallel the soul development of a vast number of individuals as revealed through past-life regression, and began putting it all together—and thus *The Psychology of Spirit* was born.

I use the method of past-life regression as taught by Marcia Moore in her now unfortunately out-of-print book, *Hypersentience*. It involves an initial guided meditation, which leads to a state of light hypnosis in which the individual is still totally in control, and can choose to come out of the trance any time. (I've had this happen!) In this state, certain neutral suggestions, designed specifically not to put any ideas at all into the subject's head, are given by the therapist which in most cases brings to mind memories of prior incarnations.

At this point I feel compelled to counter the arguments of skeptics who refuse to acknowledge the reality of past-life regression, stating that it is all either total imagination or delusion or suggestion on the part of the therapist. In the method we use, first of all, there is no suggestion given other than that clients will find themselves in a prior life. We take special care NOT to plant any ideas into the subject's mind. Marcia—as well as other past-life therapists—always believed that even if the experience is totally imaginary, it could still be valuable in shedding light on a person's problems and ways to counter them. However, though I don't do it anymore, in the past I have spent hours doing extensive research, searching through ancient tomes, newspapers and birth records in British libraries seeking to verify the existence of various past-life personalities—and have been successful in enough cases to convince me that most of these experiences, at least, are neither delusionary nor imaginary.

Over the years I have learned that in one sense, the skeptics are correct. The process of past-life regression is not infallible. Just because a person goes into a light hypnotic state and can tap into unconscious memories doesn't mean that everything he comes up with represents actual historical fact. Many people have come up with scenarios that disagree with historical fact—for instance, in a past-life experience of mine in which I telescoped two very unpleasant characters into one—but this is hardly a condemnation of either the concept of reincarnation or the past-life regression process. Human memory is faulty! How many of us, even under age regression, can remember past events in *this* life exactly as others remember them? Our memories are always tainted by later experiences, and a good past-life therapist always bears this in mind when working with a client.

Religious fundamentalists fight this idea tooth and nail—I've received enough hate mail in the past to realize this—but the fact is, the concept of reincarnation does not nullify other concepts. My guru, Swami Muktananda Paramahansa, in his book *Play of Consciousness*, revealed that in the course of his journey to God-realization he discovered that the concepts of heaven and hell, for example, were hardly imaginary, but represented real places on the astral plane. The difference between the Hindu and Christian heaven-hell doctrines is that, according to Baba, you may go to heaven or hell after death, but *you don't stay there.* After learning specific lessons from being in either place, you return to Earth and continue your journey—at least until you evolve beyond even heaven and merge with the Absolute. Nor does the concept of reincarnation negate either the importance or the divinity of Jesus, Moses or Mohammed. It only brings to light the idea that there are many Great Masters, many Sons and Daughters of God, and that whatever path an individual chooses is unlikely to be the Only True Path, but the one that works best for that individual.

A book like this is never truly the work of one person. With great love and honor I want to extend my thanks to a number of beloved friends who began this journey with me, and who have since passed on to the Higher Planes: Marcia Moore, my initial mentor; Edward Sparks, my close friend and partner in research for more than twenty years, who designed the graphics for this book; and Shaun McNamara, my friend/lover/companion/creative partner for a period of time that was far too short. I also wish to honor Robert Byron, who provided one of the sparks that got this all going, and Don Dewberry, whose initial financial sponsorship made it all possible. Above all I wish to honor my guru, Swami Muktananda, whose teachings shed light on all I discovered and whose energy kept me going (and still does) at times when I felt I no longer wanted to go on.

Other old friends who have also helped me along my path and who are still with us are Rose Sydeman, Toni, Athena and Anton Sparks, Skye Alexander, Travis, Judy and Lisa Pike, Don Bruner, Jean Lori, Tom Dye, Diane Freburg, and Robert Koch. New friends (meaning those I have known for ten years or less!) who continue with me even now whom I would like to thank are Carol Huffstickler, Tim Rayborn, Peter Ransom, Sujata, Herman and Martha Frietsch, Isabel Lennie, and Marilyn Zeff. My children, Thomas and Allan Dye and Laura Dye Meador, have always been a source of inspiration, support and encouragement to me, and are likely to continue to be so for the rest of my earthly life. There are also a number of wonderful musicians with whom I have worked, who have stayed with me through some pretty rough times to make beautiful music together, and thus have elevated my spirits and kept me going: Renée Fladen-Kamm, Nannette Silva, Paul Keaton, Stephen Prestwood, John Canepa, Victoria Varieur, Gary Sano, Barbara Jaspersen, Harvey Garn, Brad Erickson, John Harris, Tim Rayborn, Shira Kammen, Keith Bray, and John Davenport.

I like to think there is a piece of each and every one of these people somewhere in this book.

Introduction

In a lush, verdant, prosperous kingdom in ancient India lived the young, handsome, kindly King Padma, and his beautiful, beloved young wife, Queen Lila. King Padma was perfect in almost every way. He subdued his enemies as the sun overcomes darkness, making them tremble on the battlefield; he destroyed evil within his borders. He honored spiritual traditions as the trees respect the authority of the soil; holy men found themselves turning to him for guidance. King Padma was also highly learned and a master of all the arts.

Queen Lila was soft-spoken, graceful, intelligent; her smile radiated the warmth of the rays of the sun. She was highly devoted to the king and shared his joy and sorrow. King Padma and Queen Lila lived an ideal life, enjoying it in every possible and righteous way. Their love for each other was pure and intense, with no hypocrisy or limitations.

One day Queen Lila became very sad. She heard of a woman whose husband had died, and immediately became overcome with grief at the way she would feel if King Padma should die. And so she determined to perform austerities and make sacrifices to the gods, in order to ensure that she and King Padma would enjoy their beautiful life together forever.

Although the Brahmin at the castle tried to convince ha that such immortality was not possible, Lila became more and more determined. And so she began petitioning the goddess Saraswati, praying to her, making sacrifices, and performing penances, entreating that the goddess appear to her and grant her a boon.

Ultimately, the goddess did appear. Lila begged that she grant the gift of immortality to herself and to King Padma. Saraswati only repeated the words of the Brahmin, that such a favor was beyond even the ability of the gods to grant, and Lila at first was devastated. However, she finally gained control of herself and asked for two other boons instead: one, that the goddess appear to her whenever Lila asked, and two, that if King Padma should die before Lila, the queen be allowed to visit the heavens where her husband's soul reposed. Saraswati granted the bequest, and then vanished.

Many years later, King Padma died, and Queen Lila was distraught. Once more she began performing her austerities and making her sacrifices, calling upon the goddess Saraswati to fulfill her promises. The goddess appeared, and took Lila by the hand and led her into the world of the gods. Once there, she granted to Lila a vision: a vision of young lovers, all in different times and different places, all deeply devoted to each other and living beautiful lives together.

Lila was confused. Who were all these people? She turned to ask this question of the goddess.

Saraswati answered: "They are all you—you and Padma. The life your king just left was only one of many, many lives which you have lived together on this planet. There are three types of space, O Lila—the physical, the psychological, and the infinite space of consciousness. On the physical space, your husband is gone; on the psychological, you still desire his presence, but on the infinite space of consciousness, he is still one with you, and will never leave you until together you merge with Brahman himself."

Lila asked, "How can that be?"

For answer, Saraswati took her hand, and led her to a field where a bloody battle was raging. The goddess told Lila the story of the quarrel that led to the declaration of war. The two women watched as missiles bombarded the field, as spears streaked through the air, and as arrows pierced and destroyed the healthy young bodies of handsome young warriors. Lila asked: "What has this to do with my husband, who is dead?"

"Your husband's death," replied Saraswati, "is as real as this battle, which is no more real than a dream."

She then led Lila above the oceans, past the sun, through the starry universes, through all the galaxies, and Lila perceived that the souls of all the dead soldiers were traveling with them. Once more she turned to the goddess, asking, *"How can this be?"*

"During the life of the Universe," Saraswati replied, "only the infinite Brahman lives in peace. However, It still experiences the existence within Itself of all the diverse creatures. Thus all creatures exist forever in Brahman, and so how can something that always exists become nothing? How can infinite consciousness cease to be?"

"But what happens to these infinite souls?" asked Lila.

"The worst among the sinners undergo terrible sufferings in hell and then are born again in countless painful incarnations before they see the end of their agony. The lesser sinners are reborn in lives requiring hard work and struggle. The best among the righteous ascend to heaven and are later born in affluent families or children of the Brahmin. But even the righteous among the departed must pass through the realms of pain to suffer the consequences of the iniquities they might have committed."

"And how might I escape this?" asked Lila.

"Only through self-effort," said the goddess. "Self-effort is only another name for divine will. She who desires salvation should divert the impure mind to pure endeavor by persistent effort—this is the very essence of all scripture.

"In the minds of all human beings are numerous latent tendencies, the results of all their past lives, and these tendencies give rise to various actions—physical, verbal and mental. All one's actions are in strict accordance with these tendencies. It cannot be otherwise."

"But," asked Lila, "then where is freedom of action? How can I free myself from these tendencies?"

"You must learn to separate the pure from the impure. The impure have to be abandoned, and the pure tendencies strengthened. Then you will be

absorbed in the good, and the evil will weaken by disuse. By self-effort you will therefore restrain the senses and the mind, and then become liberated from the cycle of birth and death. When that happens, and only when that happens, you, Lila, will join your husband forever, in the infinite consciousness of Brahman, never to be parted again."

And then Queen Lila was gifted with a transcendent vision, a burst of light, and in that burst of light she saw a vision of her husband, and of herself, together in the pearl of light that was the heart of Brahman. Joy overwhelmed her. "Oh, great Goddess!" she cried. "I want to be with him! I want to be with him there, right now!"

"Ah, but this is a vision of the far future," said Saraswati. "Only the enlightened can reach there—and you, my dear Lila, are not ready. But your husband awaits you once more, on earth, in a new incarnation. And I will guide you, throughout your future lives, to aid you in your self-effort, in your ultimate goal that you now see."

Lila found herself in a new body, in a new palace, with a new husband, a king, whose name was Viduratha. The king stood and saluted Saraswati, who blessed him and Lila with health, long life, wealth, and enlightenment.

The above story, told in the thousand-year-old Hindu scripture *Yoga Vashishta*, hints at a very early awareness of the need for effort in overcoming psychological barriers which prevent us from being and attaining all that is possible.

Unfortunately, few of us are blessed enough to have as our therapist so exalted a being as Saraswati, the Hindu Goddess of Wisdom and Learning. In fact, most out there who claim to be able to help us along are far from it. Mainstream psychology, in particular, is almost always useless for Seekers on the Path to Self-realization. In my work and the work of all my colleagues as New Age counselors and past-life regression therapists, there is one line we hear from clients again and again: "I've been in therapy for the past three years (or two, or five, in some cases even ten) and you've helped me more in the past ten minutes than my therapist has in all that time!"

Too many psychologies suffer from a number of deficiencies. Perhaps the most destructive is that some still embrace the *tabula rasa* theory: the idea that the newborn child's mind is a blank slate, with character traits, ambitions, desires, dreams, etc., all to be written on that slate by parents, peers, society, etc. Another is that they embrace the notion of an abstract called "the norm." According to this theory, everyone who conforms to that "norm" is a proper human being and everyone who doesn't is "abnormal" and in need of being forced into the mode that this notion of "normal" requires. Thus some psychologies appear to be anti-individualism.

A third deficiency that I see in so many traditional schools of psychology is that they tend to want to classify all individuals into specific categories, or personality types, which they have observed over the years. I hesitate to condemn this tendency as a deficiency because, to be fair, the founders of these schools are using the tools they know best; however, it is inclined to be somewhat limiting. Whether the psychologist in question observes four basic personality types, or twelve, or sixteen, doesn't seem to matter; all these ideas work on some level, for many people share the same traits and therefore respond to events in similar manners. Such ideas definitely increase patients' understanding of themselves. Yet too many people see these classifications not as guidelines, but as complete windows to their natures, and thus they can become so enamored of these schools of thought that they subconsciously begin to play the roles, thereby limiting their growth rather than expanding it.

Still another deficiency lying not in the psychological school of thought itself, but in the psychologist, is the basic arrogance of some individuals who choose this way of making of living. Even in this age of many options, they tend to feel that they are omniscient, that their views are the final word, and that the patient should willingly conform to the therapists' recommendations. Not all psychologists and psychiatrists are like this; there are many who are very open-minded and up-to-date in their attitudes. In my humble opinion, the first category should be avoided like the plague and the second sought out like the Holy Grail. However, some patients, when first referred to any therapist, are too emotionally vulnerable, too desperate for help to be discriminating and thus are not in any state of mind to do any "shopping around."

This book, which grew out of twenty years of study and fifteen years of experience with past-life regression, may at first seem to be another sort of tool using categories, and in one sense it is. However, the "categories" outlined in this book are flexible. The Stages of Development (Chapter Two) represent one's position on the evolutionary cycle, which is constantly changing and therefore dynamic rather than static. The Role Functions, as determined by the Seven Rays (Chapter Three) represent such a wide range of potential that it is difficult to see them as static categories. Archetypal responses, like the Stages of Development, also change throughout the course of life.

There is a definite need within the psychological community for a psychology of spirit. The psychology of spirit traces the psychical influences beyond the material world rather than limiting its scope to the influences of society, parents, childhood experiences, and so on. It also accepts as a given the theory of reincarnation, which states that we live not one life, but many. Many mainstream physicians and psychologists, including Richard D. Willard, M.D., Raymond Moody, M.D., Dr. Bernard Goldman, and Roger Woolger, Ph.D., are now accepting the reality of past life experiences and using past-life regression in their practices. But even they are only beginning their study and observation of the psychology of spirit.

Of all the schools of mainstream psychology, the one that best fits the description of a psychology of spirit is the one founded by Swiss therapist Carl Gustav Jung (1875-1961). Jung was the first pioneer psychoanalyst to eschew the *tabula rasa* theory and accept that babies are highly individualized at birth. Jung deduced that the influences that make a person what he is mainly come not from experiences in infancy and early childhood, but from forces beyond the personal, from what he called the *collective unconscious*. He referred to the contents of the collective unconscious as *archetypes*. Jung, unlike others who call themselves scientists, acknowledged the reality of the world of mythology, psychic phenomena and astrology, which he believed had their roots in the archetypal realm.

But even Jung's theories don't tell the whole story. The influences that shape the psyche stem not only from the archetypal realm, but from a significant number of other sources at which Jung only hinted. These sources are outlined in detail in Alice A. Bailey's *Esoteric Psychology I* and *II* and Dr. Douglas Baker's *Esoteric Psychology: The Seven Rays;* but neither Bailey nor Baker offers any practical methods for putting their material to work in a therapeutic context.

Still, as New Age knowledge becomes more and more widespread, the need for Seekers to understand themselves becomes more and more acute. There is a desperate need for a transpersonal psychology that people can actually put to work for them. Austrian philosopher and metaphysician Rudolf Steiner (1861-1925) once wrote, "For every one step you make in the acquisition of occult knowledge, you need to make three towards knowing yourself."[1] In a lecture tour I took in the fall of 1991, I introduced some of the information contained in this book to my students and was amazed at how hungry they were for the information. It is a given that we all want to know more about ourselves, and it

---

1 Rudolf Steiner, quoted in Bernard Wesfield Cookson's *Rudolf Steiner's Vision of Love: Spiritual Science and the Knowledge of the Heart.* London: Aquarian Press, 1976. P.11.

also appears that few explanations are totally satisfactory, for people continue to search.

I do not say that the information in this book will prove to be "the solution"; for many people it might not be—especially since transpersonal psychology acknowledges that there are dimensions of the psyche that no one on the earthly plane will ever understand. Yet I do feel that this information goes far beyond what most popular books on psychology offer. It is the result of many, many years of research, on the part of myself and a small but tight group of counselors and researchers. We have been pooling our information and conclusions for over a decade, and for the most part the information presented in this book represents a rousing consensus of opinion.

The psychology of spirit traces, or attempts to trace, the development of the psyche from the moment the entity emerges from the Infinite. When the soul first breaks away from the Infinite, it enters into what we call the involutionary are, a term defining the process of God becoming human. It descends through the various planes of existence to the earthly physical plane, where it takes incarnation in the first of hundreds—yea, thousands—of physical bodies. It then enters the evolutionary loop, which is a fancy name for the cycle of earthly incarnations up through various stages of development until the soul has gone as far as it can on the earthly plane and moves on to the realms beyond.

STAGES OF SOUL DEVELOPMENT

The stages of development roughly parallel the concepts of "young" and "old" souls outlined in popular New Age texts such as the "Michael" material. However, progress along the loop is more complicated than these texts imply. My colleagues and I prefer to avoid the terms "young" and "old" souls or any reference to the "age" of the soul. The concept of age as we understand it is relative. A person is commonly defined as "young" or "old" by the number of years he or she has lived as compared with other people still living at the time.

The soul actually has no age. All souls have been in existence since the beginning of time. We also view the terms "young" and "old" as dangerous because of the simplistic connotations too many people attach to those terms. They seem to communicate the idea that "old" souls are "better" or more "spiritual" than "young" souls.

Rather than making use of the concept of soul "age," we prefer the term *stages of development*. The idea of stages parallels the concept of progression through grades in school. As each school child is promoted to the next grade whenever she is ready, so souls progress from one stage to the next at their own pace. Souls on Stage Three or Four are not "better" "more worthy" or "higher" than those on Stage One; they simply have completed certain levels of experience that the Stage One Soul has not and are moving on to others.

Indeed, to the hierarchical way of thinking embraced by so many people in our Western society, the entity, in its progressions toward the latter stages of development, may actually seem to regress. So-called "older souls" tend to place little emphasis on seeking employment and/or amassing material wealth, probably because they see the futility of it, while the "younger souls" seem to be full of energy and enthusiasm for climbing to the top of the corporate ladder and attaining the "American Dream." Therefore, after several incarnations of being wealthy and successful, a person may pass to a lifetime where he is more interested in pursuing his own individual interests and spiritual growth, sometimes at the cost of his own financial security.

The ultimate goal of every soul-entity moving along the evolutionary loop is to regain innate knowledge of its own divine origin—in short, to attain enlightenment or God-realization, which is sometimes called Self-realization. God- or Self-realization may be defined as a state of consciousness in which the individual lives constantly in total and complete awareness of his or her own unity with God. In the beginning, the soul entered the involutionary arc and became human in order to experience life on the lower planes, and in order to do this completely it was necessary for the entity to forget its divine origin (see Chapter One). At some point along the latter stages of the evolutionary loop, however, this awareness must be regained if the soul is to return to its ultimate Source. In the past two hundred years, we have been privileged to have among us a number of God-realized beings, including Ramakrishna, Vivekananda, Yogananda, Muktananda, and Maharishi Mahesh Yogi to use as role models.

KARMA

Our path to God-realization is retarded, however, by karma. Karma is a word that is bandied around quite a bit these days, even though some people don't seem to understand what it really means. The word comes from the Sanskrit and merely means "action." In India, there is a religious sect called Jainism whose more fanatical devotees spend their time sitting all day and all night in meditation doing nothing, not even eating or drinking, and since they must breathe, they wear a mask over their faces to avoid breathing in microorganisms in the air. They believe that if they do absolutely nothing they will create no more karma to keep them from attaining enlightenment. They seem unaware of the fact that, at least according to our research, there does appear to be something called the karma of neglect.

There are many different kinds of karma, but the most widespread meaning is the kind I like to refer to as *boomerang karma*. Boomerang karma means, simply, that what you do in one lifetime, be it good or evil, always comes back to you, often in the next incarnation. This is true. Also, most people seem to think of karma and "karmic debts" in terms of their negative aspects. But the concept of karma (see Chapter Five) is actually much more complex than that. Also involved are unfulfilled desires, incompletions, and attachments—none of which, strictly speaking, is actually negative, but still tends to bind a soul-entity to the trials and troubles of the earthly plane.

Throughout the course of progress along the evolutionary loop, the experience of each entity involves identification with the myriads of life circumstances it creates, what exactly are the karmic "debts" that it has to pay, and what is owing to it. There are no hard-and-fast rules as to what course of action the soul takes in the unfolding of its own individual evolution.

THE AGREEMENT

There is, however, the Agreement. In the early years of the existence of our solar system, when the Solar Logos (the soul of our Sun, known to ancient civilizations as Vishnu, Apollo, Amon-Ra, El, and Mabon) determined to create a world in this system, all the Light Masters or Monads (see Chapter One) who chose to participate entered into an Agreement that certain physical and spiritual laws would be obeyed for as long as the solar system was in existence.

The Agreement has been likened to a football game. Before the players ever go out onto the field, they form a pact that certain rules are to be scrupulously followed. To break the rules involves a penalty, and these rules are to remain in effect until the clock runs out at the end of the last quarter.

None of the players is actually forced to stay in the game. At any time, the quarterback can choose to stop in the middle of a play and walk off the field, and in the long run no one will have been seriously harmed. However, pros don't do that. No matter how rough the game gets, no matter how many times he is battered by the opposing team, the quarterback hangs in there, trying (but not always succeeding) to obey the rules, until the game is over.

The Agreement has also been compared to a legal contract. The terms and conditions of the contract are set out at the time of its inception, but anywhere down the line those terms and conditions can be renegotiated, and thereby the "rules" are changed.

Agreements exist on all levels. There is, of course, *the* Agreement, made between all the Light Masters who chose to participate in the evolution of this solar system. There are also "private" agreements, between different groups, nations, and individuals, in which "contracts" are made which karmically benefit both parties in some way.

To illustrate: Suppose you have a karmic relationship with an entity who feels that it is her karma to lose her eyesight. Your Higher Self makes an agreement with hers to be the instrument by which her eyesight is lost in a particular incarnation. Then, when it happens, your Higher Self decides that you have a "karmic debt" to pay for depriving that entity of her eyesight. A karmic debt may be defined as an obligation stemming from a negative act that must be atoned for if the entity is to continue to progress along the evolutionary loop.

This may seem strange, but it appears to be the way the game is played. Now remember: your Higher Self decides what karmic debts you have to pay. But the Higher Self, for the sake of the game, often allows its decisions to be guided by considerations—whatever their source, however inappropriate they may be—rooted in the human personality.

For example: My late friend and partner, Edward Sparks, was once on a lecture tour in Texas. On the way to his lecture, he drove down a quiet street in a residential district. Suddenly a little girl darted out between two parked cars and into the street, less than fifty feet in front of him. Edward swerved and slammed on the brakes, barely avoiding hitting her. He leaned out of his window and shouted, "I refuse to participate in your karma, little girl! If you want to get yourself killed, you're going to have to find someone else!" For a moment, he claimed, he saw understanding in the child's eyes, as if the Higher Self were responding to his words. Then she dissolved into tears, as frightened little girls are prone to do.

Edward may have had an Agreement, forged long ago, to take this little girl's life. However, if this is the case, at the last minute he chose to renegotiate that agreement because he did not want to kill anyone. Or perhaps the agreement was that he would teach her a lesson about darting out into the street, and he therefore fulfilled his part in full!

No soul is forced to remain on the wheel of incarnation. At any time, a soul can pull out of the game and return directly to the Infinite. Certain myths that have persisted throughout the history of the human race indicate that there may have been times when this happened, as in the story of Enoch, whom God took directly up to heaven, body and all. However, such an event is very rare. We who have chosen to play the game of earthly Incarnation agreed to play by the rules. Unlike the rules of football, however, the "rules" are somewhat flexible, and the incarnating soul—the "Higher Self" guiding each separate personality—often sets its own standards, usually in accordance with its ray vibration. The evolving entity, in accordance with these standards, creates its own rules above and beyond those covered in the Agreement. and tailors its own lives accordingly—thus making karma of "good" and "evil" at choice by each individual. What is good for one person might constitute evil for another. As the old saying goes, one man's bread is another man's poison.

The above occult truth has been distorted in recent years. In the late 1970s and early 1980s, there was a popular New Age belief that you actually create your own reality, implying that the human personality, rather than the Higher Self, was responsible for everything that happened to it, be it good or evil. This led to useless guilt on the part of Seekers who lost their jobs, were victims of auto accidents or abuse, or contracted serious illnesses. This distorted bit of philosophy implied that it was all their own fault, that there was something lacking in them that caused them to "attract" undesirable events into their lives.

In some cases the above scenario is true. The success that many have had with creative visualization in creating near-miracles in their lives attests to a hitherto unacknowledged power existing in the human mind. Also, enlightened doctors such as Deepak Chopra, Raymond

Moody and Bernie Siegel have written extensively on the power of love and the will to live to heal people whom doctors had sworn had only a short time to live.

The field of psychosomatic medicine is now accepted even by mainstream physicians who acknowledge that some mental attitudes actually cause people to create serious illnesses in themselves. Anyone familiar with law in any form is aware that there is a certain type of "victim" personality that attracts abuse or is accident-prone. This has led to the practice among judges, juries and other people involved in the legal system to adopt an inexcusable attitude called "blaming the victim." To excuse the abuser because the victim "asked for it" is to make the statement that under certain conditions, abuse is all right. I take strong issue with this idea. For one thing, "victim" personalities are in the minority. For another, even if the victim does "ask for it," the abuser does not have the right to "comply with their request." To condone this sort of behavior is to say that killing someone who begs to be shot is not murder.

But I digress. The Higher Self is bound by the Agreement. and before birth it attempts to create specific life circumstances and to foresee probable events that will serve the entity's purpose for taking incarnation in accordance with the Agreement. There is inevitably some level of uncertainty, because the Higher Self itself is still evolving and therefore incapable of foreseeing all possible contingencies. Subconsciously, the human personality is guided into those events that may fulfill the Higher Self's purpose. In that sense, we do create our own reality. But once incarnation is taken, there are in fact situations that arise over which the individual human personality and its intentions seem to have little control. "Night will follow day," says Starhawk, "and there's noth-

---

2 Starhawk, *The Spiral Dance*. 10th Anniversary Edition. New York: Harper Collins, 1991.

ing you or I or Werner can do about it."[2] It was part of the Agreement at the beginning of life on this planet that night would follow day—and we must live in accordance with that Agreement.

"If you contract cancer because a nearby factory is spewing toxins into the air," says Ken Wilber, "it isn't your bad karma. It's theirs."[3] It was part of the Agreement that the presence of toxic substances in the body would lead to disease and possibly death. The scenario outlined above by Wilber, which happens all too often in this technology-crazed society, is due to a callous lack of responsibility on the part of factory officials, not to any character flaw on the part of the cancer victim.

The idea that "we create our own reality" has led as well to a lack of responsibility on the part of those who wish to continue such harmful habits as smoking, drinking alcohol, using illegal drugs, etc. Many times my colleagues and I have confronted pseudo-New Age teachers puffing away on cigarettes. They have excused themselves by saying, "I absolutely create my own reality and I will not create that smoking cigarettes will do me any harm!" Edward Sparks always said that if you really believe that, he had a bridge he wanted to sell you—cheap. At least one of these people that we know of has already died of cancer. Again, it was part of the Agreement that the presence of toxic substances in the body could lead to disease and possibly death—and at this late date there is nothing you or I or Lazaris can do about it.

If setbacks or tragedy occur in your life, it is useless to lay a guilt trip on yourself because of it. You can only do what you do when you do it. Neither playing the victim nor indulging in useless self-blame will serve you or anyone else. In fact, believing too strongly that in some way you created a setback and agonizing over what you're doing wrong tends to

---

3 Ken Wilber, interviewed in *East-West Journal.* September 1987.

throw more blocks into your path and add to the frustration, and certainly doesn't help to create the condition you want.

The above statements call to mind the case of Kimberly Bergalis. Kimberly, as you may recall, was nineteen years old when she contracted the AIDS virus from her dentist. There is no possible way that the two human personalities involved—Kimberly and her dentist—could possibly have foreseen what happened and created the situation, either subconsciously or otherwise. However, there was apparently some kind of Agreement involved between the two Higher Selves and the Powers that Be. In spite of the tragic premature deaths of the two parties, the awareness that was spread to the entire world through this incident—that it was possible to contract the AIDS virus from a health-care worker—will probably be instrumental in saving other lives.

Yet Kimberly Bergalis—the human personality unaware of the Agreement—seems to have believed herself to be a helpless, unwitting victim of circumstance. Had she been aware—even on an intellectual level—of the Agreement, she could possibly have drawn some comfort from it. Towards the end of her life, however, she appears to have been more aware, as people approaching death often are. In her will she left $60,000 to AIDS research.

Another tragic situation that led to a higher good involves the case of Adam Walsh, the six-year-old Florida boy who was kidnapped and murdered by a still-unknown assailant in the early 1980s. Channeled information that my associates and I have received indicates that the soul who took incarnation as Adam Walsh was actually a highly advanced being. His Agreement with the Higher Selves of his parents and with the Universe was that he would make this sacrifice in order to provide help for the thousands of children who disappear every year and to comfort the parents of other murdered children. After Adam's death, his parents, John and Revé Walsh, led the charge upon the United States government, drawing public attention to the many unsolved cases of missing children, taking steps to educate children in ways to protect themselves, and working to pass stiff laws against parental kidnapping. Because of Adam Walsh's Agreement with his parents, many missing children have been found and countless numbers of others may have been saved from a similar fate. Still, there is no way that the human personalities of the Walshes could have foreseen or "created" the tragedy of losing their beloved six-year-old son.

As the Agreement stands, you can only do what your Higher Self has agreed to do. Everything that happens in the course of our lives happens in accordance with the Agreement. There is no character flaw involved. There should be no guilt. For almost everything that happens, for good or evil, there is a purpose, and there is a lesson to be learned from everything.

The Agreement—and all the lesser Agreements we form with other soul-entities throughout the course of our incarnations—is not always an easy contract to fulfill. As the rules governing football often cause players to be kicked, battered, knocked down, and otherwise injured, sometimes our Agreements can lead to inconvenience, setbacks, and even tragedy in our lives. Sometimes, as in the above two cases, they can lead to a greater good for the rest of the world. More often, however, they are meant to contribute to our own personal level of awareness. The job of the past-life therapist is to seek the ultimate karmic source of a particular situation and allow the client to see for herself how that situation affected her. Sometimes the results can be unpleasant.

PAST-LIFE CRISES—PRESENT LIFE EFFECTS

Generally, a phobia, hangup, or chronic physical dysfunction can be traced to a traumatic incident that happened many, many lifetimes ago wherein the entity's survival was somehow threatened. This incident is called the Number One incident. As a result of this incident, a decision was made—usually along the lines of "Love (or wealth or health or whatever) means death." In subsequent incarnations, whenever incidents similar to the Number One incident (called *engrams*) occur, the decision is reinforced. An engram bank is created, and the intensity of the effect of the original decision is increased until it results in a potentially severe problem.

It is accepted among most reincarnational experts that we do not carry around with us all the time the sum total of all our past-life crises. If we did, we'd all be basket cases—worse off even than Quasimodo—and there would be no human society as we know it. Rather, to trigger a hangup or phobia in the current existence, the subconscious memories of past-life crises have to be brought to the surface by a similar (or in some cases even dissimilar) incident in the current incarnation. This event is called the *keying incident*. Mainstream psychology often interprets the keying incident as the ultimate source of a mental or emotional problem. The patient looks at the incident and acknowledges its significance, and the therapist then considers the book closed. However, the psychologists don't seem to be able to explain why one child who is rescued from a fire develops a crippling phobia about fire while another simply treats it as an interesting experience. And in too many cases the problem disappears for awhile only to reappear when another similar keying incident occurs.

To illustrate, let us take an experience of my own. For many years, I had a phobia about walking down stairs. As I stood at the top of a flight of stairs and looked down, I immediately had the sensation of tumbling down, hitting the bottom and breaking off my two front teeth. I could actually feeling pain shooting up through my gums, though I would still walk down the stairs, very slowly, clinging with all my might to the banister.

I traced this hangup to an event that occurred when I was eleven years old, when my younger sister, then aged two, fell in the bathtub and broke off her two front teeth. However, my hangup was not about the bathtub, it was about stairs. And my recollection of my sister's accident did not alleviate my own fear.

Then, when I was in my early twenties and first began to explore my own past lives, I had a very vivid dream. In this dream, I was a fat, homely merchant seaman, coming home to my Chinese wife after a long sea voyage. As I approached the house where we lived, my wife came out of the door of a second-story room, saw me, and turned to rush down to greet me. She nipped at the top of the stairs and plummeted down. I called out to her: "Fish! Fish!" and ran to the foot of the stairs and picked her up. She raised her head slowly and looked at me. I saw that her two front teeth were broken off.

I awoke from that dream with a totally new awareness of why I had felt the way I did about stairs. The mishap that happened to my past-life spouse was the Number One incident; my present-life sister's falling in the bathtub was the keying incident. From the moment I realized the truth, I was no longer afraid to walk down any staircase.

An interesting epilogue to this story is that a few years after I had this dream I attended a therapy group, where I told my story. One of the women in the group told me that her maiden name had been Herring, and throughout her years in school everyone had called her Fish. When she was five years old she had fallen down a flight of stairs and broken off her two front teeth. Later, after the session was over, she told me China and its culture had always fascinated her.

Needless to say, I was quite excited by this validation of my dream. I never saw the woman again. But apparently there was no need. Our relationship in the merchant seaman lifetime had been a good one, and its completion in this life apparently rested only on her reaffirming my belief in the reality of my experience.

Of course the above example is a relatively simple one, and past-life therapists more often encounter problems that are much more complex. For a moment, let us imagine that I never had the dream, and that in my future lives several other similar incidents occurred which added considerably to the engram bank. Several incarnations down the road, the hangup could have increasing until it resulted in a serious condition such as agoraphobia, or fear of going out. It would have taken extensive past-life and follow-up therapy in order to enable me to let the hangup go and continue on my path to self-realization.

Guilt may also be connected with problems that are rooted in past lives. A client, whom I'll call Jane, came to me once at the end of her rope because her marriage was breaking up. Jane's husband had developed an attachment to an orphan named Louise and insisted upon adopting her, even though Jane was somewhat repelled by the child and was dubious about accepting her into their family.

To please her husband, however, Jane agreed to the adoption and made a valiant effort to treat Louise the same as she treated her own three natural children. However, Louise seemed to sense Jane's antipathy to her and allied herself with Jane's husband. Jane's husband saw the child as an innocent and his wife as the persecutor. It was at this point that Jane came to me for past-life therapy.

I took her through two separate regression sessions, during which she experienced several lives. In all of them Jane found Louise—sometimes as a man, sometimes as a woman. In every single one of these lifetimes, the relationship between them had been an antagonistic one. After about the sixth lifetime in which hostilities between the two entities had occurred, I was beginning to feel desperate. I then decided to take Jane back into a lifetime in which the relationship between her and Louise had been a good one, and planted that suggestion into her mind.

Jane saw herself as a man, sitting in a tavern somewhere in medieval England, drinking tankard after tankard of coarse ale, apparently drowning his sorrows and complaining to the landlord about a person he referred to as "Jason." I asked Jane to tell me more about Jason, and the quiet answer came: "Ann and I were going to be married. But Jason came and stole her. I'll never, never, never forgive him."

I then asked her who Jason was in the current lifetime, and she replied, "Louise."

I cringed. This was a lifetime in which the relationship had been a positive one? I brought Jane out of that lifetime and asked some questions of her Higher Self. In spite of my suggestion, the Higher Self had not taken Jane to a period in which the contact had been pleasant, but to the Number One incident in which the hostility between these two entities had initially been created. Apparently, subconsciously, Jane was still sticking to her vow that she would never, never, never forgive Jason. I planted the suggestion that perhaps, in light of the situation, now was the time to forgive him.

Jane was so overwhelmed by the information revealed in that regression session that she took a long walk to clear her head and sort out her feelings. She returned about two hours later, experiencing a mixture of relief and apprehension, determined to work things out with her adopted daughter. She telephoned me later, saying that she had managed for the first time to look Louise in the eye and say with all sincerity, "Louise, you are my daughter, and I love you.

However, it takes two, and apparently Louise was not as willing as Jane to let go of her hostility. In spite of Jane's efforts, the enmity continued, and eventually Jane's marriage broke up. Jane's three natural children stayed with her, while Louise went to live with her adopted father.

The above case history illustrates not only the power of guilt in causing current-life neuroses, but of *incompletion* and *attachment*. An *incompletion* is a pressing situation that has never been resolved—in common parlance, unfinished business, a "loose end" that was never tied up. Incompletions can involve unfulfilled dreams and ambitions or tasks that were undertaken but never finished—as in the case of a thirteenth-century English pilgrim who made a vow to visit the Holy Land but died on the way and never made it. In the current life, he was constantly traveling, searching for something, but was never really sure what it was. In Jane's case, the incompletion involved the ill feelings surrounding the relationship between Jason/Louise and herself. Most modern metaphysical teachers now accept that we are here on Earth to have relationships and learn from them—and therefore Christ's message of "Love your neighbor" represents one of the highest spiritual truths ever bestowed upon human beings.

You don't necessarily have to *like* your neighbor, or approve of everything he does, or enjoy his company. But you are in Agreement to care about his well-being to the same extent that you would care for your own, or that of a member of your family. Even though Jane knew she could never truly like Louise, her ability to set aside her antagonism and say truthfully that she loved her hopefully completed the relationship for Jane—even though Louise did not return her feelings.

Now if Jane were truly complete with the experience, she would be totally freed from the bonds forged by the continuous hostility generated by this relationship. To return to our football-game analogy, the quarterback can now walk off the field. However, if Louise does not at some time in this lifetime complete it within her, in future lifetimes she may find herself continuing the pattern—but with someone other than Jane.

The case of Jane and Louise also illustrates the power of attachment to contribute to psychological problems. Even though life on Earth may involve several millennia of human embodiments, it still encompasses only the blink of an eye in the history of the Universe. Hence we should not become too involved with anything associated mainly with existence on this planet.

The Qabbalah holds that there are 613 experiences that we must complete on this planet before we can move on to the higher realms. A beautiful story from the Qabbalistic tradition expounds upon this aphorism. There was once an entity who, from the start of his earthly evolution, had always chosen to incarnate as a rabbi. From lifetime to lifetime he grew, completing each of the 613 "requirements" appropriately in each existence. Then, in his 613th incarnation, he suddenly broke from his pattern and came back as a power-hungry merchant enmeshed in the lusts of the flesh. He spent his entire lifetime drinking, whoring, conning, stealing—even participating in murder.

So, you ask, how could an entity who spent 612 lifetimes as a rabbi suddenly turn into such a monster? He had completed 612 of the "required" experiences. The 613th he still needed to complete was repentance. He had spent all his previous lifetimes being so good he had nothing to repent.

Thus is the power of the Agreement. We all have agreed to play certain roles and fulfill certain functions.

ATTACHMENTS

When the soul completes the involutionary arc and takes incarnation on Earth, it seeks to enjoy every possible facet of life on this plane. Inevitably attachments result. Entities experiencing attachment tend, life after life, to recreate situations in which they have felt comfortable in previous existences, even long after the lesson dictated by that situation has been learned. If the Qabbalistic tradition represents the truth, then we only need live a maximum of 613 lives. But our research reveals that we live many, many more than that. In some cases, people even live thousands. One reason for this is *attachment.*

Attachments can involve relationships, places, social or political positions, specific experiences, or material wealth. The mythical rabbi mentioned above was so attached to his role as a rabbi he postponed a vital earthly experience until the very last. Jane, over a period of centuries, had become attached to her subconscious conviction that the soul who had been Jason was her enemy.

FORGIVENESS

Instead of giving in to considerations based on long-dead events, it is best just to let them go. The best way to do this is through the process of forgiveness. If we are to release all our karma and move more rapidly along the evolutionary loop towards God-realization, we have to do a lot of forgiving. We live hundreds and thousands of lifetimes on this planet; throughout the course of those lifetimes, we do a lot of bad things, and a lot of bad things are done to us. We develop a lot of attachments and are faced with many incompletions. If every single one of these elements had to be resolved, we would be compelled to remain in earthly incarnations for longer than the 15 billion years which scientists project as the lifespan of our solar system. At some point we'd have to end up like the more fanatical Jains because they are right in one sense: Any kind of action creates karma of some kind.

Forgiveness provides the only foolproof way out. Ideally, you should be able to forgive yourself and everyone else you have ever known in all your incarnations without knowing your past lives or the sources of them. But sometimes the entity has been so deeply scarred, and the considerations run so deep in the subconscious, that a blanket declaration of forgiveness simply isn't enough. Past-life regression may be necessary.

This statement calls to mind a case of a fifteen-year-old star female athlete who could never get along with her father. The friction between them was starting to affect the psyches of everyone else in the family, so I was called in to perform a regression on the daughter.

She found herself in England in the early nineteenth century, the eldest daughter in a large family. Her father—the same entity who was her father now—was a sea captain who was constantly away from home, sometimes for years at a time. While the father was gone, this entity had to take over running the family, and she was so young she sometimes felt overwhelmed by the responsibility. During the course of the father's long absences, the mother became seriously ill and eventually died; the house had to be sold, and the children were all placed in different homes. The eldest daughter blamed her father for all her misfortunes.

I said to her, "Forgive your father. It's the only way to let it all go."
She was silent.
"Forgive him," I repeated. "He didn't know. Forgive him."

Again she was silent.

"Forgive him," I went on. "Say the words, 'I forgive,' even if it's a lie."

Her face contorted into a frown, and she opened her mouth as if to say something, then cried out, "I can't! He did it all! It was all his fault! I can't even pretend to forgive him!" Tears began to flow from her eyes.

I then planted the suggestion that she would forgive him when the time was right and brought her out of her regression. She immediately threw herself into her father's arms. She remained there for several minutes, weeping copiously. In spite of her words, some level of forgiveness had been reached.

While their relationship never became totally tranquil—they are both too high-strung and too much alike for that—at this point, thirteen years later, they do seem to be friends, at least most of the time.

In the case of Jane, it was necessary for her not only to forgive Jason/Louise, but herself—because she had clung to and re-created the antagonism throughout so many centuries. The process of forgiving yourself, with or without the help of past-life therapy, is one of the most powerful tools you can use to give yourself a tremendous boost towards the ultimate goal of self-realization.[4]

BREAKING THE CHAIN

Releasing attachments, completing incompletions, and making it OK that unfulfilled desires were never fulfilled are also powerful tools in aiding one's progress. Attachments—particularly those regarding relationships—are best handled by realizing that everyone you've ever known will always be with you in some way, for did we not all come from the same source? Incompletions can be dealt with by completing

---

4 For a more detailed analysis of the benefits and process of forgiving yourself, see Edward Sparks' chapter, "Forgive Yourself," in *Your Future Lives* (West Chester, PA: Whitford Press, 1988).

the experience within yourself. For example, let us take the case of the pilgrim who never reached the Holy Land. In this life the entity could complete the experience by actually taking that pilgrimage, or, if financial considerations or family responsibilities made it impossible, he could complete the experience by learning as much as possible about the Holy Land he once wanted to visit.

Unfulfilled desires can sometimes be completed by guided fantasy. Let us say that a young girl always wanted to be a gymnast, and was working toward that goal when she was struck down by polio. The desire still exists, but the young woman wants more to work towards spiritual progress and avoid having to come back and fulfill that desire in future incarnations. The best way for her to fulfill that desire may be to go ahead and create in her mind the fantasy that she did become an Olympic gymnast—and possibly follow it up by finding another young girl who wants to be a gymnast and doing everything she can to help that person attain her dream.

But every person is different, and the path to forgiveness and to releasing attachments is unique to every individual. The rest of this book will analyze the differences between individuals and give everyone an idea of how to approach those differences.

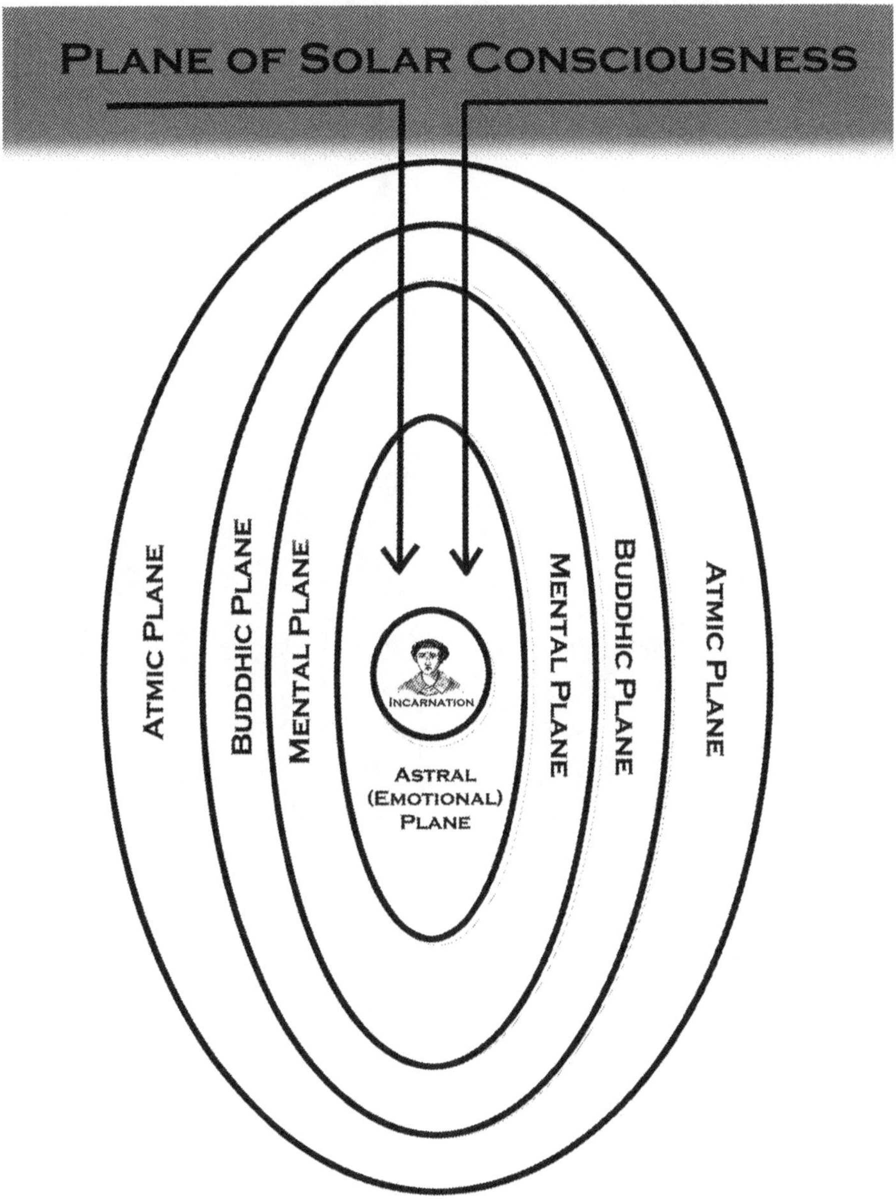

PLANE OF SOLAR CONSCIOUSNESS

ATMIC PLANE

BUDDHIC PLANE

MENTAL PLANE

INCARNATION

ASTRAL
(EMOTIONAL)
PLANE

MENTAL PLANE

BUDDHIC PLANE

ATMIC PLANE

THE INVOLUTIONARY ARC

ONE

The Involutionary Arc

God Becoming Human

It has long been a given among proponents of the perennial philosophy that we all came from a single Source and are trying to find our way back to that Source. The process of reincarnation represents our attempts to find our way home, so to speak.

But how did we get to Earth in the first place? This question is largely ignored, in religious teachings, in schools, even among the most enlightened therapists and practitioners of past-life regression. Yet logically it would seem important for us to be as aware of where we came from as of where we are going.

Perhaps part of the difficulty in studying how God became human is that we are dealing with matters far beyond the conceptual ability of most people on Earth. Many great minds throughout the centuries have had revelations of the process, but even they often had problems expressing what they saw. The story of Lucifer, in the Bible, for example, could well represent an ancient memory of the soul's involution—but when expressed in words it reads more like an interesting fable. The Tibetan Book of the Dead contains a detailed explanation of the involutionary cycle, as do ancient Hindu scriptures, but knowledge of these up until recent decades was reserved for those who were already considered initiates. In her *Book of Divine Works,* Vision One, Section 10, the Christian mystic Hildegard of Bingen (1098-1179) gave a brief outline of the involutionary arc—though it is admittedly colored by medieval Christian theology.

We must bear in mind that when we who are incarnate on Planet Earth describe the involutionary arc, we are forced to speak in symbols. We are attempting to define the indefinable, to attach labels to that which is elusive and subtle, and thus our words can only give a vague, rough approximation of the truth. The reason for this is we are dealing with descriptions of divinity in time and space, neither of which is an absolute, and our explanations come off appearing to be linear when, in fact, they are not. "Being" is not linear, it is timeless, and until human beings become consciously aware of their own divinity it will be hard to perceive anything except in terms of time. Time is a function of the brain and therefore our language is linear, but the cycles we are trying to describe are not. Thus we have a problem with communication right from the start. Still, readers can gain a rough picture of the processes I am trying to describe if they remember that I am attempting to put into words that which is too subtle to be accurately translated.

Our work with past-life regression indicates that it is possible for people to remember their experiences on the involutionary arc as well as their past earthly incarnations. These experiences explain why past-life regression sessions often turn up what appear to be illogical anomalies. For example, a person recalls being a great Master with total Divine Awareness and fantastic powers in an ancient long-gone civilization such as Atlantis or Lemuria or perhaps on another planet. Then he finds himself several thousand years later incarnated as a primitive shaman teaching his fellow tribe members how to make a fire. My associates and I have successfully taken people all the way back to the Big Bang, and their regression material has helped to shed light on the involutionary process and experience.

IN THE BEGINNING

The one question that no one—not regression subjects, not trance channels, not even the Great Masters—seems to be able (or willing) to answer is why we are here. Why would Brahman, the source of all being, decide to expand Itself and create all the pain and suffering that comes with life on the material plane? We have no idea—though some thinkers have tried to make educated guesses. According to the Qabbalah, the Creator needed entities on which to bestow his benefi- cence as the Absolute. bestowed Its light on the Creator. The most pop- ular educated guess appears to be the following: boredom. God had existed for eons of time and had become totally bored and had nothing to do; therefore, out of sheer ennui, He/She/It exploded into billions of particles.

Some of these fragments became galaxies, nebulae, great suns. Some became planets, some became asteroids and moons. Some of them became the small life energies that are now you and me and all the liv- ing creatures throughout the Cosmos, throughout and transcending the limits of space and time. Ever since then what we have all been trying to do is get back together again. I later discovered—quite on my own, though Carl Sagan also pointed it out in his wonderful television series, *Cosmos*—that this particular idea is a direct parallel to the physicists' theory of the Big Bang origin of the Universe as well as the ancient Hindu theory of the Days and Nights of Brahm. At the dawn of each Day of Brahm, God—or Brahman—expands into a myriad of life forms and creates the game called the Universe. At the end of that "day"—15 billion years—Brahman pulls all those life forms back into his own being and rests for another 15 billion years. Then we get to start all over again.

Again, the term Brahman is only a symbol, a convenient handle that human beings can use to focus our perception. You cannot name the unnamable; by giving it a name you limit it, and Brahman is limitless. Still, we will use, for convenience, the term Brahman—perhaps more accurately named THAT, or, as in modern Western metaphysics, the One About Whom Naught May Be Said.[5]

In the beginning there was only the One, but in the early morning of the Day of Brahm (at the moment of the Big Bang) the One became Two. We now know these two as the forces of Yin and Yang, or Shiva and Shakti as the Hindus call them. Yin represents that which is dark, receptive, feminine; Yang is the light, the aggressive, the masculine. All polarities are rooted in the forces of Yin and Yang—male/female, light/dark, good/evil, positive/negative, matter/antimatter. Please bear in mind that these polarities were created for the sake of the game, and that all are a part of THAT—even the good/evil polarities. Evil was created so that there could be good. Brahman exists outside of both.

Regression material relating to the Big Bang is extensive, but all transcripts tell basically the same story. The following transcript from a regression session is typical:

> I feel as if I am spread throughout the Universe, as if my Being is one with it I am the Universe...
>
> What happened? I appear to be flying through space and time. I am still the Universe, but I am something else as well. I feel as if I were falling...

---

5 See *A Treatise on Cosmic Fire* and the rest of the highly advanced series of books channeled by the Tibetan Master Djwahl Khul through Alice A. Bailey. Also see *The Secret Doctrine* by Mme. Helena Petrovna Blavatsky and *Anthropogeny: The Esoteric History of Man's Man's Origin* by Dr. Douglas Baker. (Hert, England: Little Elephant c. 1975.)

This statement seems highly significant to me because the subject was a young Korean immigrant who had only been in the country seven years and had spent that entire period in college, majoring in physics. He claimed he had never in his life read anything about Western metaphysics.

The two forces then became three—the Three Primary Rays (see Chapter Three), knowledge of which has survived in the consistent tradition of Trinities existing in most earthly religions. Ancient Hindu scriptures refer to the first trinity as *sat-chit-ananda* (being, consciousness, and bliss) and Western metaphysics refers to it as life, consciousness, and form. The divinities of mythology include the ancient Indo-European trinity of Varuna, Indra, and Mitra, the Hindu trinity of Brahma, Vishnu, and Shiva, the pagan trinity of Father, Mother, and Child, and, of course, the Christian trinity of Father, Son, and Holy Spirit.

The Three Primary Rays then projected themselves first into Four, then into Seven (again, see Chapter Three) and the Seven became billions. The rapidly developing physical Universe of galaxies, nebulae, stars, and planets was paralleled in the spiritual world by the myriad fragments of Brahman. These fragments are called Light Masters or Monads.

I find it fascinating that this concept parallels in many ways the Big Bang theory of the origin of the Universe. According to modern cosmology, in the beginning there was only one force, the cosmic egg, which scientists find it impossible to describe. Then a tiny fluctuation agitated the cosmic egg, and it broke into two forces, which are called the *strong force* (Yang)[6] and the *weak force*[7] (Yin). According to author/physicist John Boslough the strong force was an amalgamation

---

6 My parallel.
7 My parallel.

of the strong nuclear force, the weak nuclear force, and electromagnetism. The weak force was none other than our old friend, gravity.

Then as the baby Universe evolved, the two forces became three—the strong nuclear force, gravity, and a new amalgam of the weak nuclear force and electromagnetism. When the weak nuclear force and electromagnetism parted company, there were then four forces.[8] No parallel can yet be drawn for the Seven, though it is probably just a matter of time until it is. Still, according to Boslough, physicists now believe that the interactions between the four primary forces created the various nuclear reactions—centering on the polarity principle, of attraction/repulsion—that gave rise to all the different forms of matter and energy in our Universe.

THE BIRTH OF OUR PLANET

The developing planets in this system were originally part of the Sun God Monad, yet other Light Masters were attracted to this system and chose to become anchored in the planets. Among them was a yin, Third Ray entity who attached Herself to the third planet out from the Sun. This Monad was the soul of our Earth, the Planetary Logos, known to mythology as the Great Mother, Gaia, Lakshmi, Ceres, and Danu, and to modern metaphysics as Sanat Kumara. Mother Earth did more than anchor Herself to a heavenly body. She decided to create a world.

At that time the planet was a rather barren place, with a dense atmosphere composed mainly of nitrogen. The planet itself consisted mainly of rock, but it was very active, with volcanoes erupting all over the place, every minute of every day. This volcanic activity led to the saturation of

---

8   John Boslough, *Masters of Time: How Wormholes, Snakewood and Assaults on the Big Bang Have Brought Mystery Back to the Cosmos.* London: Dent, 1992. PP. 147-148.

the primordial atmosphere with hydrogen and oxygen, which combined to form water vapor.

One day the volcanic activity slowed to a crawl, cooling both the planetary surface and the atmosphere above it. Then it rained—steadily, constantly, for hundreds of thousands of years, until the primordial oceans were formed. Afterwards there appeared the first life forms, and thus began the cycle of physical evolution of life on Earth.

All the evolving life forms on this planet were originally—and actually still are—projections of the Mother Earth Monad.[9] However, as they began to evolve, other Monads became attracted to the planet. They began to feel the first stirrings of desire for experiencing life on the lower planes of existence. They then descended from the Divine or Logoic Plane onto the *Causal* or *Monadic Plane,* called the *Chikhai* in the Tibetan Book of the Dead. Over a period of eons, each developing life form, or *family,*[10] was anchored by a specific Light Master or Monad.

Once each Monad had "adopted" a family and sought to guide its evolution, it began to divide into soul groups—or group souls. Contrary to the opinions of some metaphysical groups, there is no difference at all between a soul group and a group soul. All entities on this planet were originally part of a single Monad, be they animal, crystal, or human entities. Some group souls—such as the human—individualize faster than others, such as the so-called "subhuman" animals (I prefer the term "nonhuman"). But eventually all do individualize, and afterwards, all do ultimately return to their source. Soul groups are said to come into existence on the subtle level or atmic plane, which is

---

9 This statement calls to mind the words of a beautiful chant used in many feminist circles: "We all come from the Goddess, and to her we shall return."

10 I use the term "family" here to mean the biological classification ? as in kingdom, phylum, class, order, family, genus, species and subspecies.

referred to in the Tibetan Book of the Dead as the *Chonyid* or *Shambhogakaya*.

DO HUMANS REINCARNATE AS ANIMALS—AND VICE VERSA?

At this point I wish to digress a little. Although classical Hinduism maintains that "bad karma" can cause a human being to reincarnate in the body of an animal, few serious Western metaphysicians accept this idea. However, the reverse is widely believed in Western metaphysics. This popular tradition maintains that animal life forms are "less evolved" than humans, that they possess no individual essence, but belong to a sort of mass soul, and that they eventually reach a point where they "break away from the group soul" and begin reincarnating as humans. Our research indicates that this is not the case.

What our research reveals is that every species of animal is under the domain of a particular Light Master and always remains a part of that specific Monad. This means, for example, that the Monad of the cat family takes Her entities through the various Stages of Development (see Chapter Two) until they become the ultimately evolved cat and return to Her.[11] Each species, then, is on its own individual path of spiritual evolution, seeking to return to the unity of its original Light Master.

This conclusion is not only based on the fact that my colleagues and I are all animal lovers. We admit to a certain prejudice. But animals do

---

11 The Monad of the cat family is a yin, Third Ray entity, and is referred to in Egyptian mythology as Bast, the Cat Goddess. For dog lovers, the Light Master of the dog family is a yang. Second Ray entity, and was immortalized by the Egyptians as Anubis, the Jackal God. We believe that the various animal gods of the ancients were our ancestors' way of honoring the Light Masters of the animals who served them so well.

have a special beauty and grace all their own, and the domestic animals in particular are capable of an exalted form of unconditional love that most humans lack. In recent years much has been observed of the almost avataric effect that a dog, cat or horse can have on a depressed or ailing human being. Not only that, in some mythologies—particularly the Australian and Native American—animals, rather than being considered subhuman creatures incapable of thought, are regarded as the teachers sent by the Great Spirit to guide the human family.

But perhaps the most significant indication that animals do not evolve into human beings is that in all our years of experience, in all the thousands of regressions we have performed—and in the experience of every regression therapist we have known, worked with, or even heard of—nobody in all the vast number of subjects, which must at least approach 100,000, has ever recalled a lifetime as an animal. We have taken subjects through various stages of the involutionary arc, all the way back to the Big Bang, but never has anyone reported having been an animal. They always find themselves in a body that is unmistakably human.

Our reply to those who point to such occult classics as *The Secret Doctrine* and the Alice Bailey books, which refer to the process of animals becoming human, is to remember that both these great series were channeled, and with all channeled material there can be problems with transmission, or with the difference in language used. Also, other passages in the Alice Bailey books, which relate to the history and development of human beings on this planet, seem to contradict this idea, as they do not mention any period of time in which human souls inhabited the bodies of animals other than the remote animal ancestors of human beings.

Therefore, it is quite possible that these statements are the result of misinterpretation, and do not mean that animals actually cross over and enter the human species, but that they become human*like*. Animals go through a process known as individualization, which animal man once went through (see Chapter Two for a more detailed description of this process) and which every species will eventually undergo—but still they remain a different species, distinct from humankind in every way. Once individualization is complete, the animals then begin their own specific path up the evolutionary loop, just as humans do. This has already happened with whales and dolphins, and according to most occult literature will soon happen with the domestic animals—cats, dogs, elephants, horses, and so on. In my experience, at least with some domestic animals, it has already happened.

This pretty much shatters the theory that all other life forms on Earth exist for the benefit of humans. This point of view is extremely arrogant, selfish, and "species chauvinistic," to quote the late science writer Isaac Asimov. The animals are on their own path of spiritual evolution. We, as beings gifted with upright posture and opposable thumbs—and thus with a distinct physical advantage—have a responsibility to aid them in their spiritual progress, even as the Great Masters such as Jesus and Buddha had a responsibility to us. We should treat them, then, as we would like the Great Masters to treat us—in accordance with Christ's message of "Love your neighbor as yourself," and, "As ye have done to the least of these my brethren, so ye have done it unto me."[12] End of sermon.

BECOMING HUMAN

Somewhat late in the course of the evolution of life on Earth, after the extinction of the dinosaurs and the first flourishing of mammals, a yang, Fourth Ray entity took an interest in an intelligent ape-like species that was just beginning to swing out of its original arboreal home in the African jungle and learn to walk upright so that it could

---

12 Matthew 25:40.

use its hands. The entity decided to create a superspecies—and thus marked the beginning of the human race.

Many of our subjects, when taken back through past-life regressions, recall the experience of the separation of the soul group from the Monad. Witness the following excerpt from the regression of a thirty-eight-year-old private investigator:

I'm in heaven. It is all light and music here. I sense the presence of God, and of several angels like myself. We are all one, and yet we are not. I can't explain it

...I'm falling; I've been cast out. I'm falling down to Earth. I feel intense sorrow from the separation. The light is all behind me; I'm spinning down into the dark.

This man associated his experience with that of Lucifer and came out of his regression actually believing that he was the Devil. It took me at least an hour to convince him that this was highly unlikely to have been the case.

From a thirty-two-year-old jewelry and dress designer:

There are many of us here and we are all going in one direction. Everything around us seems blue. I'm happy. What an adventure! I'm excited about going down to earth...I'm alone, but the others are still with me. I can't explain that.

I eventually find myself in a room. I'm a child; my mother looks lovingly down upon me. I am surprised; intrigued, fascinated. This is all so new.

I find it interesting that one of these people was totally unwilling to split from the soul group while the other thought it a great adventure. Our files reveal many different reactions to this experience—all reflecting the fact that the soul group was separating into individual entities, each with its own unique reaction.

THE BUDDHIC PLANE

Once the soul group has divided, the individual entities descend to the Buddhic plane—or the Realm of the Higher Self. On this level, the soul is still totally conscious of its divine origin, possesses a vast cosmic awareness, and rests in the security of that knowledge. The descent of the entity onto the Buddhic plane marks the first appearance of what we could call an earthly body, or vehicle. The Buddhic vehicle, however, is so subtle in nature that it would be virtually impossible for anyone now in incarnation to perceive because of the present rate of vibration of earthly matter.

It is on the Buddhic plane that many seem to have taken incarnation in ancient civilizations such as Atlantis or Lemuria. In those days, according to occult sources, the world was not as dense as it is now, and therefore it was possible for entities on the Buddhic level to make appearances on earth. This explains the conundrum that researchers often confront when they regress subjects who recall being an extremely powerful being on an exalted level of consciousness in one lifetime and a primitive Neanderthal tribesman hundreds of thousands of years later. Witness the following statement:

> I'm in Lemuria, so long ago I can't really count the years. I'm a woman, at least six feet tall, with chin-length reddish hair. All the little people evolving here look me up to as a goddess. They are very small, like Munchkins, and their faces look like the statues on Easter Island. They consider me a goddess because I have great powers. I can heal; I can materialize objects; I can levitate. My name is Jaluyana.
>
> ...I'm flying up over the country. It is very beautiful, with tall grasses that are conscious and move on their own. As far as I know, I'm the only one like myself around. It's nice to be worshipped, but I'm lonely.

The woman who was the subject of this regression was, in a later session, told to go to her "first incarnation" on the planet, and found herself in early Europe, in the Upper Paleolithic era, thousands of years later. The only explanation for this inconsistency is that Jaluyana was an involutionary entity.

From a thirty-nine-year-old nurse:

I'm in Atlantis. I'm a young woman, a member of the priestly class and I work in the library. There are all kinds of wonderful scrolls and books here, containing the history of the world from the beginning of time.

There are others like me here. I keep the information, but I also am the information; I seem to know instinctively all the knowledge that is kept here. I know the secrets of the crystals, and the other ancient truths. I live a calm, quiet, peaceful life. Each of us wears a color in accordance with our function here in the library. My robe is green. Green is one of the highest of colors.

After the Buddhic experience is complete, the entity then projects itself onto the lower planes—the higher mental, the lower mental, the astral, the etheric, and finally the physical. At each level it acquires another body, each more dense than the previous one.

I have often been asked about the channeled teachings of alleged Ascended Masters which state that the soul has the capacity to divide and subdivide endlessly, like an amoeba, so that many people can share the same past-life experience. I am not familiar with the teachings in question, but I have a feeling they are misinterpreted. Our research reveals that the soul dividing and subdividing can and does happen—*but only on the involutionary arc*. Once physical incarnation occurs and the entity enters the evolutionary loop, the emphasis is not on separation, but on getting back together. There is little if any drive to create new fragments to enter into a myriad of new bodies; the drive is to *transcend* the need for physical bodies and rejoin those from whom we were separated in the process of involution. Occasionally, in times of great planetary or personal need, a phenomenon called *parallel selves* arises, when the soul takes incarnation in two places at once, but according to our research, this phenomenon is somewhat rare.

THE FOUNTAIN OF OBLIVION

Between the astral and etheric planes, the entity passes through a point which I call the "Fountain of Oblivion." This term is borrowed from the Oz books by L. Frank Baum. The Fountain of Oblivion stood outside the gates of the Emerald City, and anyone who drank from it automatically forgot everything about his past—including his name and where he came from. I use the term to signify the point at which the veil is dropped and the entity loses all knowledge of its divine origin.

There does, however, appear to be a minute number of souls that never fully received the impact of the Fountain of Oblivion and who retain some subconscious knowledge of their divine origin, buried away in a deep recess of the mind. These people generally compose the ranks of the pioneers of mysticism, psychism, and new religious movements. When I began working with past-life regression in the mid-1970s, nearly everyone I regressed appeared to fall into this category. Now, of course, the benefits of past-life regression are known to nearly everyone and practically no one new who comes to my colleagues and me now seems to be one of these beings. However, this is merely an interesting aside; it does not really matter. The New Age is about reawakening knowledge of the divine origin of every life form—whether or not a grain of such awareness remains from the passage through the Fountain of Oblivion.

THE PLEROMA STAGE

After the Fountain, the entity then enters the *pleroma* stage, where it "floats" through the etheric plane on earth with no conscious awareness of anything except a vague sense of unity with its environment. Many people remember the pleroma stage. Consider the following regression transcript from a twenty-five-year-old female singer/songwriter:

There's a bird flying overhead. But I am the bird, at least I'm flying with it. And I'm also the tree, and the ground. But I'm not really centered into any of them. I seem to be everywhere. It's a great feeling.

Then I rise into the air and explore the leaves higher up in the tree, and watch the birds. They don't seem to be aware of me.

At some point during the elemental stage, the entity proceeds to take incarnation. The involutionary arc is complete, and the entity is ready to enter into the evolutionary cycle. This will be covered in the next chapter.

STAGE FOUR: CENTAUR

The search for inner peace begins. The beginnings of a sense of unity with all Creation, and awareness of the benefits of serving others. Psychic abilities may manifest. The quest for enlightenment begins, though it may at times battle with residual desires for sensual pleasures. First stirrings of self-healing and full chakra openings. Chakra correspondence: Heart.

First awareness of the God within.

STAGE THREE: HIGH EGOIC

The flowering of civilization. The beginnings of desire for worldly attainment. Desire for ego-gratification at all costs. Firm belief that the individual has all the answers and the game of "mine is better than yours." Desire for power and control. The growth of pragmatism. Chakra correspondence: Solar plexus.

STAGE TWO: EARLY EGOIC

First stirrings of karma. Awareness of the entity as an individual. Sensual gratification primary motivation. Love present as a selfish form of attachment. Flourishing of organized religion. Beginnings of writing, recordkeeping, history, commerce, agriculture, architecture - and war. Chakra correspondence: Sexual center.

STAGE ONE: PRE-EGOIC

First incarnation on the earthly plane, and the beginnings of the evolutionary loop. No memories of previous loops or lives, or of the Divine Origin. Fear the predominant emotion. Love and compassion totally absent in the earliest incarnations. The birth of speech, toolmaking, music, art, horticulture. Chakra correspondence: Root.

STAGE FIVE: GURU

Much negative earthly karma released and very little being acquired. May achieve total past life recall. Nearly full psychic awareness and growing sense of unity with the inner God. Almost full development of the eight chakras. Incapable of violence against other life forms. Some need for ego gratification, which can be be the last earthly hurdle to overcome. Chakra correspondence: Throat.

Last stage requiring earthly incarnation.

STAGE SIX: EARLY LIGHT MASTERS

They have begun to touch the face of God and are not yet complete with their karma but are very close. The beginning of a sense of power from the open chakras. Near-complete power over the material world. Release of almost all earthly desires. God-realization. Chakra correspondence: Brow.

STAGE SEVEN: FULL LIGHT MASTERS

The purpose of this stage in the Aquarian Age is to set an example for the masses by attaining a Christlike existence and lifestyle. Total forgiveness, near perfect physical body. Reunion with the soul group. Beginnings of solar consciousness. Chakra correspondence: Crown.

STAGE EIGHT: COMPLETION

The finishing of the loop in the Aquarian Age. Completion of all karma and the choice of accepting the role of the Boddhisattva or moving on to join the Absolute. Reunion with the Monad. Total solar consciousness. Chakra correspondence: Alta major centre.

STAGE NINE
THE PATH TO
THE UNKNOWN

STAGES OF DEVELOPMENT

TWO

Stages of Development

Human Beings Rejoining God

Almost from the beginning of psychoanalytic theory it was apparent that the human personality goes through changes in its psychic structure throughout the course of its life. The newborn infant, it was determined, reacts differently to events and happenings in its life than the six-month-old, and certainly much more differently than the adolescent or adult does. Freud, with his emphasis on the Oedipus complex, was the first to make this observation. A young male child may fall in love with his mother, while the older child or adolescent still may secretly bear strong attachments to his mother, but simultaneously feels a powerful drive to break from her—and this is the side of him which he emphasizes, both publicly and to himself.

This is only one example of a change in consciousness over the course of development. Other examples are legion, and for this reason Freud's successors saw the need for a separate school of thought to define these changes and how they affect the growing personality, therefore dictating how the therapist should deal with each individual. Among the pioneers of this concept were Carl Jung, Jean Piaget, Silvano Arieti, Heinz Werner, and H. L. Russell. The result of their research and observations is called *developmental psychology.*

Because it was found to be universally applicable and useful, developmental psychology flourished, and it is still used today by therapists who work with children. Developmental psychology traces the changes in the psyche from birth to the attainment of adulthood and covers such diverse factors as cognitive evolvement, learning theory, moral maturation, psychosexual stages, motivational, affective, and intellectual progress, as well as role appropriation.

In recent years, psychologist and Buddhist scholar Ken Wilber has taken developmental psychology beyond the limits of the mainstream and into transpersonal realms, using his knowledge of Eastern philosophy to expound upon the growth of spiritual potential in the human soul in addition to all the matters outlined above. While other developmental psychologists concentrate on progression from the earliest moments of life to maturity, Wilber continues, tracing the human potential for spirituality from maturity to beyond death. His theories were first publicized in his monumental work, *The Atman Project.*[13] Wilber takes his view a step further by projecting his conception of the stages of development onto the development of the human race as a whole, in *Up from Eden.*[14]

---

13 Ken Wilber. *The Atman Project.* Wheaton, IL: The Theosophical Publishing House. 1980).

14 Ken Wilber, *Up From Eden.* (New York: Harper & Row. 1985).

When I first became acquainted with Wilber's work, I was struck by the parallels between Wilber's stages of development and the "ages" of the soul put forth in metaphysical works such as *Messages from Michael* by Chelsea Quinn Yarbro[15] and Alice A. Bailey's *Esoteric Psychology I and II*. I then drew upon my years of experience with past-life regression and realized that the soul, as well as the race and the personality, also goes through various stages of development from the point of incarnation through attainment of full solar consciousness. I went to my files and studied my case histories carefully; the idea of stages explained many puzzling anomalies that had come up throughout the course of my work.

Why, for example, did most of my clients find it difficult to identify with their incarnations as primitive humans—and why were physical and emotional problems rooted in those incarnations so hard to get rid of, whereas those from later incarnations sometimes disappeared as if by magic? Why was it that clients who in previous incarnations had been kings, generals, abbesses, and successful merchants seemed to lack the drive in their current incarnations to seek out the vast successes attained by their former personalities? Why did they allow themselves to become enmeshed in financial insecurity when three or four lifetimes ago they had fulfilled every person's dream of success? And why did these same people, when taken back two thousand years or more, recall lifetimes in which they indulged in the rankest kinds of physical pleasures, sometimes involving blatant cruelty? I began to view my case histories—and the current incarnations of friends, associates and clients—in a new light.

I came to the conclusion that the stages of development of the soul, while roughly paralleling those of the personality and the race, were

---

15 Chelsea Quinn Yarbro, *Messages from Michael*. (New York: Berkley. 1980)

ever so slightly different. My friend and colleague, Edward Sparks, when reviewing my observations, noted a distinct parallel between the stages of development and the chakra system—the seven traditional chakras and the eighth, or *alta major* center, in the base of the skull. Everything seemed to be coming together. And I found myself having much greater success with my clients.

I therefore came to believe that knowledge of the Stages of Development is vital to our understanding of ourselves and others. An individual on Stage Two is going to react differently to events, problems, relationships, and other stimuli than a person on Stage Three or Four. When guiding clients through past-life regression, it is important at least to make an educated guess as to the stage of the personality the client is recalling, because in order to clear a particular trauma completely both the therapist and the client need to know how the past personality reacted to the Number One incident causing the trauma, and to the engram bank that probably resulted from similar incidents In subsequent incarnations. The best way to discern the stage of a past personality is by noting the behavior and attitudes described by the client—and to use a lot of intuition.

One modern school of psychology with which I have always disagreed strongly is behaviorism. Founded by the late B. F. Skinner, behaviorism holds that treasured human concepts such as freedom, dignity, love, honor, respect, and so on are all illusory and the only true reality in human life is observable behavior. To me this philosophy represents the most negative and pessimistic approach to human beings that could ever be conceptualized, and I am hard pressed to envision any therapeutic benefits such an approach could possibly have. Yet in determining the stage of development and Ray vibration of a client, I find myself constantly using one of Skinner's methods—careful and detailed observation of a client's behavior. I maintain that all inspired theories probably contain at least a portion of the truth. Perhaps B. F. Skinner keyed into the idea that the only sure key to a person's inner nature lies in observable behavior—an insight colored in his conclusions, no doubt, by the fact that he was a confirmed atheist.

It is important for any kind of enlightened psychotherapist—past-life or otherwise—to know the client's stage of development. However, in most cases this is not difficult. Most people who voluntarily approach psychotherapists are on either late Stage Three or early Stage Four. The confusion that leads a person to seek more understanding of herself almost never appears before late Stage Three, and by late Stage Four most individuals have probably come to terms with their situation in life and forgiven themselves and everyone else—and hence have little need for past-life regression work.

Spiritually speaking, the stages of development can help many followers of revived old religions to understand the history of their "new" faiths. Modern Goddess worshipers, for example, often are bothered by the idea that their ancient forebears who practiced the religion of the Great Goddess might have made use of blood sacrifice—human *or* animal. Some seem to feel that if ritual killing were practiced in Old Europe, it invalidates the entire worth of worshipping the Great Goddess. So in their writings they often take a defensive standpoint and deny that such sacrifices ever took place—in spite of the archaeological and anthropological evidence which, though admittedly inconclusive, indicates that such sacrifices might indeed have taken place.

However, when one realizes that the ancient practitioners of this religion were most likely on Stage One or Two—periods in history when fear and survival were the driving forces in the human psyche—one can understand a little better why the ancients might have done this. There were no meteorologists to warn them of killer storms, no seismologists to prepare them for earthquakes, no Josephs to inform them of impending famines. Their fear of such phenomena, coupled with the drive to survive at all costs, along with their self-centered attitudes, caused them to treat the Great Mother the way they would treat a human enemy: bribe her with valuable gifts. And to their minds the most valuable gift was blood.

The neo-pagans who now worship the Great Goddess are probably mostly on Stage Four, which, as we will see, involves an awakening of the soul to certain levels of spiritual truth. Stage Fours are aware, either consciously or unconsciously, of the fact that the only sacrifice God or Goddess requires of human beings is the sacrifice of the idea of sepa-rateness from God/Goddess—and all paths lead toward Unity with the Absolute. So honoring the Great Mother or the Great Goddess, as well as drumming, dancing around the fire and chanting the names of the Goddess is as valid a path to enlightenment as any—whatever our long-ago ancestors may have done.

The Stages of Development of the soul, as drawn from my many psy-chological and metaphysical sources and my own experience with past-life regression, are as follows.

STAGE ONE: PRE-EGOIC

This stage marks the first appearance of the soul into incarnation. The entity is fresh from the *pleroma* stage and, in spite of the fact that it now inhabits a physical body, still sees no difference between itself and the world around it. This is basically the stage of "animal man," and the entity's primary focus is to learn about the world and how to survive in it. Therefore the ego, here defined as a sense of individuality, is virtually nonexistent. Apparently at this stage the entity is intended to get to know the world rather than to know himself. There have been few if any past lives and therefore the person has minimal experience or memory. Because of this, there is little capacity for acknowledging the input of others. These factors, along with the lack of a sense of uniqueness, ren-der the differentiation of an individual ego virtually impossible, and so I refer to Stage One as the "Pre-Egoic" stage. The dominant emotion at this stage is fear—fear for the entity's own survival. Stage One can last for many, many lifetimes. The first few levels of Stage One are called the *uroboric substage.*

In the uroboric substage the entity possesses no time-consciousness. The entity has no sense of the beginning and end of anything; there is only now. Therefore, though the person may pick up a stick to aid him in digging a hole, or a stone with which to kill an enemy or food-animal, toolmaking skills do not exist because he has no sense of the idea of beginning a tool and finishing it unless there is a more advanced soul around to teach him. Stage One souls can be taught simple skills, but do not always retain the knowledge for any lengthy period of time.

In Stage One, on the uroboric level, the entity at first views the world from the standpoint of a sense of unity, seeing himself as one with everything around him, but this pre-personal sense of unity is not to be confused with the transpersonal unity that exists before the involutionary process or as the cycle of evolution comes to an end. Eventually, the entity develops a sense of "me" and "not-me," and views himself as virtually alone and very special, and the world (and everyone else in it) as something hostile that threatens this "me" and its survival. For this reason, fear becomes the dominant emotion.

Because of the lack of ego differentiation, because of the pre-personal sense of unity with his surroundings, the Stage One soul on the uroboric level does not see any difference between waking reality and the world of dreams. For him, the monster who threatens him in a dream is as real as the bears of the forest. Therefore in the uroboric substage there is no sense of other worlds beyond our own, nor is there any sense of deity.

There are very few Stage One souls left on the planet right now, although a few may still exist in remote areas. In the early part of the twentieth century, the mystic T. H. White was visiting a Tibetan monastery. The monks told him of the existence of a primitive tribe they referred to as the "Snowmen" (not to be confused with the Abominable Snowmen or Yeti). According to the monks, the Snowmen were human beings with potential for spiritual development, but they were so totally overwhelmed by fear that they probably wouldn't be able to explore that potential for centuries. Most of the people now living on Planet Earth went through Stage One, particularly the uroboric substage, in the Paleolithic or Neolithic periods.

At this point the entity is only just beginning to explore his sense of himself as an individual, and therefore the ego is not differentiated from the pre-personal self. Because of this lack of ego identity, anyone taken back through past-life regression into this stage finds it a difficult experience to relive. This can prove unfortunate because most of our serious hangups, as well as chronic physical problems, the ones we have the hardest time exorcising, have their origins in the uroboric substage. They are difficult to alleviate because at the uroboric level, any traumatic experience is much more devastating than it would be at a later stage. Such an experience was always complicated by an overwhelming and intense fear for survival.

For example, in later stages marked by a fully developed ego, loss of one's mother produces grief, but most people at these levels know that they will be able to pick up the pieces and go on. For a being at the uroboric level, however, who is accustomed to depending on his mother for his survival, loss of the mother indicates that without her he can no longer survive. Whether or not the person eventually does manage to survive is immaterial; the psyche is indelibly marked not only by the grief that accompanies a traumatic loss, but by the fear for one's own survival generated by that loss. Entities on the uroboric level are incapable of looking back and realizing that their fears were groundless because there is no sense of time and little memory.

This substage actually parallels the newborn infant stage. As the newborn infant has no sense of time, when he sees his mother leaving the room in his mind she is gone forever—and the resulting fear creates an intense fear for his own survival. For the soul-entity on the uroboric substage, any traumatic event in his life has the same effect. In other words, if he is caught in a fire or swept away by rapids he has no sense of its ever being over. Even if he runs or swims for his life, in his mind the fear and pain are a permanent part of his life. This is further complicated by the fact that the current personality with a fully differentiated ego often has a difficult time identifying with a pre-Egoic individual—though such people seem to know the person they are tuning into is them. Often, ridding oneself of the engram banks generated by a Stage One traumatic event requires help from healers in other fields. I once worked with a young woman in her late twenties named Ardith, who since a serious automobile accident had been plagued by severe back pain. Nothing seemed to help—not chiropractic adjustments, not medication, not even painful surgery. She turned to past-life regression as a last resort. Her regression revealed that her back problem had its roots in something that had happened to her back in "cave man" times, when she was still on the uroboric substage. Her previous personality had been male, about nineteen years old.

> I find myself standing outside my cave. I am terrified. I know there are others here, but I don't know who they are. I only know I'm afraid of them.
>
> ...It's our enemies. They belong to a neighboring tribe. They know I'm alone and they're chasing me. I trip and they find me. They are piercing my back with their spears, again and again. Then they leave me in my pain. It took me a long time to die.

Ardith reported that the feeling of fear she had experienced in that life had permeated the very being of her previous personality. She also said that at first she had found it "very hard to be there."

Though Ardith's back pain was eased somewhat by her regression work, it did not go away. She still had to pay regular visits to the chiropractor and take medication in order to go about her life without pain.

Another client was on the verge of divorce. His wife adored cats and felt incomplete without their company. Yet this man—a big, strapping football-player type—was terrified of cats and froze up whenever one came near him. Naturally, he didn't want cats around.

But his wife saw his fear as irrational and his refusal to allow her to have a cat as selfishness.

In order to save his marriage, my client resorted to past-life therapy. Regressions revealed that as a Neanderthal huntsman, he was hunting with his twin brother when the latter was killed by a huge cat-like animal. While my client reported a memory of running as quickly as he could back toward the cave, he said he could never get over the idea that the cat would eventually come back to get him, too.

This experience, like all Number One incidents, was reinforced in many later lives. In one, he was a sacrifice in Egypt to the cat goddess Bast; in the seventeenth century he was a woman accused of being a witch and subsequently burned simply because the "witch" owned a pet—a black cat. When he awakened from his regression, my client was so overwhelmed by the fear generated by the Number One incident—and its carryover into other lifetimes—that I had to leave him alone to sit for half an hour to allow it all to dissipate.

While his fear of cats had not totally disappeared, at least he was aware of the reason for it. He was determined to deal with his fear rather than knuckle under to it, and so he allowed his wife to adopt two kittens. Eventually he discovered that he liked the little creatures, with their soft fur, affectionate and playful nature, and loud purrs. Only the direct experience that cats weren't so bad after all served to finally exorcise the fear that had plagued my client since the Paleolithic era.

One psychological hangup that virtually everyone suffers from, that almost always has its roots in the uroboric substage, is the consideration, "Whatever I love dies." This consideration appears to be at the bottom of so many relationship problems that it seems to be almost universal. As a significant percentage of our clients come to my colleagues and me because of problems in either current or past relationships, I find it necessary to emphasize the karmic source of this consideration for at least eighty percent of my clients.

Apparently, many times, in the course of cave-man incarnations on the uroboric level, virtually everyone experienced the death of a mother. Or, she went out of the cave and never returned, and the child was left to survive on his own. The intense fear for one's own survival that follows loss of the mother—the only being those in the uroboric substage come close to feeling love for—is beyond the scope of our present imaginations.

The seed of fear planted by this Number One incident in the psyches of those long-ago children is reinforced incarnation after incarnation, because unless one dies shortly after birth it is practically impossible to go through life without losing many people one loves. Eventually what seems to result is an unwillingness to enter into a relationship that involves true intimacy. Hence, the vast number of unhappy marriages, shattered friendships, and the skyrocketing divorce rate.

This consideration is very, very difficult to expunge. Past-life regression, followed by counseling by an enlightened therapist or by one of the many fine psychotechnological seminars on relationships that are available today, can be helpful—but often, no matter how much the individual works at exorcising this fear, a trace of it always seems to remain. However, the knowledge of the past life experience can provide a focusing point (or a copout, if you prefer) for understanding one's reactions when the excitement that heralds the start of a new relationship is all too often followed by the panic symptomatic of the fear of intimacy.

The second substage of Stage One is called the *typhonic* substage. By the typhonic substage, the entity is totally aware of the existence of others, but still has not developed a true sense of love or trust for them; the person's view of the world is still basically "me" and "not-me. The entity perceives others as mere extensions of himself, and has no concept that they may have needs or desires of their own. Selfishness dominates all relationships; the entity wants only to impose his will on others.

The primary mover in the being's psyche is still instinct, but use of a rudimentary intellect does gradually increase, at a pace peculiar to each individual. This substage parallels the level a child reaches at the age of about six months. Though fear is still a dominant factor, it no longer is the sole or primary emotion; the individual begins to experience other elementary emotions such as rage, greed, pleasure, and desire. The predominating drive in typhonic personalities is still survival, but the increasing awareness of the pleasure and desire principles gives rise to the need to seek physical pleasure and to gratify one's desires. Rapidly developing memory skills lead to a rudimentary awareness of the past and some sense of history, but there is still basically no sense of the future beyond a day or so.

By this time, therefore, the individual has learned that if he sets out to make a tool, he will finish it. If the mother, or another familiar companion, leaves the cave, he knows she will return. However, it is only in the latter levels of this substage that a true sense of time—and possibly outgrowths of this such as storytelling—emerge.

In the early days of animal man, it was the typhonic substage that gave rise to the existence of the *shaman*. While some sources maintain that the shamans were the first great Masters, this is a misconception. The great Masters such as Jesus or Buddha have completed the process of evolution; the original shamans had only begun it. The shamans were, however, according to Ken Wilber, the first successful practitioners of kundalini yoga, and the first to be aware of a guiding intelligence beyond themselves.[16]

How did the kundalini initially become active in these primitive tribesmen? There are many different theories. First of all, it has been speculated that in the typhonic substage of development, the entity is

---

16 Wilber, *Up From Eden*, p. 112.

aware that the dream life is different from the waking life. To the typhonic soul, the dream life is still as real as the waking, but he is aware that it is *different*. A potential typhonic shaman may have discovered the phenomenon of the lucid dream, in which the dreamer controls his dreaming experience. Therefore he may have drawn the conclusion that he can control his outer environment in a similar way—and possessed enough personal power and charisma to convince his fellow tribesmen that he has this power. This may have given rise to such phenomena as bone-pointing, in which members of a primitive tribe firmly believe that if their witch doctor points his bone at them, they will die immediately—and so they do!

Another theory is that the potential shaman had what is now known as a near-death experience, and thus was awakened to knowledge of worlds other than the physical one. Still another idea is that the original shamans were habitual consumers of psychedelic plants, which increased their abilities to see beyond the material. Or it is altogether possible that the original shamans belonged to that small group of entities who never fully passed through the Fountain of Oblivion. Or it could have been all of the above.

The healing abilities of witch doctors are said to arise from the phenomenon of autosuggestion and from primitive herbalism. How they attained the knowledge that certain plants cure certain diseases is a mystery. Some speculate that the Powers that Be gave a hint in that parts of the plant resembled the organs whose ills they cured. Other scholars theorize that the shamans observed the effects of the consumption of these plants upon animals. Both these theories may have hit upon part of the truth, but there has to have been some intuition involved. The chance of hit-or-miss experimentation resulting in such a miraculous herbal pharmacopoeia as is known to even the most primitive of remote tribes today would appear to be slim indeed.

Many of my clients with acute psychic abilities trace their origins to Stage One lifetimes on the typhonic level. The following excerpts are some examples.

From a woman who had always possessed a powerful imagination and a rich dream life, and who began working as a psychic at the age of twenty-seven:

> I am the tribal medicine man...We live in a desert area, with red cliffs all around. I am tall, lean, hawk-nosed, handsome; I wear nothing but a loincloth. I spend most of my days alone, searching for rocks, shells, plants in the desert. There is someone who follows me around—I guess he's something of an apprentice, but I don't seem to pay much attention t him, or to anyone else for that matter. The only face I can focus on is my own. I can read oracles in the fire, and it scares everyone else in the tribe. I seem to like that.

From a teacher of Silva Mind Control:

> [In answer to a question about the mother] I don't know who she is; I don't seem to care. I only care about the medicine man. I follow him everywhere; I love the headdress he wears; I love all the necklaces he has around his neck—beads and shells and claws. I want to be just like him, to learn everything he knows. He doesn't seem to like me much, but he is flattered by my attentions. I tell him that I will be just like him, that one day I may even be better. He seems to think that's funny, but I don't. I want to become the best medicine woman there is.

This client seemed to see her studies of Silva Mind Control as continuing her efforts to become the best possible medicine woman.

Once the lessons of awareness of self and separation of ego consciousness are learned, the entity goes through the process of individualization. This process represents the emerging of the soul from the pre-personal sense of unity and initiates the entity into the world of apparent separateness and individuality. The entity has accomplished the task of getting used to the physical world and begins the long journey back to the Divine. "A Son of God," says Djwahl Khul, "is born." The entity, in short, has experienced the world of nature and is now ready to experience himself.

STAGE TWO: EARLY EGOIC

The entity, having passed through the individualization process, is aware of herself as an individual and is just beginning to glory in her new self-awareness. The first levels of Stage Two are called the *membership substage*.

As the ego is thoroughly differentiated at this point, the individual is totally aware of the presence of others, though she perceives them as "me" and "many other me's." After the process of individualization, the entity no longer experiences the primordial sense of unity with the environment and is totally aware of her apparent separateness from the rest of the world. Still, in the membership substage of Stage Two, the entity sees herself less as an individual with an intrinsic value as such and more as a member of the group. The good side of this trait is that the membership substage marks the first appearance of social consciousness, an awareness of the need to work for the good of the group, whether it be a tribe, a town, or whatever. The downside is that the individual is incapable of realizing that the interests of other individuals within the group may differ from hers, and therefore the person is shocked and often enraged when other members of the group do not share her interests, opinions, or needs, or make her the center of their universe. Conflicts can lead to violent arguments or even to bloody combat.

Once the individualization process is past and the ego is fully differentiated, the entity starts to develop its own unique brand of intellect. Intelligence varies of course with the individual, but for the most part, it has increased enough so that the person is capable of learning, retaining and using skills. In most cases, however, these skills are mainly imitative, and though the person may be an industrious and productive worker she rarely uses her own ingenuity to expand upon the basic learned skills or create new methods of working. Exceptions usually include Third and Seventh Ray types (Sages and Artisans) or any individual who karmically has chosen the path of exceptional intellect. But in any case, the entity operates less on the level of what is good for her as an individual and more from the consideration that the group—the tribe, village, or whatever comes first.

Often societies whose members are primarily operating from the membership level have strict rules regarding what is best for the group. There is little freedom, as there is not yet any concept that the individual has the capability to make her own decisions. Many taboos still practiced even in our "advanced" societies—such as the incest taboo— have their origin in membership societies where strict taboos were observed. One especially repugnant taboo was practiced in some ancient Celtic societies, where it was considered a heinous crime for the woman of a family to let the home fires go out. If she slipped up in this way, she was burned to death in a wicker basket.

At this point, the soul has acquired some karma, particularly if the individual's Stage One personalities expressed their fear through violence and sadism. In fact, Stage Two is where the soul acquires most of its so-called "negative karma," because the Stage Two soul is primarily concerned with itself. The membership substage has been compared to the "Terrible Two" stage in the development of the human personality, when the child's favorite words are "I," "me," and "mine." The early Stage Two soul, unconsciously reveling in her new knowledge of her own uniqueness, tends to take what she wants and couldn't care less if her needs and desires differ from those of others. In fact, the basic worldview of the soul on the membership level is that everyone in the world is just another "me" and therefore should need and want everything "I" want.

All Stage Two souls attract what is at least in their minds a lot of negative karma—but whether the majority of it involves murder and mayhem or not-so-serious peccadilloes depends basically on the Ray type.

(See Chapter Two). Souls derived from the First and Fourth Rays (Kings and Warriors) tend to be more aggressive and therefore more apt to resort to violence in order to take what they want. Second, Third, Fifth, and Seventh Ray souls (Priests, Sages, Scholars, and Artisans) are more reserved by nature and therefore are much less inclined toward violence than their First and Fourth Ray cousins. When operating at the Stage Two level, Priests, Sages, and Scholars tend to take what they want by deviousness rather than overt aggression.

Sixth Ray souls (Devotees) are, by definition, those who seek a person or an institution to serve. Therefore, whether they resort to violence or con games depends on the nature of the person or institution they serve. A Stage Two, Sixth Ray type could go from one incarnation as a Tibetan monk who spends all his life meditating on the face of his beloved Master to a subsequent incarnation as a soldier in the army of Genghis Khan—and his "negative karma" would be tailored accordingly.

This is not to say that some Kings and Warriors do not live reserved lives and acquire karma from those lives, or that Priests, Sages, Scholars, and Artisans do not live lives as murderers. They do. But these incarnations are in the minority. Because of the basic nonviolent nature of the Second, Third, Fifth, and Seventh Rays, however, one life in which violent deeds are committed often creates more guilt—and hence more "negative karma"—in the minds of Priests, Sages, and Scholars than two such lives in the minds of Kings, Warriors, or Devotees who adopt the creed of a bloodthirsty master.

A great many physical problems seem to be rooted in guilt, less because of actual crimes committed than over one's inability to do what the Stage Two mindset dictates she should. The following is an excerpt from the regression of a gentleman in his late forties (apparently a Second Ray soul), a schoolteacher who loved his work and his students, but who found his congenital deafness (total in one ear, partial in the other) impeded his ability to serve his students as well as he would have liked. He therefore sought to find the karmic source of his deafness and, hopefully, to heal it.

His regression revealed the following:

> I'm a priest. I'm in prison, in Spain during the Inquisition. I have been here for months.... They take people out and torture them, innocent people. I can here them screaming in pain, begging for mercy, but no one heeds them. It just goes on and on, night and day, and nothing can stop the screaming. And I can't help them!

Apparently his Higher Self, having mercy upon him, shut out the cries of the torture victims by taking away his sense of hearing.

I suggested to my client that he was no longer in that life, nor were the torture victims, who were probably now all reincarnated in new, healthy bodies, and that there was no longer any need for him to shut out their cries. I then took him through a healing meditation for the ear, and afterwards informed him that he should do it for himself every day. I spoke to him about three months later when I ran into him on the street. He informed me that he had finally been able to take the hearing aid off his good ear—and put it on the ear that was previously totally deaf.

The dangers inherent in membership consciousness involve mainly a misuse of the growing sense of good and evil. Traces of fear and distrust remain from Stage One, and are focused on fear for survival of the group rather than the individual. This is combined with the Stage Two tendency just to take whatever is wanted. A philosophy of "us versus them" appears—"us" representing good and, "them" being evil—therefore justifying mass murder and theft by "us" against "them."

Though most souls now living on Planet Earth went through the membership substage during the early days of civilization, Stage Two souls at the membership level still exist today. Some that exist in remote areas continue to pursue their way of life the way their ancestors did, causing no problems to other communities.

Others, however, can and do pose problems. There are entire nations (mostly in underdeveloped areas of the world) that are still composed predominately of Stage Two souls, some on the membership level—and relations between these nations and the governments of the more highly developed countries pose a diplomatic enigma to world leaders. Social conditions in these countries have changed very little since the early days of civilization, and thus the spiritual development of many of their citizens has been retarded because of the continuous necessity to concentrate on survival. Some prime examples are the countries in Southeast Asia—Cambodia, Laos, Vietnam—which caused so much tension throughout the world in the period from the mid-1960s to the early 1970s. One of the reasons the Vietnam war lasted for over thirty years was because the people didn't have the ability to communicate. There was no adjustment, no give and take, no real negotiation—possibly because the nations involved were still caught up in the "us versus them" way of thinking—and many so-called "First World" (Stage Three) countries exacerbated the situation by making use of it to suit their own ends.

There are also the primarily membership-oriented societies that exist in our inner cities, where membership consciousness takes the form of gangs. Highly fanatical religious groups try to push their ideas on others, often feeling perfectly justified in persecuting those who do not accept them, are another example. After an especially horrendous epidemic of gang murders in Southeast Los Angeles in 1989, a young man involved with one of the gangs in question was interviewed on the six o'clock news. When the reporter asked if he felt any pangs of conscience over the murders, the young man shook his head. "It's a matter of survival," he declared. "It's us versus them."

Another television interview in that same year centered on a certain foreign-born family that belonged to a rigid religious sect. The parents murdered their eldest daughter, on the grounds that she wanted to become an American and therefore rejected her family's religion.

Family members questioned in the course of the interview stated that they had no problem with their young relative's murder. Because she was not a dutiful daughter, they stated, she deserved to be killed.

Like this religious sect, some ghetto gangs follow a very strict code of conduct. Such gangs have been known to punish errant members as horrendously as boys from rival gangs—even as the ancient Celts would burn a woman to death if she let the home fires go out. For this reason, one's leaders and authority figures are often feared as much as one's enemies.

Extreme racism or religious prejudice, practiced by modern-day cults such as the Ku Klux Klan or various racist-fundamentalist religious groups, is a direct reflection of attitudes peculiar to membership societies. The overwhelming conviction that "we" are good and "they" are evil, and that "God is on our side" still leads to incredible atrocities that the groups inevitably feel are totally vindicated—particularly when compounded by the same horrendous fear that dominated in Stage One and which can be keyed in by reinforcing events, such as a calamitous raid by "them." While a few of the members of these groups aren't necessarily on the membership level, the social conditions in which they grow up can cause them to respond to Number One incidents in long-ago lifetimes in which they were on that level, possibly when "we" were wiped out by "them." Response to this Number One incident could well have been triggered in the current life by racist or religious attitudes dominating the community into which the entity was born.

And yet the concept of right and wrong—and therefore of "sin"—is also very strong, so at the end of the membership substage guilt for atrocities performed by "us" against "them" often remains, taking the form of "negative karma" in later lifetimes.

At mid-Stage Two there often appear one or more lifetimes in which the entity, having broken through the limitations of the membership substage, seems to spend her time doing exactly what she wants—sowing wild oats, so to speak. These lifetimes are spent primarily enjoying sensual pleasures—drinking, overspending, gluttony, promiscuity. The purpose of these lifetimes is apparently to satisfy the thirst for physical pleasure so that in later lives one can concentrate more on developing the intellect and intuition. Sometimes it satisfies the drive, more or less; sometimes it doesn't, depending on the entity's capacity for attachment.

Witness the following transcript of the regression of a talented and successful artist:

I'm a traveler, somewhere in the Middle East. No, I don't seem to be going anywhere in particular, I just wander. Right now I seem to be in the middle of a marketplace. [Laughs] I just shoplifted a gold medallion from one of the merchants here and I'm going to sell it to another!

…There's a girl here. She's the daughter of a merchant. Her name is Cassandra. I think it's you. She has her eye on me, and I like her too. We sneak off to her tent and spend the day together…No, it wasn't any great romance, just a passing thing. But I liked you, nonetheless. I'm spending the evening drinking, in some son of tavern. There's a musician there playing the flute, and someone telling stories like the Arabian Nights. It's nice. The next day I move on.

[Asked if this lifetime contributed to his artistic talent] I don't think so. I think I spent my life just the way I spent that one day I just told you about. I steal to get money, then spend my time drinking and whoring. (Laughs) It wasn't a very productive life, but I sure had a great time!

[Asked if this way of life had any moral implications for him] I really don't think so. Too many other people were doing just the same thing. I didn't think I was doing anything more wrong than anyone else was. The merchants were con men, so they deserved to be stolen from. I never took a woman who didn't want me. And the drinking hurt no one but me. I think the main purpose of that incarnation was just to have a good time…

The latter levels of Stage Two are called the *early mental* substage. On this level, the entity leaves the security of membership consciousness and begins to think for herself. The entity finally is totally aware of

herself as a unique individual, with talents and abilities that can benefit her as well as the rest of the group.

An important development in the early mental substage is the realization of one's own niche in society. A soldier who is good at fighting
takes pride in himself as a soldier and starts thinking of himself as "a
soldier." A cook does the same; as does a shoemaker, scribe, or king. The
positive aspect of this tendency is that the person develops self-worth
and a sense of pride. The downside is that the individual becomes
attached to her niche; hence so much of the "reverse snobbery" that can
exist among the working class, especially in some European countries,
making it appear unthinkable to try to raise oneself beyond one's station in life.

The acknowledgment of oneself as a unique individual leads to the
acknowledgment of others' uniqueness and their accomplishments.
Hence the desire nature, formerly focused mainly on gratifying physical
needs, becomes transmuted into love. The desire for the companion-
ship of those whom one respects leads to friendships; desire for a wife
or husband leads to romantic love. A sense of respect and awe (rather
than fear) for those who have accomplished more than the entity leads
to love and loyal service for one's overlord, rather than forced servitude.
By the same token, betrayal can lead to intense hatred and falling back
upon the tendencies toward violence, which for many comes with Stage
Two.

The majority of the souls in the world reached the early mental substage when language skills flourished to the point where history was
being recorded. This is the first appearance of awareness of the distant
past and the far future. However, it is at the point of the early mental
substage that our estimates of the majority of the souls on this earth
break down. Again, most of the souls now on Planet Earth went
through Stage One in "cave man" times; most went through the membership substage during the early days of civilization. However, every
soul advances at its own pace, according to its own karma and level of

attachment to the status quo. Therefore, even though most of the souls now on Planet Earth entered the early mental substage at the time of the beginning of history, a significant number of souls incarnate today are still operating on that level.

The early mental substage is marked by the beginnings of differentiated ego states. The entity is beginning to absorb and manifest attitudes and behavior patterns from other people around her, such as parents and other role models. She finally sees herself as a unique individual, separate from the group as well as from the rest of the world, with a value all her own. In some, depending upon Ray vibration, karma, and attachment, there is developed the "I'm great" syndrome. The individual has lived many lifetimes, and traces of these personalities and their experience remain in the subconscious and can be activated by similar events in the person's life. The early mental substage parallels the point at which the child starts to show curiosity and to show off for her mother—generally at about ages three or four.

During my Hollywood years many of my clients were aspiring actors, actresses, musicians, and so on. As is well known, it is very difficult to succeed in the entertainment industry, and sometimes it involves compromise as well as dedication and determination. I was often amazed by the number of hopefuls who would deliberately turn down or subconsciously blow incredible opportunities that any aspiring entertainer would have given his eyeteeth to have.

I found that most of these career blocks could be traced to lifetimes in the early mental period, where the person was a member of the working class and was totally satisfied with her niche and content to stay there. Now, after many subsequent incarnations, subconsciously they were still clinging to that comfortable niche they were so proud of long ago—but which, for them, had long since become redundant and obsolete.

Career blocks dating from the early mental period can sometimes be as difficult to exorcise as hangups dating from Stage One, particularly if this determination to keep to one's place persists throughout several lifetimes. However, it can be done if the person genuinely wants to break free. If the client isn't successful at letting go of this attachment, perhaps she needs to acknowledge that deep down she really doesn't want to be what she thinks she should want to be.

Witness the following regression excerpt from an aspiring young actress who had a way of getting sick or otherwise excusing herself whenever she had a major audition or other opportunity:

My twin sister wants to marry the master's son. I'll tell you a secret, it's not her he loves, it's me. He just wants her because she looks like me. But they'll never let him marry her; she is only the daughter of a tenant farmer.

[Asked if she would have married the master's son if she could] Of course not. I am only the daughter of a tenant farmer. It wouldn't be right.

[Asked if she would prefer to be in the same social class as the master's son] That won't happen. I could never be good enough to be in that class.

Apparently she had carried the latter consideration over into her current life, believing she wasn't worthy to be a successful actress.

From an aspiring rock musician:

I'm a soldier, in the army of the king of England. I'm just a simple peasant boy, a foot soldier who wants to fight as hard as he can for his king. We're marching into battle…I fought well; I did both myself and my king proud.

…The king wants to reward me for my valor. He wants to knight me! But I don't want to be knighted! I'm not a knight; I'm just a simple foot soldier. [Asked why he didn't want to be a knight] I don't know…

[Long pause, then tears] It's the fucking horses, man! I've never been able to bring myself to ride one. I'm terrified of them! If I become a knight I'll have to ride, and I'm afraid! But I can't insult the king. *I have to let him knight me…*

One tends to wonder if this client's previous personality had really been that afraid of horses or if he simply wanted to avoid the responsibility of being a knight. His fear of horses (and presumably of responsibility) and the resulting determination to remain in his place were still keeping him from reaching his goal of success as a rock musician. After the regression, he took a good long look at what was holding him back. He then admitted that he had never cared for horseback riding and probably never would. But there was no need to allow that particular dislike to keep him from achieving his goals any longer. Once he acknowledged that, his career began to take off. He is now quite successful, playing in a band that tours Europe often as the opening act at concerts for established stars.

During the early mental period, particularly in Second and Sixth Ray types, religious faith can grow by leaps and bounds, and the sense of deity becomes clear. Even though religion at this point is probably marked by dogma and prejudice, the growth of faith is a step in the right direction. It promotes a sense of avoidance of sin, of the growth of self-control over the baser desires of the flesh. Therefore when the entity has reached the full sense of ego-self that is developed in Stage Two, she undergoes the process known as the First Initiation. The First Initiation signifies that the entity has rejected domination of the soul by the lower needs of the body and aspires toward purification. It goes without saying that few, if any, of the soul-entities reaching the end of Stage Two actually fulfill this standard. More often than not they don't, and even after they move on to Stage Three, they can and do fall back into the patterns of greed, licentiousness, power plays, and so on. However, at the end of Stage Two, the entity has to express a willingness to work in that direction and make a vow to that effect in order to qual-ify for the First Initiation. It is interesting to observe how Stage Three souls reconcile this vow with the drives that still rage within the desire nature.

STAGE THREE: HIGH EGOIC

By this time the ego is in full flower, and the entity is enjoying his indi-viduality. He sees himself as special, unique, immortal, invincible—and lives his life accordingly. Stage Three is characterized by ambition coupled with a powerful desire to attain all the finest material rewards of earthly existence and to fit in with the rest of the world. The attitude most characteristic of Stage Three is, "My way is the only way."

Depending upon Ray vibration, the energy of the Stage Three soul often appears to be limitless. Stage Three souls are the movers and shakers of the world, and have been referred to as the "architects of civilization." They are the entrepreneurs, the world leaders, the pioneers, the builders, and the conquerors. Stage Three is a time of adventure, when the soul begins to take the risk of moving into new territory. Having found their niche in late Stage Two, these entities now move on to assume monumental tasks in the physical plane, and sometimes they set goals for themselves that are virtually impossible to reach. They become aware of a hunger within, of a need to seek and find something they do not possess. This hunger actually represents a restless and impatient need to complete the cycle and once more unite with the Infinite, but these souls are not yet aware of that. They are still too enamored of their own egos, which came to full flower at the end of Stage Two, and they focus that hunger on accumulating worldly wealth.

At this stage of development, the game of karma is in full sway, and whether the entity allows himself to advance through the hierarchy and reach the goals he has set for himself depends on Ray vibration, attachment, and karma. This concept cannot be stated quite so simply as: If positive karma outweighs negative karma, he advances; and vice versa. This is true—but there are other factors involved. Again, remember that the word karma means *action*. All the unfulfilled desires, all the attachments and incompletions that have been festering in his mind since experiences on the previous two stages now come to the forefront. The entity rushes to take care of everything at once, in a vain attempt to satisfy his inner hunger—but in the course of doing so, he continues to create karma.

The "my way is the only way" consideration is so powerful that it permeates every facet of Stage Three existence. Hence the domineering parent who demands that his children live their lives the way he wants them to, without any consideration of what they may need or want—even after they become adults. ("I know what's best for you!") Hence the little old lady who obstinately clings to using an old-fashioned wringer washer when a new, more modern washing machine would be a lot easier on her. Hence the stubborn businessman who sticks with the old ways of doing business, ignoring the bright young employees who propose newer, more efficient methods that would save him money. Hence ultra-conservative politicians who seek to maintain the status quo at all costs, and gain public support by appealing to their constituents' basic fear of the unknown.

These politicians sometimes use their speechmaking skills to create in the minds of their people frightening future scenarios that could come into existence if new ways and ideas are adopted. On the other hand, there is the radical politician who almost fanatically promotes new programs—all reflecting conditions that he himself wants. Even in cases where a majority of the people initially opposes such programs, an especially charismatic politician can eventually win them over and convince them that what he wants is best for them, too.

The first few levels of Stage Three are called the *questor* substage. The questor's primary characteristic is curiosity and an intense desire to learn. The entity seeks to take advantage of the niche secured in late Stage Two and use his new self-awareness to propel himself into a prominent position which he feels he deserves.

Whether the Stage Three soul chooses to express this energy—the blatant promotion of self-interest—through parenting, business, politics, or education depends on the Ray vibration. Also, the need to hang onto the status quo at all costs is not typical of all Stage Three souls; whether they manifest this need or not depends upon their own levels of attachment, as well as their individual karma. The main drive of the

Stage Three soul is to accomplish what he wants. This may involve clinging to the past, or it may involve building a new world tailored to his own personal ideals. A good example of the latter condition is Adolf Hitler, a Stage Three, First Ray soul, Seventh Ray personality who had a vision of a whole new world peopled by supermen. He also possessed enough personal magnetism to convince many people in Germany that his ideal was worthy enough to justify war, murder, annihilation, and the risk of their own death.

The Stage Three soul perceives others in the world as unique individuals like himself—but more often than not refuses to acknowledge the worth of their uniqueness. The Stage Three entity is mainly concerned with bringing others around to his point of view. He is capable of love, though it is generally a selfish, conditional love. He sees other individuals as support systems for himself and for the promotion of his own ways. If the individuals he wants to support him have doubts about him, he charges ahead like a ram in order to change them and get them to adopt his ways. He rarely questions his own motivation—for in his mind he is always right.

Even if an exceptionally intelligent Stage Three soul acknowledges that someone else has a valid point of view, that acknowledgment is only at an intellectual level. Deep down he still believes that his own point of view is always the only correct one.

On Stage Three, the entity becomes increasingly aware of his own intellectual abilities and gains a strong sense of pleasure and satisfaction from using them. He begins to enjoy being in the limelight, and, depending upon Ray vibration, seeks the best possible path for him to take in order to keep on being in the limelight—thereby setting himself apart from others. As the entity continues on the questor level, the desire to make the most of his talents in order to advance himself intensifies until he reaches the point where his main drive is to "reach the top" at all costs. The questor substage has been compared to the period in which the child is in grade school—observing, learning, and beginning to assert and express himself.

Sometimes Stage Three considerations—particularly the more self-ish ones—can lead to intense guilt in later lives on more advanced stages of development, and therefore to "negative karma" which creates problems in the current life. Consider the following regression material from a twenty-six-year-old singer/songwriter, apparently a late Stage Four, First Ray soul, Third Ray personality recalling a Stage Three incarnation as a king who took his realm by conquest:

> I had several incarnations as a leader. I was a lieutenant in the Mahabharata war; I was a king in an ancient civilization. I was acknowledged as a great teacher in another. I was always striving, trying hard to be a good leader and to have people acknowledge me as such. But I wasn't about to let these people get to me. I was the rightful king—no one else.
>
> Some of them came over to my side and were loyal to me. Others weren't. So I punished the ones that weren't. I took their land and gave it to my followers. I taxed them heavily. Sometimes if they rebelled actively I even killed them. But I tried to be fair. I was actually a pretty successful king—no one was afraid to go out at night under my rule...

This client's first regression into this lifetime proved to be a real shock for him; it was difficult for him to believe that he could ever have been that ruthless. In the current incarnation, he seemed to have retained the latter personality's desperate desire to be fair while at the same time lacking his drive.

A second client recalling a Stage Three incarnation—as a Celtic king in the Dark Ages in Britain—experienced blatant betrayal by many whom he loved, including his own son, toward the end of his reign. The pain he underwent in that lifetime became a Number One incident—and so it gave rise to the consideration, "success brings betrayal." This led to his constant, subconscious sabotage of his own ambitions in all existences, including the present one. However, having acknowledged this consideration, he has hopefully become to terms with his former personality's pain and will be able to complete his unfinished business in this incarnation.

Traumas and inappropriate decisions made in Stage Three are easily exorcised. Sometimes problems acquired on the Stage Three level, brought to the surface by past-life regression, seem to disappear overnight. For instance, one of my clients had a ten-year bout with intense back pain, which she had acquired at the age of nineteen by foolishly attempting ballet movements she was not conditioned for. However, under past-life regression, she discovered that the source of her back pain was rooted in a Stage Three experience when she had fallen off a ladder while surrounded by enemies and had been left by her comrades to die. Once this memory was brought to the surface, the back pain virtually disappeared. Since this regression (which took place in 1979) she has not experienced low back pain unless there was a definite reason for it—such as too much strenuous exercise. Contrast this case with that of Ardith, who acquired her back pain on Stage One, and even past-life therapy could not totally exorcise it.

Stage Three souls who have actively chosen the path of introvertedness find satisfaction of their Stage Three ambitions through self-acknowledgment—in the good feelings that result from a job well done. Entities whose karma doesn't allow great success often expend vast amounts of energy striving for it, but are constantly frustrated. This frustration can cause problems in later lifetimes by giving rise to low self-esteem, which can limit the entity's spiritual progress.

For example, take the client referred to on page 45 who strove for success as a king. In the very lifetime in which his Stage Three ambitions were fulfilled, he committed a vast number of cruelties in the course of his conquests. In subsequent incarnations—including the current one—he found his successes constantly frustrated because he still had not forgiven himself for those cruelties. This tendency also spilled over into his spiritual life. He seems determined to make up for the material successes that had karmically been denied him. Therefore, in spite of an almost irresistible pull toward the spiritual life, he continues to persist in striving for worldly and financial success in a Stage Three manner—even though it appears to those who know him best that he is merely going through the motions. At the same time, he does not seem to have totally forgiven himself for the cruelties, because he still stops just short of attaining his worldly goals.

The late Stage Three substage is called the *dictator* substage. It parallels adolescence in human development, when the individual is becoming involved with the outside world, finding it exciting, and striving to be the best he possibly can. On this level, *if Ray vibration and karma render it possible,* and the world is willing, the entity's worldly ambitions are usually fulfilled. Wealth is amassed; fame—or at least acknowledgment in one's field—may result.

Oddly enough, the higher the level of success, the sooner the entity becomes uncomfortably aware of the futility of it. As the entity progresses though the dictator substage, a part of him becomes aware that he is never satisfied, no matter how large a store of wealth, possessions and fame he accumulates, and he begins to wonder exactly what it is that will bring the contentment he seeks. He starts to notice that there are many around him who are much less fortunate than he, and guilt begins to creep into his thought patterns.

The more successful of these late Stage Three souls—such as Bill Gates and Donald Trump—become active in charity work, donating huge sums of money to good causes. Sometimes they even set up their own foundations for the benefit of their fellow beings—which is actually not a bad way to ease their guilt karma.

Toward the end of Stage Three, the entity seems to realize that worldly gain will not satisfy the hunger within, but a part of him loves all he has managed to amass and continues to pursue more—often repressing his growing sensitivity and social consciousness in the process.

There comes a point on very late Stage Three when the entity's growing social conscience becomes too powerful to ignore. At this point the entity may acknowledge his guilt by choosing to give up everything and live like one of the underprivileged masses. This often happens to children of mid- or late Stage Three parents who have been given every advantage throughout their lives. Needless to say, this upsets the parents tremendously. Consider the following excerpt from the regression of a ten-year-old Stage Four boy:

> My name is Josh, and I live in New York. My family is very wealthy; my father is an entrepreneur. He wants me to enter the family business, but I don't belong there. I put off making any commitment to him until World War II breaks out.
>
> I become a journalist, and am sent to Europe to cover the war there. I send home some wonderful stories, and win an award. My father is very proud of me. When I come home, he hails me as his famous son and boasts about me to all his friends. Then he starts in again about my joining the family business. But I've seen too much, too much pain and suffering in Europe throughout the war. I can't bury myself in a protected little hole while there is so much suffering going on. So my father disowns me.
>
> [Moved up ten years] I've become a barber, and I'm back working in New York. I didn't inherit from my father—it was almost as if he was determined to get even because I didn't do what he wanted. But I don't mind. I have a nice wife, and a lovely daughter, Edith Ann...I died in a street accident. I was run over, I think by a taxicab.

Experiences such as this were common in the late 1960s, when many upper-middle-class children were overwhelmed by guilt and spiritual hunger and gave up all the advantages their parents had slaved to give them and joined communes or devoted themselves to spiritual or charity work. It has been speculated that this pattern emerged from conditions experienced during World Wars I and II, when so many died in battle. In their immediately following incarnations they fanatically promoted "peace through flower power."

The above type of behavior—the rejection of a way of life devoted to worldly gain—represents the culmination of the Stage Three experience. The individual does not have to resort to such extremes as the young New York journalist, or the hippies of the sixties, but the rejection has to be genuine. Sometimes it is marked by a religious conversion and a renewed interest in the church or other spiritual groups, especially in Second and Sixth Ray types. (There can be, however, still a bit of the Stage Three mindset in that the person's religious attitude might be stated as, "My god is the only god.") Some people (particularly Third, Fifth, and Seventh Ray types) throw themselves into the study of art, music, history, and so on—to the exclusion of all other interests. First and Fourth Ray types usually gravitate toward political activism.

Stage Three marks a pivotal period in the evolution of the soul. Remember, in the beginning the entity broke away from the Infinite in order to experience existence on the lower planes. Stage Three marks the culmination of that experience, and once this stage is completed the soul is free to concentrate on returning to the Infinite. Until the Stage Three experience is totally complete, the soul will not be able to move on—and therefore we sometimes find souls on Stage Four (such as the young man referred to on page 45) and even on early Stage Five who still have not completed the Stage Three experience. This does not necessarily imply that they need to cast off or shelve their spiritual aspirations and return to the mindset of the entrepreneur. Such a course of action would be impossible, as the entity has evolved beyond that mindset. But the entity needs to acknowledge the incompletion, and either find some sort of middle ground where he can pursue some degree of worldly success without compromising his spiritual ideals, or else accept and become comfortable with the fact that he never reached the heights of worldly success he once desired and recognize that in the higher realms to which he aspires, the attainment of worldly success is irrelevant. In this situation, self-forgiveness becomes vital,

Most of the souls now incarnate in the Western world are operating on the Stage Three level. The high degree of economic development and the complexity of our social and political systems reflect Stage Three values. However, a significant percentage of the children born since the mid-1960s are Stage Four, which foreshadows a paradigm shift and a change in world values.

The results of this are already being seen. The "voluntary simplicity" lifestyle being adopted by many who are disillusioned with the work-work-work-spend-spend-spend ethic of the post-Depression era (much to the despair of our Stage Three politicians who define world prosperity and well-being in terms of economic growth) and the shift from the immediate material desires of man to the more far-reaching well-being of the environment reflect the coming change in values. The next twenty-five years are sure to see vast changes in the dominant structure and attitudes of Western society.

Once the entity has reached the end of Stage Three he undergoes what we call the Second Initiation. At the time of the Second Initiation, the entity acknowledges that worldly desire no longer dominates his focus of endeavor, and that he wishes only to concentrate on working for the good of the Whole. The entity has attained a profound knowledge of the earthly plane and now aspires to work toward development of the higher nature, toward a deep universal love, and toward service to the world. In the course of the Second Initiation, two metaphysical truths are revealed to the entity: (1) the existence of the astral plane and the power of the mind over that plane, which can then spill over into the physical; (2) the law of cycles and of karma. Previously, in late Stage Three, the entity may have heard about these concepts and possessed an "intellectual" awareness of them. However, true understanding is only conferred at the time of the Second Initiation, when a commitment is made to spiritual progress.

The final two earthly stages of development are devoted to releasing worldly attachments, completing one's karma, and serving the life forms on this planet so that one may evolve beyond the need for physical incarnation and move on. In the course of human development, a Stage Four soul rarely operates from that level before the age of twenty-one, and Stage Five souls usually attain that level of awareness at around twenty-eight to thirty. Hence all the traditions of the great religious leaders such as Jesus, Buddha and Zoroaster, who became aware of who they were roughly at the time of their thirtieth birthday.

STAGE FOUR: CENTAUR

Stage Four is called the Centaur stage because the symbol for the centaur is half animal, half god—and thus the Stage Four soul could well be described. Stage Four marks the first appearance of higher mystical and visionary abilities.

There is no longer any desire to change others or to force them to adopt the individual's attitudes, values, and lifestyle. Rather, the soul on the centaur level appreciates differences between individuals and likes to learn from those whose cultural backgrounds, education, and lifestyles are different from hers. The sincere social conscience developed in late Stage Three is still in evidence, but there is little, if any, guilt involved.

Sensitivity in the Stage Four soul is highly developed. Consequently, some, particularly Third, Fourth, and Seventh Ray types—may possess exalted musical, artistic, or literary talents. Because of the secret of the astral light revealed at the Second Initiation, the person usually exhibits the beginning of some psychic talents, and is able to train and focus her extrasensory perception, hopefully (though, unfortunately, not always) along constructive avenues. The Stage Four soul may have remarkable insights into the psyches and motivations of others, and hence can be an excellent psychotherapist.

The first levels of Stage Four are called the *early centaur* substage. The early centaur level is the most difficult of all to get through. Soul entities on this level are committed to the Path, but to some degree are still attached (depending, of course, on the individual) to the material wealth and worldly attainments to which they aspired while on Stage Three. There can be an extreme sense of ecstasy over the new worlds the soul is discovering; the awareness bestowed at the Second Initiation, that these worlds are real, can lead to great happiness. Yet the early centaur soul still lives in the material world, and to some degree must conform to the values of that world. This leads to frustration, discontent, and unhappiness, as well as to a need for escape. As a result, there are more alcoholics on the early centaur level than on any other.[17]

In fact, the early Stage Four soul often feels like a fish out of water. In families where Stage Three souls predominate, a child on the early centaur level is conditioned to see herself as a freak. Her Stage Three parents and siblings often view her sensitivity and awareness as "strange" and make powerful efforts to get her to be more like them. The entity, overly sensitive to her family's unhappiness with her attitudes, often tries desperately to conform to what they want in order to keep them happy. Yet the path she has chosen will not be ignored, and so she finds herself walking a tightrope, trying to live in two worlds—and, in the earliest levels of this stage, often not having much success at it. Sometimes the family forces the child to go into therapy (probably with a Stage Three soul practicing psychiatry) and she ends up on tranquilizers, often brainwashed into agreeing that she is in fact "strange" and must conform to what is "normal." In extreme cases, particularly where

---

17 I was asked once if there were many drug addicts on the early centaur level. There are some, of course, but not quite so many as one would expect. Drug use is the mode of escape used more by Stage Two and Three souls. The Stage Two souls now living in our inner cities who seek escape prefer crack because of its instant high and ready availability. Stage Three souls go for cocaine and prescription medications such as Quaaludes or Valium because of the glamour element involved. For the most part, early centaur souls seem to prefer alcohol.

mystical tendencies are apparent, the person can be branded as "schizo-phrenic" and may even be forced into shock therapy or into the use of antipsychotic drugs.

To the world at large, then, the soul on the early centaur level may seem "messed up"—more messed up, in fact, than her Stage Three friends and neighbors. Unless the level of attachment is still strong, the early centaur soul has evolved beyond the need to seek acknowledg-ment in the world of business. However, she still loves her material comforts enough to strive for financial success in spite of the fact that she probably hates her job, loathes the boredom of routine work, despises the lack of ethics and the moral compromises involved, and hates being taken away from the spiritual studies she loves so much. The happiest of early Stage Four souls are generally found in the fields of science, engineering, education, and the arts, for these fields tradition-ally require fewer moral compromises than the business world. These fields are also less concerned with the stockpiling of wealth and more with accumulation and dissemination of knowledge. However, even these souls eventually wish for more time to pursue what they perceive as their true purpose in life—their spiritual studies and service to humanity.

Early Stage Four souls are particularly vulnerable to pseudo-gurus and to distorted New Age concepts that are roughly based on ancient truths but misunderstood and misapplied. Inevitably the pseudo-gurus are discovered to have feet of clay; the new concepts are discovered to be lacking. At this point the entity may experience what St. John of the Cross referred to as "the Dark Night of the Soul." According to St. John, the evolving soul experiences initial elation at the first revelations of spiritual knowledge, but later plunges into extreme depression when she finds she still must deal with the problems and concerns of the world around her.

If the entity does not receive spiritual guidance, this immense disap-pointment can cause the Dark Night of the Soul to last for several incarnations. More often than not, however, the pull toward spiritual progress and world service is too strong to allow the entity to persist in the Dark Night for very long. Most early Stage Four souls do manage to find some kind of guidance—either through reading, or through the church or other spiritual sects (such as Transcendental Meditation or Siddha Yoga), or through a psychotechnological school of thought such as Silva Mind Control, The Forum, Omega, Actualization, or Making Love Work.

There is a danger in becoming involved with psychotechnologies or spiritual sects, even those run by true Masters. The danger involves the possibility of getting stuck in that one school of thought and falling back on the old Stage Three attitude of "my way is the only way." "Getting stuck" in this manner can give rise to the cult mentality, and can lock a person into one particular way of thinking instead of allowing her to progress. This tendency can be counterproductive, resulting in a standstill instead of the progress the person wants.

I once had dinner with a young woman whom I'll call Claire, who worked for Dr. Barbara de Angelis as program director for Making Love Work. Claire was expected to attend seminars and actively participate along with the students. She told me that she believed in Dr. de Angelis's work and planned to continue her work as program director, but had already told Barbara that she would not be participating in any more seminars. "If you go to too many," Claire related, "you tend to undo all the good work you've done. You become a professional crier, creating shit in your mind so that you can show everyone else how to let theirs go." The best way to progress both spiritually and intellectually is not to become locked into any one school of thought, but to take what each has to offer, make it work for you, and then move on.

Swami Muktananda, the world-famous guru who popularized the ancient Hindu practice of Siddha Yoga, used to kick overly enthusiastic devotees out of his ashram and insist that they take their newfound knowledge out into the world and put it to work for them. In the course of his work, Muktananda went on three world tours, visiting areas in different parts of the world for as long as six months at a time. He had a remarkable memory for faces; in his travels, he recognized people he had met previously, even though several years had passed since his last visit. "Why are you all here still practicing Siddha Yoga?" he would ask. "I thought you'd all have progressed beyond it by now!"

As mentioned before, the Stage Four entity's drive toward spiritual progress is too strong for most centaurs to resist. Contrary to the fears of Stage Three parents who fear their centaur children have been brainwashed by a cult and are trapped for life, studies have demonstrated that most Seekers who join cults leave voluntarily after two or three years—and most do so with no sense of bitterness. Rather, they report fond memories of their lives with their comrades and feel the sect to which they once belonged contributed greatly to their sense of self-worth and spiritual well being. They leave not necessarily because of disillusionment (though a degree of that may be present), but because they feel it's time to move on.

No amount of brainwashing (and few sects actually indulge in such a practice) can overcome the drive of the Stage Four soul to progress. In many cases, once the specific angst of the early centaur soul is overcome, this drive can be so strong that the entity goes from the Second to the Third Initiation in a matter of a few short years. The late centaur stage, which immediately precedes the Third Initiation, is marked by a release of attachment to outgrown values, forgiveness of oneself and of others, and acceptance (at least at this period of time) of the fact that one is different, that one will never again fit comfortably into the mainstream of society. Once these considerations are released, the entity is free to develop in any way she sees fit—through service, education, artistic expression, and/or spiritual practices. The Third Initiation marks such an important milestone in the progress of the soul that some people sense a heavy change approaching and actually sabotage their own progress. "Getting stuck," as outlined above, can be one type of sabotage, as the entity convinces herself that she is progressing while actually she is at a standstill.

Seeking enlightenment in dangerous ways is another form of sabotage. One famed pioneering metaphysical teacher, whose impact is still being felt in the New Age movement more than thirteen years after her death, managed to convince herself that psychedelic drugs would be a great boost to her progress and her students'. In the end, she only succeeded in becoming addicted and eventually dying of an overdose, thereby sabotaging both her own progress and her mission.

Other entities fall back upon incompletions from Stage Three and become caught up once more in the drive for material success, to the exclusion of artistic or spiritual pursuits. But again, the drive to progress is usually too strong, and the entity eventually does undergo the Third Initiation.

The Third Initiation has also been called the Transfiguration. The spiritual intuition is awakened completely. The soul is flooded with light from above, and the entity falls under the influence of the Monadic Ray. The entity vows to use her psychic faculties to help the race, and is therefore granted true knowledge of the creative process of thought-form building, the transmission of energy from the Higher Self to the physical body via the chakras, and the secret of raising the kundalini. The entity is now ready to move on and enter Stage Five.

STAGE FIVE: GURU

At this stage the entity is not yet totally aware of his divinity, but is strongly aware of the inner god and has an innate rather than an intellectual concept of the universal god. Stage Five marks the first appearance of power at will over the material world. The visionary and mystical abilities which began their development on Stage Four have reached an exalted level, and at some point will culminate in God-realization. Even in souls whose Ray vibration usually inclines otherwise, exceptional artistic and musical talents may appear as a result of the intense awareness of the fascinating world beyond the physical, as well as the "music of the spheres". There is no remaining desire to stockpile worldly power or wealth, though there is no attachment to poverty either, and the person can live equally comfortably in either a shack or a palace. While Stage Five souls sometimes form marital relationships, sexual desire is falling away, and on the final levels of this stage all sexual activity ceases.

Individuals operating on the Stage Five level are almost always extremely attractive, in both physical appearance and personality, for at this point they have acquired a great deal of inner beauty and it shines through to those around them. They are magnetic, charismatic; their conversation is captivating. They usually find themselves surrounded by people who wish to draw upon their vast stores of knowledge— which can prove frustrating to these people because their desire for enlightenment usually inclines them toward solitude. The Stage Five soul rarely seeks employment, preferring to take his chances with poverty rather than become enmeshed in the mundane concerns of others, although some earn their livings as writers, musicians or artists. Some, who are especially close to the earth, work as gardeners, while those attuned to animals may work in stables or on farms.

Although these individuals may be dedicated scholars, writers, or teachers, the desire for intellectual achievement gradually begins to fall away, as earthly knowledge seems to lose its significance in light of awareness of the vastness of Creation. The Stage Five entity perceives others primarily as incarnations of God, even though he is totally aware of their humanness and the resulting personality quirks. His level of awareness enables him to see into the hearts even of total strangers, and therefore he is a master psychologist, possessing uncanny knowledge of exactly how to deal with every individual he meets. Stage Five souls may embark upon specialized social programs designed to alleviate specific societal ills, but for the most part the Stage Five soul is an educator, whose social conscience is expressed primarily as an altruistic love of all life forms.

The success of a Stage Five soul in reaching his goal of independence from earthly concerns depends mainly upon the level of completion of karma and acceptance of self-worth. Attachment, if it still exists at all, is minimal, and eventually is finally released. By this stage the Ray vibration is inclining towards its highest mode of expression. Depression and perhaps nostalgia are the last neurotic ways of escape available to Stage Five souls. They usually tend to come when the entity's highly developed sensitivity tunes into the overwhelming concerns of the world and he feels a restlessness to pass on to the higher planes.

The entity may choose to become a spiritual teacher, or guru, particularly in the *guru/teacher* substage where he may still be somewhat extraverted and socially inclined. A caution arises at this point. By Stage Five the ego is highly refined—and yet so long as the entity is incarnate on the physical world, there is always the chance that he will revert to long-outmoded patterns of behavior and become enmeshed in egotistical attitudes. This has happened to a number of popular gurus.

What apparently happens is this: the guru takes his innate knowledge and what he learned from his own particular Master into the world and brings it to the masses. He—or she as the case may be—attracts numbers of followers, who virtually worship at his feet. For most guru/teachers, this represents no problem; the more enlightened among them caution followers against directing so much devotion toward another human being, even them. But a few fall into what I call the "Stage Five Trap." When followers hail such a person as the Great Master, he starts to think, "I am the Great Master!" Rather than spreading his knowledge, as he had originally intended, he decides that only those who are "deserving"—like himself—should have access to it. He also begins to fall back into the Stage Three consideration of "My way is the only way." This can mark the beginning of what is now referred to as a "cult"—and the dangerous practices associated therewith.

Anyone who becomes involved with a guru/teacher whom they suspect of having fallen into the Stage Five trap in most cases should move on. However, remember that even though a guru/teacher has become once more enmeshed in his ego, his teachings, and the advancement gained through them, can still be valid. Also remember that at this point the soul is so highly developed that the guru/teacher usually realizes his mistake—generally within a few short years—and comes out of the trap. Falling into the "trap" may constitute a karmic lesson that he has to learn. (Remember the story of the rabbi on page xxxvi?) It is not for us to pass judgment on these advanced beings; we can only take what they have to offer and tailor our own behavior so that it best serves our own development.

Eventually the entity reaches the *guru/saint* substage, often in the same lifetime. At this point the guru may have followers, but he does not actively seek them; nor does he spend much time talking. He prefers to spend his time in solitude and silence, seeking his own enlightenment. Usually he has highly evolved disciples who have been with him for years to whom he passes the torch of guru/teachership. He possesses great powers over the physical world, but rarely chooses to use them.

He is aware of the cosmic Plan and capable of operating totally on the Buddhic plane. He is able to operate the Buddhic vehicle and uses this capability both to serve those still incarnating on the lower planes and to continue evolving himself toward the ultimate Reunion. Eventually he moves on to the Fourth Initiation, also known as the Crucifixion. At the Fourth Initiation, the entity lays his all on the altar of sacrifice, renouncing friends, family, intellectual achievement, character, even his perfected self, all in the interest of continuing on to the Ultimate Reunion.

Once a soul has taken the Fourth Initiation, there is generally no need to take further incarnations on the physical plane. However, the entity may choose to do so if he feels he still has an earthly mission to fulfill—or if he chooses to assume the role of the Boddhisattva, who continues to incarnate on Planet Earth until all life forms who entered into incarnation on his cycle have attained enlightenment and moved on.

STAGE SIX: EARLY LIGHT MASTERS

Because of the paradigm shift and the world changes that are going on even as I write, the twentieth century has seen the incarnation of an unusually high number of Stage Six souls. Although there is no way that most of us can judge the level of such high souls with total accuracy, the consensus of opinion seems to be that such great spiritual teachers as Yogananda, Muktananda, and the Maharishi were at least on Stage Six. Other Stage Six entities continue to serve the human race, but they do it from the higher planes by working through the hearts and minds of people still incarnating on earth. It is these entities that the occult teachings refer to as "Ascended Masters." The Stage Six soul is totally enmeshed in universal love, and lives in a constant state of God-realization. Such individuals may not be totally complete with their karma, but they are very close. Few earthly desires remain to them—and those that do still exist involve matters such as having a successful seminar. The entity possesses near complete power over the material world, but hardly ever uses it.

At the end of Stage Six, the soul group reunites. If the entity wishes, she may undergo the Fifth Initiation, but there is no real need for it. The entity moves on, desiring only the Ultimate Reunion.

STAGE SEVEN: FULL LIGHT MASTER

Stage Seven marks the reunion of the Monad. All karma and forgiveness relating to the evolutionary cycle are complete. The entity then moves faster, onward and upward to the Ultimate Reunion.

There are records of only a few Stage Seven souls ever taking incarnation on Earth. These Monads include the Christ, who incarnated as Lord Krishna and Jesus of Nazareth; the Buddha, who assumed the body of Prince Siddhartha Gautama; and the Great Goddess, known primarily as Queen Isis and the Blessed Virgin Mary. According to occult tradition, the Christ and the Buddha were among the first groups of entities to complete the involutionary arc and take incarnation on Earth. The Christ made the most rapid progress along the evolutionary loop of any soul ever on this planet, with the Buddha following closely behind—eons ahead of all other earthly entities. Both chose to assume the role of the Boddhisattva.

The Great Goddess has never entered onto the involutionary arc, though she has taken incarnation when necessary. She is a projection of the Goddess Kundalini Shakti, the primary yin energy of the cosmos, who has anchored herself to this solar system. She is not to be confused with the Planetary Logos. The Great Mother and the Great Goddess are two separate Monads.

The work of the Stage Seven Monads on this planet is primarily to give the opportunity for the masses to attain a Christlike existence and lifestyle. If the entity desires, at the end of this stage it can undergo the Sixth Initiation, but again, there is no need.

STAGE EIGHT: COMPLETION

The entity has reached the level of full solar awareness and exists in a level of serenity, bliss and total peace. We who are still incarnating on earth cannot imagine what happens to the entity on Stage Eight and beyond. It may decide to stick around and re-enter the involution/evolution cycle, or it may move on to galactic consciousness, but then we cannot be sure. It is for this reason that we call the Path beyond Stage Eight the Path to the Unknown.

Knowledge of the Stages of Development can be of great help for psychotherapists, social workers, and others who are dealing with the lives and psyches of people. It is vital for such people to know that you cannot change anyone's basic viewpoint. Mainstream psychiatrists, most of whom are operating from Stage Three, seem to be obsessed with turning everyone into a Stage Three person living according to Stage Three values. This cannot be done. All stages of development represent important realms of experience that everyone on this planet goes through and must go through at their own pace in order to experience life on Earth to the fullest.

It is important for a confused Stage Three to be able to get rid of most of his hangups so that he can work on being a successful Stage Three; this is a pivotal point for the soul-entity. But the other stages and their values should be recognized, too. The real estate broker who quits her stressful, boring job in Sacramento and moves to Yelm, Washington to be near Ramtha is not insane, abnormal, or incompetent. She is probably an early Stage Four just learning to put aside worries about financial insecurity and concentrate on spiritual development rather than material success. Once she has taken all she needs from Ramtha she will most likely move on to a new teacher and a new school of thought.

Social workers dealing with citizens of our inner cities who may be operating on Stage Two can gain a distinct advantage from knowledge of the stages of development. For example, if a social worker is attempting to rehabilitate a member of a gang, it helps to know (judging, of course, by behavior and attitudes) if the gang member is simply a bored early Stage Three seeking a support system, or if he is operating from Stage Two, membership level.

In the former case, it can be fairly simple to find the individual a new focus for his energy and channel him into seeking a more productive support system. In the latter case, it will be virtually impossible to take the person away from his gang. No matter what the social worker says, no matter what the courts order him to do, the person sees his gang as an extension of himself. If the social worker, or anyone else, tries to rip them from him he will view the social worker as the enemy and resist anything she says. The best course of action for the social worker in cases like this is to try to reform the whole gang. This may sound like a task of Herculean proportions, but it has been done quite successfully.

A priest who had once been a gang member in a New York ghetto returned to his old neighborhood after completing his studies and becoming ordained. Although his old gang was now composed almost entirely of younger people, he still felt a need to help them. Rather than try to force the gang into a mode of behavior that was foreign to them—convincing them all to join the mainstream and get jobs—he turned the entire gang into a successful semi-professional basketball team. They loved it—and him!

In doing this, the priest wisely allowed the group to make the most of their membership consciousness and channel their "us versus them" point of view into healthy competition rather than into murderous gang wars. In the same way, the founder of the Harlem Boys' Choir took gifted boys from the ghetto before they had a chance to become involved in the gang scene and encouraged them to make full use of their talents in a membership context.

I insert a caution here. I say each person's stage of development is best discerned by careful observation of attitudes and behavior. Note the word *careful*. It is not safe to make quick generalizations based on the person's station in life. Hindu tradition tells of how saints often disguise themselves as beggars in order to test the hearts of their devotees. I once was acquainted with a very old soul—late Stage Four or early Stage Five—who had taken incarnation as a homeless black man in the drug-ridden neighborhoods of Venice, California. He participated in the drug culture along with the Stage Twos, but at the same time watched over them. He made certain they had blankets at night and spent the money he earned cleaning windshields to buy food for them as well as himself. And he gave them guidance and a shoulder to cry on whenever they needed it.

Therefore, it is a mistake simply to assume that an inhabitant of the inner city is operating from Stage Two and tailor one's dealings with him accordingly, nor is it safe to accept that any person employed by a prestigious corporation is automatically on Stage Three. Remember the rabbi! No matter how overworked we are, no matter how strong the pressure from higher-ups, all of us who make a career of handling the human psyche—psychotherapists, social workers, psychics, priests, or spiritual counselors—must take the time to know our clients, to sense their specific needs, and to treat them properly as individuals. Awareness of the stages can be an invaluable tool.

THE SEVEN RAYS

Ray	Vibration	Hindu Name	Qualities of God & Human Ideals	Worldly Manifestation	Role Function	Definition of Role Function
First Ray	Will or Power	Iccha	Freedom	Government	King	World leaders; history-makers. Those who assume authority through knowledge and unselfish power.
Second Ray	Love-Wisdom	Jnana	Unity	Philanthropy	Priest	Humanitarians; philanthropists. Those who aspire to serve a higher being or ideal.
Third Ray	Active Intelligence	Kriya	Comprehension	Philosophy	Sage	Thinkers; teachers. They who express themselves through seeking and disseminating knowledge.
Fourth Ray	Harmony through Conflict	Maya	Harmony	Synthesis	Warrior	Leaders; pioneers; conquerors. Those driven instinctually to command and explore.
Fifth Ray	Concrete Knowledge or Science	Sattva	Truth	Science	Scholar	Gatherers of knowledge; observers. They who prefer to live life vicariously rather than through direct experience.
Sixth Ray	Devotion or Idealism	Rajas	Goodness	Religion	Devotee	Servants; followers. Those who seek a person or institution to serve.
Seventh Ray	Ceremonial Magic	Tamas	Beauty	Art	Artisan	Magicians; artists. Those driven instinctually to create that which is perfect.

THREE

Role Functions

The Influence of the Seven Rays

Awareness of the Seven Rays goes back to Vedic times. These seven primordial impulses underlie all existence, at least in our solar system. Everything within our comprehension vibrates to at least one of these Rays.

According to modern Western metaphysics, the Rays are said to stream from the seven stars making up the constellation of the Great Bear. The seven stars of the Great Bear represent the seven head centers of The One About Whom Naught May Be Said—as the Absolute[18] is

---

18 With all due respect to HPB and AAB, I wonder if this is really the Absolute we're talking about. Since those ladies were still writing, we have learned so much about what a vast Universe this is. I wonder if these seven stars are actually the head centers of a Galactic Logos?

referred to in the works of Mme. Helena P. Blavatsky and Alice A. Bailey. Each Ray is analogous to a force stemming from the One, and have all been in existence since the first few seconds after Creation—or, in the terminology of modern physics, the Big Bang.

The Rays are the governing forces surrounding all facets of existence—whether it be spiritual, physical, intellectual, emotional, or otherwise—and, in our Universe, nearly everything can be explained in light of its Ray vibration. Study of the Rays can give us all a better understanding of ourselves as immortal entities, and also of everyone around us.

In our solar system, there are seven heavenly bodies upon which there is not, and never has been, any aboriginal form of physical life. They are the Sun, Mercury, Venus, Jupiter, Saturn, Uranus, and Neptune.[19] The only life that has ever existed on these orbs is the soul that animates the heavenly body itself—and so, in the beginning, because there was no risk of harm (in the form of energy overload) to developing life forms, these planets[20] were chosen to serve as the channels for the Seven Rays.

The Rays, therefore, pass through the bodies of the seven chosen planets and are deflected to Earth, where their energies color all life forms on the planet, from subatomic particles to Monads. The Tibetan Master Djwahl Khul calls the Rays "the seven emanations of spiritual energy, issuing forth from God at the beginning of an era of creative activity."[21]

The concept of the Rays is hinted at in various Hindu scriptures, including the *Upanishads* and the *Bhagavad-Gita*. In Chapter Seven of

---

19 It is interesting to note that my sources do not include Pluto on this list. Physicists will scream in protest—but apparently modern occult literature implies that there is or once was at least one aboriginal form of life on Pluto.

20 Even though the term is not technically correct, for convenience, in esoteric lore as well as astrology the Sun is referred to as a planet.

21 Alice A. Bailey, *Esoteric Psychology II*. (New York: Lucis, 1940.) P. 202.

the *Gita,* Lord Krishna refers to the eightfold division of his manifestation, including earth, water, fire, air, ether, manas and buddhi. The
eighth division is *ahamkara,* or the "I-making": in other words, the primordial energy beyond all Creation. Other Vedic scriptures refer to the
seven principles: *iccha, kriya, manas, maya, sattva, rajas,* and *tamas.* The
correspondence between these seven principles and the Rays is shown
in the table on page 65.

Knowledge of the Rays was not restricted to the Hindus. There are
also indications that at least one medieval Christian mystic was aware of
their existence. Abbess Hildegard of Bingen (1098-1179), in her *Book of
Divine Works,* Vision Two, describes a vision of a human figure and several animal heads surrounded by a ring of fire, held in the arms of God.
From the Ring of Fire seven rays streamed toward the human figure.

> Above the head of this human figure the seven planets were sharply delin-
> eated from each other…All the planets shone their rays at the animal heads as
> well as the human figure…The seven planets signify the seven gifts of the Holy
> Spirit, which exceed all human reason…[22]

But the concept of the Seven Rays was not popularized until the
nineteenth century, when Madame Helena Petrovna Blavatsky wrote of
her own visions of the origin of the Universe in *The Secret Doctrine:*

> There are seven Forces in Man and in all Nature…The Seven Beings in the
> Sun are the Seven Holy Ones, self-born from the inherent power in the Matrix
> of Mother-Substance. It is they who send the seven Principal Forces, called
> Rays, which, at the beginning of Pralaya, will centre into seven new Suns for the
> Manvantara. The energy from which they spring into conscious existence in

---

22 Hildegard of Bingen, *Book of Divine Works. With Letters and Songs.* Matthew
   Fox, ed. (Santa Fe, NM: Bear & Company. 1987.) Pp. 25ff.

every Sun is what some people call Vishnu, which is the Breath of the Absoluteness. [23]

Except for the Hindu references, Madame Blavatsky's vision bears such a powerful resemblance to Hildegard's it's uncanny.

I have often been asked what benefit could possibly be drawn from studying the Rays. My response is that aside from any potential intellectual enlightenment regarding the nature of the Universe, studying the Rays can bestow a keener understanding of the human race and the individuals that comprise it. Since the Rays permeate every life form within their sphere of influence, the human psyche is similarly affected. Every soul-entity came to Earth vibrating in harmony with at least one of the Rays.

I say "at least" because, according to my sources, everyone is under the influence of three Ray vibrations. The first is the Ray of the Monad, or the Light Master that gave rise to the soul group. It is said that each Monad, no matter what its particular Ray vibration, projected itself into seven soul groups, each under the influence of one of the Rays.

The "Soul Ray," then, is the Ray of the soul group. When the soul group projected itself into separate entities, each then remained true to that vibration, and will do so until the reunion of the soul groups within the Monad. After the Third Initiation, each entity begins to vibrate to the Monadic Ray as well as to its own Soul Ray.

With each incarnation, the entity comes under the dominance of still another Ray: the Personality Ray. The influence of the Personality Ray only lasts for as long as that particular incarnation—although, of course, the entity will probably repeat the experience with each of the

---

23 Helena Petrovna Blavatsky, *The Secret Doctrine*. Wheaten, IL: Theosophical Publishing House, 1974. P. 35.

Seven Rays many times in the course of its earthly evolution. Now it is totally possible that a Third Ray entity springing from a Third Ray Monad will fall under the influence of the Third Ray in a particular incarnation, and thus will become what we call a "pure Third Ray type." This actually happens quite often. The only exception we have to this rule is the First Ray. There are very, very few pure First Ray types now incarnate on Earth.[24]

In recent years, a popular way of learning about the ancient wisdom has been through "channeling" of information from alleged Ascended Masters. One particular channeled source who appears to incorporate the Rays into his teachings is Michael, channeled by a group that prefers to remain anonymous. Michael's teachings emphasize what he calls roles in essence. According to Michael, from the time an entity separates from the Infinite to the time it reunites, its role in essence does not change; the soul-entity's experience is always colored by its role in essence.

Not surprisingly, the roles in essence are seven in number. Michael refers to them as King, Priest, Sage, Warrior, Scholar, Slave, and Artisan. It seems obvious to me that these are merely exoteric terms for the Seven Ray types. Apparently the entity Michael (probably a reunited Stage Seven Full Light Master) forebears mentioning the Rays and their higher, more metaphysical implications to avoid rendering his ideas too complex. He seems to prefer to concentrate on their

---

24 It has been said that all Monads fall only under the influence of one of the three primary Rays: The First. Second and Third. However, the same sources also say that the Monad of the human race is Fourth Ray, which is an apparent contradiction. I can find no reference in any source which explains this anomaly, nor can I come up with any answers other than the following: Perhaps the Light Masters which attach themselves to stars and planets are only of the first three Rays, while those who control the life forms can be of any Ray vibration.

earthly manifestations so as to make this information more accessible to people just beginning their study of the psychology of spirit.

I have no problem with this, nor do I have a problem with any of Michael's teachings regarding the seven role functions. I do, however, object to the term "slave" for Sixth Ray types, as I feel it has too many negative connotations. I prefer the term "Devotee." (See table on page 65)

Various theories have been put forth whereby each individual can discern his or her Soul or Personality Ray through astrology, numerology, the Tarot, the pendulum, and so forth. I have explored these theories and found them weak and lacking in substance—except for the Alice Bailey school of esoteric astrology. Not all that many people practice this school of astrology, however, as Bailey's book on the subject is so difficult to read.

As with the stage of development, the best way for anyone not schooled in Bailey's practices to judge either his or someone else's Ray vibration is by carefully studying attitudes and behavior. Once a person has studied the Rays and their corresponding role functions thoroughly, it should be fairly easy for the discriminating individual to spot the Seven Ray types in this way. What is more difficult, however, is determining whether the dominant attitudes and behavior reflect the Soul Ray or the Personality Ray. For this, you would almost have to turn to someone like famed astrologer Alan Oken who actively teaches and practices esoteric astrology.

Past-life regression, of course, can help. I find that when I regress an individual through a long series of previous lifetimes, certain behavioral patterns persist from incarnation to incarnation in spite of vastly different life circumstances, astrological influences, and the stage of development of each personality. Generally these reflect one Ray and one Ray only, and this, of course, is logically the Soul Ray. Behavior and attitudes that seem to manifest only in individual incarnations reflect Personality Ray influences.

Study of the Rays can be a valuable aid in understanding why each person behaves as he or she does. It gives a broader understanding of individual behavior and its appropriateness. But, perhaps more importantly, it gives an overall picture of the role that the entity chose to play when it manifested on this planet and therefore can discern what lifestyles and careers are appropriate. It also demonstrates the best way for that entity to work toward a better world and toward ultimate enlightenment.

RAY ONE: THE RAY OF WILL OR POWER

Role Function: King

Not all First Ray souls incarnate as actual kings. Most soul-entities, regardless of their Soul Ray, assume that role, or a similar one, on occasion. For the true First Ray soul, whatever life circumstances the entity finds himself in, he will always want to take control. Most of these people are quite charismatic and they are generally successful. Examples of First Ray souls are Eleanor of Aquitaine, Lorenzo di Medici, King Edward III and Queen Elizabeth I of England, Martin Luther, Catherine the Great, Napoleon Bonaparte, Adolf Hitler, John F. Kennedy, and Jesus of Nazareth.

First Ray souls constitute a significant number of world leaders and other historymakers. They are characterized primarily by strong willpower and instinctive leadership abilities. They tend to view the world as their realm, and almost always find their way fairly easily to the forefront of their chosen field. If a King works as a garbage collector, he is the best and most innovative garbage collector in the county and is perfectly capable of dealing in a powerful and effective manner with any problems that arise, or with difficult clients—even other Kings.

Kings possess exceptional courage and vision, and appear to be born with incredible "people skills." They almost always inspire trust and loyalty in all they touch—even those twisted souls like Adolf Hitler. First

Ray types are firm in their convictions and will stick by them in spite of criticism or censure. They are also virtually fearless. They are strong and steadfast, often driven to defend the weak, put down oppression, and impose order upon chaos. Kings are capable of creating paradigms, ideologies and social systems that serve people well, and therefore their creations and influence last for generations—sometimes for centuries.

The First Ray soul is capable of powerful affection, passion, and sensitivity, though at times he is neither able nor willing to express them. One-on-one relationships are often difficult, since Kings always expect to be the center of the emotional stage and are bewildered when other people around them tire of playing a secondary role. Kings know how to bring out the best in their companions and to fire the enthusiasm of others, as well as to temper justice with mercy. Kings have powerful beliefs about their own destinies and success, and they are so confident in their beliefs that no amount of criticism or disinterest from others can sway them from it. They respond powerfully to music, art, and literature, and if other influences dictate, they may be composers, artists, or writers.

The First Ray, however, is also associated with destruction. In its highest manifestation, destruction involves that of old, outmoded political, economic, or social structures in order to make way for newer, more enlightened ones that accelerate the spiritual evolution of life on this planet. "Do not think I have come to bring peace to the world," said Jesus of Nazareth. "I have not come to bring peace, but a sword. For I am come to set a man against his father, and the daughter against her mother...And he that taketh not his cross and followeth after me is not worthy of me."[25]

---

25 Matthew 10:34-25.

In unevolved souls, particularly those on Stages One and Two, the destroyer aspect of the First Ray often manifests itself through tyranny and annihilation. The unevolved First Ray soul can be marked by cruelty, hardness of nature, and a powerful desire to impose his will upon others. He takes whatever he wants without conscience, often by means of violence and cruelty, destroying everything that stands in his way.

The ambition of Kings knows no bounds. They possess a pride so powerful it is virtually impossible for them to keep it in check. Sometimes Kings are so convinced of their own importance and ultimate destiny they feel they shouldn't have to work to achieve their goals. In their minds, they have already attained them—and, needless to say, this attitude actually obstructs their abilities to make their dreams a reality. Such a conundrum can be very hard on their families and friends. First Ray arrogance, willfulness, and anger are legend, and Kings can be frustratingly stubborn. A King's worst weakness is self-pity—which he indulges when others do not share his inflated image of himself.

A typical example of a First Ray soul is William I of England, called William the Conqueror. As a child he had to suffer the stigma of illegitimacy, but he never doubted for a moment that his ultimate destiny was to be a world leader. When he reached his majority, he was constantly battling to retain his hold on his dukedom in Normandy, and yet always seemed to win over his antagonists. Neither his youth nor his illegitimacy seemed to matter to those who threw their lots in with him. They seemed to accept without question the fact that their fortunes were assured if they followed him.

William's conquest of England marked one of the most significant transitions in the history of Great Britain—in fact, in the entire Western world. He felt that he and he alone was entitled to the throne, and so he gathered a massive army (for the time) and engineered a remarkable crossing of the English Channel, horses and all, in longboats. His army swept over that of Harold Godwinson and virtually wiped them out.

Afterwards there was nothing and no one to stand in the way of William's taking the crown. Three years later, when barons in the north of England tried to overthrow him, William, angry and weary of treachery, raged through the north and massacred every living thing he could find. From then on there were no more rebellions.

During peacetime, William devoted himself to building cathedrals, promoting education, and establishing a strict but fair system of law and order. He did away with the death penalty, preferring to back up his reforms with more horrendous punishments such as blinding, dismemberment, or castration. William was so successful in implementing his program of law and order that it was said that a virgin could walk alone through a forest at night carrying a purse of gold and no one would dare to molest her.

William, like all First Ray souls, inspired an intense loyalty in the people around him. His family—his mother and two brothers, and later his wife—stuck by him loyally until late in his life, when his self-centeredness finally wore their patience thin. His passions were intense; he loved his wife, who stayed in Normandy throughout most of William's reign, yet he had an equally beloved Saxon mistress who remained in England and gave him a son and daughter in the course of their long relationship. William doted on his children, but when his eldest son Robert decided to rebel against him, William's wrath knew no bounds. He fought against Robert's rebellion with as much fervor as if he were fighting recalcitrant earls. Later, however, he forgave his son, and restored his birthright to the dukedom of Normandy—though he chose to leave England to his second son, William Rufus, who had always been loyal to his father.

William died after a twenty-year reign as a result of an accident while fighting in Normandy. His three loyal sons and most of his lifetime lieutenants were at his side.

Surprisingly enough, all of England mourned him. "King William," it was written, "excelled in wisdom all the princes of his generation, and among them all he was outstanding in the largeness of his soul."[26] Hence, William the Conqueror presents a prime example of a First Ray soul. Our research reveals that he was probably Stage Three, with a Fourth Ray personality. The fact that even today William is still regarded as one of England's greatest kings demonstrates the occult aphorism that the power of the Will (no pun intended!) can long survive death.

The First Ray soul needs to cultivate patience, tact, sympathy, sensitivity to the needs of others, humility, and tolerance. When placed in a position of leadership, he needs to curb a tendency to be less than diplomatic if he wants to appeal to everyone. In the New Age, it is the First Ray souls who will charge ahead and plow the field so natives of other Rays can move in and plant the seeds that will bring about the paradigm shift and, finally, the Aquarian Age. The best way for the First Ray soul to approach self-realization would be by sheer force of will.

RAY TWO: THE RAY OF LOVE-WISDOM

Role Function: Priest

Priests are primarily humanitarians at heart. You will find Second Ray souls in just about every profession that involves service to either an ideal, such as religion, or to one's fellow human beings. Priests are known for their compassion and unfailing energy directed toward service. Examples of Second Ray souls are John Calvin, Joan of Arc, St. Dominic, St. Francis of Assisi, Pope Paul VI, and Gautama the Buddha. Not all Second Ray souls are religious figures; however, Second Ray

---

26 William of Jumièges, *Histoire de l'abbaye royale de Saint-Pierre de Jumièges par un religeux benedictine de la Congregation de Saint Maur*, ed. Julien Loth, 3 vols. (SHN, 1872-1875.) Vol. 11, p. 145.

energy can be very powerful when directed along artistic lines. Frederic Chopin, Hector Berlioz, Richard Wagner, Oliver Goldsmith, and Francisco Goya were all Second Ray souls. When Second Ray energies are misdirected, however, they can produce disastrous effects. Pharaoh Ramses II, the Emperor Nero, Oliver Cromwell, and (according to some sources) Saddam Hussein are all examples of Second Ray souls—probably operating from Stage One or Stage Two.

The Second Ray soul is distinguished by its innate desire to seek knowledge and wisdom. Priests constantly seek truth, but never seem to find it. Priests are eternally dissatisfied even with their highest achievements; no matter how admirable their accomplishments or how deep their knowledge, their minds are forever fixed on the unknown, forever striving for whatever is just out of their reach.

The Stage One or Two Second Ray soul tends to seek knowledge blindly, without concern for others. In fact, coldness and indifference can mark unevolved natives of this Ray. Remember that Stage One souls have no sense of love, and Stage Two love is primarily selfishly motivated. But toward the end of Stage Two and into Stage Three, the entity becomes awakened to the loving side of this Ray and begins to feel the first glimmer of compassion and humanitarianism. At this point they may start to work toward the ideal of universal brotherhood, though they may be limited by the Stage Three attitude of "My way is the only way," and thus make little progress toward a true understanding of the ideal until they pass through the Second Initiation.

Shortly before and just after the Second Initiation, Priests stop thinking of others primarily in terms of their own selfish needs. They then begin to experience an intuitive sense of union with everyone they meet, becoming as involved in the lives and purposes of others as they are with their own. Second Ray types possess an instinctive sense of universal love, and doing things that help to better the lot of other life forms gives them far more pleasure than doing for themselves. They have little inclination toward entertainment and pleasures of the flesh, but will gladly do whatever is within their power so that others may enjoy life. Priests can lose or give away fortunes without regret, drawing intense pleasure from the fact that somehow, somewhere, the fruits of their efforts are making others happy.

On very late Stage Three and early Stage Four this can result in fanaticism and become a twisted form of self-sacrifice that in the long run accomplishes nothing. Priests, especially those on the late dictator and early centaur levels, need to grasp the true sense of Christ's statement, "The poor you will always have with you."[27] Or, put into modern language, "You can't save them all." Ridden with guilt from subconscious memories of earlier stages of development when they sought knowledge for their own sakes and ignored the needs of others, these Priests will sometimes go to ridiculous extremes to try to pay off all their karma at once.

A tale is told of the poet and playwright Oliver Goldsmith, who, on one cold and frosty night in London, looked out the window of his rooming house and saw a beggar dressed in the thinnest of rags, shivering as he passed by. Moved by the pauper's plight, Goldsmith immediately tossed all his bedding out of his window. The beggar was moved by the gesture and waved his thanks, losing no time wrapping himself in the pile of quilts—but Goldsmith then spent the night shivering in the cold.[28]

On the surface this may sound like a noble sacrifice, but ultimately such a gesture accomplishes nothing. It does not help to eradicate misery; it only transfers it from one person to another. You are not easing the ills of the world when you help someone else by making yourself

27 John 12:8.
28 Ernest Wood, *The Seven Rays: A Theosophical Handbook*. Wheaton, IL: The Theosophical Publishing House, 1972. P. 87.

miserable. If you give your last five dollars to a panhandler and go hungry yourself, you are weakening your cause by limiting your abilities—through hunger, cold, or whatever—to move on and work hard to accomplish whatever needs to be done.

Second Ray souls on the late dictator and early centaur levels do tend to make overwhelming personal sacrifices for the sake of their ideals. Properly channeled, this inclination can accomplish much in helping all life forms on this planet and working toward the true ideals of the New Age. However, Priests need to be aware of the fine line dividing true self-sacrifice and foolish self-deprivation. The rule that seems to work best is this: *Never give away more than you can afford without causing hardship to yourself or your family.*

The wisdom and love inherent in the nature of Second Ray souls endows them with initiative, tact, and foresight, which can result in outstanding diplomatic skills. Priests, therefore, make excellent ambassadors, teachers and counselors. Second Ray politicians, unlike those on the First Ray, are motivated by an innate need to serve rather than to take power, and so they can make first rate senators, representatives, members of Parliament, and governors. In order to be truly effective at the top, however, as presidents, prime ministers, and so on, it is best if there is some First Ray influence—either through the Monadic or Personality Ray.

Evolved Second Ray souls generally are quite successful in personal relationships. Their loving nature, coupled with the desire to serve as well as innate tact and consideration, in most cases can render Priests near-ideal partners—unless they are among those who ease their guilt by impoverishing themselves, as the story of Goldsmith illustrates. In the latter case, the partner may feel abused and frustrated if the Priest gives away funds meant for the rent, groceries, and other household necessities.

Some of the most beautiful personalities are evolved Second Ray souls. Calm, poise, intuition, inner strength, patience, endurance, loyalty, and sweet temper make Priests dependable companions and employees. In preparing for the New Age, Priests can serve best by studying the scriptures and esoteric teachings until the wisdom contained therein becomes part of their very being, representing not simply an intellectual awareness, but a spiritual way of life, which can then be passed on to other Seekers along with the love so typical of the Second Ray.

The best way for Priests to seek enlightenment is by taking, in some form, what is known in India as the path of Raja Yoga. Raja Yoga involves aspiring to the highest, most altruistic and most harmless way of life.

RAY THREE: THE RAY OF ACTIVE INTELLIGENCE

Role Function: Sage

This is the Ray of the abstract thinker, of those who take knowledge and turn it into entertainment. Sages generally have powerful imaginations. They can use their imaginations to grasp the essence of a truth and make it accessible to those who are less able than they. Third Ray souls make excellent novelists, poets, teachers, actors, and filmmakers, and, if there is also Fourth or Seventh Ray influence, artists or musicians. Famous people vibrating to the Third Ray include George Frederic Handel, King Charles I of England, Wolfgang Amadeus Mozart, King Louis XIV of France, Miguel de Cervantes, Giacomo Puccini, Luciano Pavarotti, and Ronald Reagan.

Sages generally are overwhelmingly idealistic, which makes them dreamers and theorists. They are perfectly capable of seeing both sides of a question, which can cause them problems when it comes to making decisions. Their understanding and comprehension of facts is first rate, but they are less interested in facts for their own sake than for the bearing they have on overall awareness. They are philosophers, who seek not so much to satisfy the intellect (which is never satisfied) but to quell the hunger of the soul for spiritual nourishment.

For this reason, Third Ray souls are often very organized, and can put knowledge to great practical use for the benefit of everyone around them. They are always careful to know all their facts before making decisions or stating opinions. Their vision is expansive, and they are capable of postulating great change and reform—and if they are also under the influence of the First Ray they have the will and power to implement these changes.

Scientists vibrating to the Third Ray generally prefer expansive fields such as physics, astronomy, or cosmology rather than more limited ones like chemistry or biology. They are much more open-minded than scientists on other Rays, and probably are responsible for many of the more innovative theories. However, undisciplined types in all professions do tend to diversify too much, to take on too many intellectual problems, and to see too many different sides of them, therefore scattering their energies and postponing finding a solution. The Third Ray soul has a lot of different interests and wants to pursue them all. This tendency is hardly ever overcome, because, frankly, Sages don't want to overcome it. They love everything they do too much to drop anything. Therefore, it is imperative that Third Ray types learn to budget their time carefully.

Not that this would be difficult; when it comes to finding ways to cram everything they want into their lives, Sages can be very innovative and disciplined. They have a powerful ability to apply their considerable intelligence to any matter or activity and to adapt, innovate, and diversify. Third Ray types generally have strong constitutions and are less likely than natives of other Rays to suffer physical or nervous breakdowns. However, they resent stress of any kind being inflicted upon them because it interferes with what they wish to do. Sages can be very insecure, as their imagination and intelligence sets them apart from everyone else, making them feel like freaks. Insensitive parents, siblings, teachers, and other contemporaries (particularly those on Stage Three who are affronted by the Third Ray soul's lack of interest in the general activities of mainstream society) tend to seize every opportunity to reinforce the Sage's awareness that she is different. Such criticism can create a negative self-image.

Third Ray types generally have rich inner lives and enjoy their own company. They are rarely social butterflies, preferring the company of a few close friends who share their interests rather than a wide circle of acquaintances. Sages are partial to animals, and tend to be very concerned about their welfare and their spiritual progress in this world. In fact, they often prefer the company of animals to that of people.

On the lower stages of development, Third Ray souls have a hard time dealing with the complexities of their own minds. They tend to be quite sensitive to subconscious influences and somewhat shamanistic. Many unevolved Sages cannot handle these forces and are frightened by them; some even become suicidal, or, depending upon their culture, put out their own eyes or ears to stop the visions or voices.

Third Ray types are known for their ability to use their intelligence to manipulate people. An unscrupulous Sage has no reservations whatsoever about conning people—and the more advanced the soul, the more skilled the con artist. There is little vindictiveness in the advanced Sage, however. While Third Ray souls on Stages One and Two (and sometimes Three) can be cold and selfish, capable of robbing anyone, as the soul advances spiritually her con games are almost always centered on what she considers "unworthy people who can afford to lose it." In other words, she becomes a Robin Hood.

Other negative tendencies that Third Ray souls need to curb are intellectual pride, reclusiveness, stubbornness, lack of attention to detail, and absent-mindedness. Sages need to work on developing sympathy, common sense, devotion, and tolerance. In the New Age, Third Ray souls will be invaluable in formulating ways to practically apply the exalted ideals formulated by New Age thinkers. The best way for Sages to seek enlightenment is through Jnana Yoga—or the path of the intellect. In this way they can study metaphysical concepts until they reach an innate understanding of the world beyond the physical and of the Path they must rake to reach the higher stages.

An example of a Third Ray soul is Mary Shelley, author of *Frankenstein* and wife of the poet Percy Bysshe Shelley. She was probably early Stage Four, with a Sixth Ray personality, for throughout her life she was more dedicated to promoting the talents and abilities of others than to advancing her own. Oddly enough, in spite of the critical acclaim and fame accorded her for *Frankenstein,* she still preferred to dedicate herself more to perpetuating Shelley's memory.

Even as a child she felt different; whenever an insensitive friend or sibling taunted her or, in later life, abandoned her, Mary felt it was because of some innate character flaw in her. In spite of a certain bravado which she assumed in social situations, she never quite felt equal to the others around her. She was a gifted painter as well as writer, yet she always felt inadequate in the presence of the other talented people in her circle—her parents (celebrated authors William Godwin and Mary Wollstonecraft), her stepsister Claire Clairmont (an exceptional singer) and even a hack like Leigh Hunt, not to mention such geniuses as Shelley and Lord Byron.

Yet those who knew her—including Shelley and Byron—acknowledged her brilliance and often consulted her on matters such as grammar, word usage, and historical accuracy (Mary was a skilled historical researcher.) Her social skills (the Sage's talent for manipulation) often managed to keep the friendship of the two geniuses intact, even when their high-strung egos threatened to break them apart.

After Shelley's death in Italy, Mary returned to England. Because of her beauty and accomplishments, she was considered a "catch" by the men of London society, and she received (and turned down) several marriage proposals. *Frankenstein* had been reprinted several times and turned into plays. "I came home [from Italy] to find myself famous," she wrote.

Her other novels, though never as successful as *Frankenstein,* sold well, and publishers solicited her to write essays on the private lives of Shelley and Byron. She began going out more socially and meeting other famous literary figures, among them songwriter John Howard Payne "Home Sweet Home") and American author Washington Irving. Her self-esteem and level of contentment was higher than it had ever been before in her life. Yet strangely enough, her Sixth Ray personality caused her to consider her years with Shelley and Byron as the best, and she often looked back nostalgically on those years, actively promoting Shelley's work and bringing it to the public. Some critics have suggested that if it had not been for Mary, Shelley's work would have passed by unnoticed. Mary died of a stroke at the age of fifty-four, calling Shelley's name to the last.

RAY FOUR:
THE RAY OF HARMONY THROUGH CONFLICT

Role Function: Warrior

The Fourth Ray is the Ray of passion. Natives of the Fourth Ray are known for their powerful affections, physical courage, quickness of intellect, and dedication to a cause. Warrior energy can produce stirring works of art, music or literature, particularly in the later stages of development. When complicated by selfishness or anger, however, Warrior energy can turn to cruelty and sadism. Examples of Warriors include Julius Caesar, Queen Boudicca, composer Francesco Landini, Ivan the Terrible of Russia, Igor Stravinsky, Clara Barton, Pablo Picasso, Elizabeth Cady Stanton, Theodore Roosevelt, Mao Tse-Tung, and rock musician Sting.

The Fourth Ray has been called the "Ray of Struggle," for natives of this Ray seem to be constantly faced with difficult choices. The passions of the Fourth Ray soul seem to constantly pull it in two directions. On the one hand, these individuals are inclined toward pursuing the desires of the flesh, to a love of ease and sensual pleasure, toward indolence and procrastination, and toward a hedonistic tendency to live solely in the present. On the other hand, Warriors are strongly drawn to causes that excite their passions and ignite their inner fires, ever urging them to action. For this reason, the Fourth Ray is one of the most difficult, and life for the Warrior can be fraught with inner conflict. Warriors tend to carry a great deal of inner anger within them even under the best of circumstances, and when the frustrations mount too high they can snap and wreak havoc wherever they go. Witness the life stories of Queen Boudicca and Ivan the Terrible.

The Warrior tends to charge ahead in life, heedless of danger to himself or his followers. He can become a dashing military hero who leads his platoon to win against seemingly insurmountable odds; he can become a crusader for social reforms, willing to take on a lost cause. But he can also devote his life to the pursuit of pleasure and become a ne'er-do-well. In the early stages of development, Warriors can be bullies, deliberately inspiring fear, sometimes becoming little tyrants. In late Stage Two and throughout Stage Three, they are the patriots and crusaders who fight for their nation or religion at all costs. Warriors also make excellent athletes. Female warriors on Stages Two and Three, particularly those with Fifth and Sixth Ray personalities who accept the sex stereotypes imposed by society, may become physical education teachers.

In the latter stages, where they begin to pull their energies away from the physical world, they sublimate their drive into creative accomplishments. Music produced by Fourth Ray souls (such as that of Landini and Stravinsky) is powerful, though often loud and dissonant. Many modern heavy metal and rap musicians are Fourth Ray souls on early Stage Four, expressing their inner anger in music that listeners either love or hate. Artists vibrating to the Fourth Ray have a powerful sense of color, but in some instances their drawing skills range from the vague to the outright defective. Not only Picasso, but George Frederick Watts, Salvador Dali, and Paul Cézanne were Fourth Ray souls.

Poets and novelists on the Fourth Ray have brilliant gifts for metaphor and picturesque word painting; witness the somewhat bizarre modern poetry of Warriors Gerard Manley Hopkins and T. S. Eliot. Many writers of romantic or historical novels are Warriors, including famed English author Barbara Cartland. However, the Fourth Ray tendency to charge ahead without thinking may lead to inaccuracy of detail.

Warriors can be very charming and charismatic. They are generally captivating conversationalists, particularly from late Stage Three up. They have a way with words and an appealing sense of humor, but, often their inner conflicts cause them to retreat into gloomy silences, which can appear frightening to those around them.

On the surface, it might seem that armies would logically be full of Warriors, but this is not always the case. We do find Warriors in law enforcement and in the ranks of military officers, but the actual fighting forces are almost always composed primarily of Sixth Ray types. Many Stage Two and Three Warriors become mercenaries, as their inner drive and anger must find expression, whether or not their own countries are at war. Warriors sometimes make excellent negotiators, and therefore can do well at formulating peace treaties.

An excellent example of a Fourth Ray soul is King Richard III of England. A late Stage Three Warrior with a Second Ray personality, Richard spent his early life dedicating himself to the cause of putting his elder brother, King Edward IV, on the throne. As many Warriors will, he distinguished himself brilliantly on the field of battle and gained the respect of both his brother and all the people of England. During the struggle for the throne, Richard supposedly was responsible for murders and executions of Edward's rivals, though actual historical records do not bear this out. It is likely that he knew about the murders, but played no role either in planning them or carrying them out.

After Edward's throne was secure, Richard recreated to his lands in the north of England, returning to court only when his brother needed him. He was interested in artillery and constantly followed the improvements in its use, exploring the possibilities of increasing the use of cannon and even of primitive muskets in the English army—although he didn't live long enough to implement the reforms he dreamed of.

In 1483, Edward IV died, and his eldest son and heir unfortunately was only twelve years old. Richard was named as the boy's regent. However, the prince, now King Edward V (Stage Three, Fifth Ray soul, First Ray personality), was a formidable young man who did not know his uncle well and who also tended to fight for whatever he wanted. Richard, concerned for his position, charged on ahead as Stage Three Warriors will, doing whatever was necessary to insure his position while at the same time convincing himself that what was best for him was also best for the young king and for England.

Unfortunately, this course of action included executing many of the young king's trusted retainers. Young Edward, needless to say, was appalled at this, and stored it away in his mind for future action. Richard, too late it might seem, realized the folly of his ways, recalling similar events in English history when a regent did away with a boy king's friends—only to find himself facing exile or execution when the young king reached his majority.

In a panic, Richard trumped up a charge of illegitimacy against his nephew and dethroned him, taking advantage of the situation in order to further his own ambitions. He declared himself the rightful king—quite unjustly. Edward V was imprisoned in the Tower of London. Sometime in the summer following this coup, the young king, along with his younger brother, disappeared, and the two boys were rumored to have been murdered. History has drawn the conclusion that Richard was responsible for the murders; however, recent research, both historical and metaphysical, indicates that this was not the case. Nonetheless, even if he allowed his nephews to live, there is no doubt that he robbed them of a throne that was rightfully theirs.

Richard reigned as a Warrior would, showing skills at negotiation and an interest in building up the army. His two-year reign was plagued by rebellions, however. It appears that Richard, whose Second Ray personality caused him to experience extreme spiritual anguish over his treatment of his nephews, as well as intense pain over the premature deaths of his wife and son, actually gave up. He led the charge valiantly at the Battle of Bosworth, fighting Henry Tudor, whose claim to the throne was weak. Richard fought on, even after the battle was lost and he had been deprived of his horse and dealt several wounds. His body lashed out at his attackers even after the deathblow had been struck. According to some sources, his final battle and death were probably a relief to him. He lived his life in true Warrior manner.

The Fourth Ray soul needs to overcome self-centeredness, inordinate indulgence of passion, indolence, extravagance, and a tendency to give in to panic and start worrying. Warriors need to work toward developing serenity, confidence, purity, selflessness and mental and moral balance.

The role of the Warrior in the New Age centers on using their drive and passion to fire up the less confident and dedicated. They can do this through active reaching or through art. They approach enlightenment through cultivating self-control, possibly through the martial arts or Hatha Yoga, thus gaining a much-needed balance between their two warring natures and allowing the higher knowledge to flow in.

RAY FIVE:
THE RAY OF CONCRETE KNOWLEDGE OR SCIENCE

Role Function: Scholar

This is the Ray of science and research. Natives of this Ray are dedicated to finding and collecting information, and often they possess vast stores of it, both in the form of huge personal libraries and in their own heads. The main problem with Scholars is that they tend to get caught up in their world of facts and figures and become observers rather than participants in life. Examples of Fifth Ray souls include Marcus Aurelius, the Roman Emperor Claudius, Gioacchino Rossini, William Shakespeare, Leonardo da Vinci, King Charles II of England, Ludwig van Beethoven, Peter Ilyich Tchaikovsky, Giuseppi Verdi, Woodrow Wilson, author Brad Steiger, and actor Leonard Nimoy.

Fifth Ray souls live so much in their heads that they rarely come down to Earth, and they are happiest with their noses buried in books or sharing the information contained in those books. No Scholar, regardless of the stage of development, lacks curiosity. All Scholars on all stages possess keen intellect, a need for great accuracy in detail, and an orderly, businesslike mind.

The Fifth Ray soul will make untiring efforts to trace the most minute of facts and to verify every theory. Scholars are orderly, punctual, forthright. Their research is always accurate, no matter how outlandish their facts might seem. They possess great common sense and are very practical. They are truthful, sometimes to the point of bluntness. They derive great pleasure from disseminating the information they uncover, but unless there is also an influence from the Third, Fourth or Seventh Ray they can be extremely long-winded, pedantic, and somewhat dull, though clear and understandable. Indeed, without some influence from one of the above three Rays the Scholar's work will be technically correct but lacking fire and color.

On the earlier stages of development, even with influence from the Third, Fourth, or Seventh Ray, the music, poetry, painting and sculpture of Fifth Ray types may tend to be masterpieces of technique but lacking in originality. However, as the soul progresses along the evolutionary loop and sensitivity and awareness increase, Fifth Ray entities can approach transcendence. Some of the greatest of artists have been Scholars, so apparently many evolved Fifth Ray types choose to come in

with influence from the Third, Fourth, or Seventh Ray in order to produce great works of art that are rich in detail and accuracy and full of
feeling, emotion, and sensitivity.

Once the facts have been collected, many Fifth Ray types are at a loss
as to what to do with them. They may simply abandon their notes for
that project and move on to the next stint of research. In these cases,
however, they make excellent partners for Third, Fourth, and Seventh
Ray souls who dislike collecting facts and prefer to dive right into the
creative work.

With many Scholars, the drive to collect facts is so strong that these
individuals actually prefer their private realm of knowledge to the real
world. They become observers, living life vicariously rather than as
participants. Their emotions will always be subdued, even when under
the influence of other Rays. Their enthusiasm for their work is genuine, but low key. Fifth Ray types dislike favors, honors or flattery, preferring to continue their work without interruption for what they
consider "trifles."

Fifth Ray souls, needless to say, make excellent journalists and
researchers. They also can be highly skilled chemists, laboratory techni-
cians, surgeons, and engineers. When influenced by the Third, Fourth,
or Seventh Ray—especially in the latter stages of development—they
can be excellent writers, teachers, and artists.

The poet Lord Byron was early Stage Four, Fifth Ray soul, Fourth Ray
personality. He exhibited intense curiosity and a remarkable memory
from an early age. As his lame leg prevented him from actively playing
with other children and caused him to be the target of cruel taunts from
neighborhood boys, so he lost himself in his world of study and observation. When he was six, he wrote a short piece about a butterfly with
which his later friends were quite impressed, but which has since been
lost.

After he had inherited the baronetcy from a great uncle, Byron was
known for the vast amount of detail he remembered from his early

childhood. His relationship with his mother (and consequently with all future women) was strained. Lady Catherine Byron was never known for her intellect, and it irritated her to have her "little lame brat" reciting lists of things he had learned in school. Byron began seriously writing poetry in his early teens. To prove he was not handicapped by his lameness, he threw himself into athletics, becoming an expert boxer, swimmer and cricket player (with another boy running for him).

A bright young man, with extreme good looks and magnetism in spite of (or perhaps partly because of) his deformity, the adult Byron had more money than he'd ever dreamed of, enough female admirers to rival any modern rock star—and nothing to do with his time. So he created a lifestyle for himself, studying European culture and history and writing poetry on the one hand, and chasing women and creating scandal, in accordance with the drives of his Fourth Ray personality, on the other.

At times his scandals drove him away from his homeland, and he took advantage of these periods to learn firsthand about the countries he had heretofore experienced only in books. He became fascinated with the Albanian culture and fought enthusiastically in their revolution. One of his most famous portraits, in the National Portrait Gallery in London, shows him in Albanian dress. Later he was nicknamed "Albé" by Mary Shelley and her stepsister Claire Clairmont because he loved to sing Albanian folksongs—which were actually not much more than wild howls.

He returned to England, only to become involved in a scandalous affair with his half-sister. While most of Byron's entanglements with women were superficial, unmarked by any passion or deep love (at least on his side) this one seems to have been the exception to the rule. Perhaps it was the forbidden nature of the relationship that appealed to him; Byron's attractions to women were always directly influenced by their availability. In order to quell the rumors about himself and his sister, Byron married—an intelligent woman, a "bluestocking" whose intellectual talents he probably enjoyed, at least in the beginning. The marriage very quickly soured, however, and Byron once more fled to the continent of Europe.

In Geneva, Switzerland, he fell in with the poet Shelley, his wife Mary, and Claire Clairmont. Byron had had a brief affair with Claire before he had leaving England, but had rapidly tired of her. Now, however, he was feeling lonely, abandoned, and in need of love, so he allowed himself to be pressured into resuming the affair.

His primary interest, however, was in Shelley, whose level of brilliance and education matched his own and in some ways surpassed it. For hours the two great poets would roam the countryside around Geneva, sharing their thoughts and trading facts. They would explore the lake in Byron's boat, leaving Mary and Claire to fend for themselves. In the evenings the four of them, along with Byron's private physician, John Polidori, would dine together, again trading facts and sharing viewpoints. Byron became quite impressed with Mary as well as with Shelley; for a young woman of only eighteen years, her knowledge was extensive.

The Geneva circle fell apart when Claire announced that she was pregnant by Byron. Claire's possessiveness repulsed Byron, however. Rather than be pressured into a relationship he didn't want, Byron made arrangements to provide for the child with the condition that Claire relinquish all claim to it. The former friends then went their separate ways, the Shelleys to northern Italy, and Byron to Venice, where he began a life of drinking and debauchery. He gained a great deal of weight and lost his good looks.

A few years later, in Pisa, Italy, Byron joined forces with the Shelleys again. Byron had refused to visit them as long as Claire was with them, for he no longer wanted anything to do with her. But by this time Claire had left the Shelleys and taken a job as governess. Byron enjoyed being with Percy and Mary again, and once more they spent hours together, trading facts. Byron was becoming more reclusive than the Shelleys remembered, spending hours in his study, reading and writing letters and poetry. Once more he was involved in a rather superficial relationship, with Italian Countess Teresa Guiccioli, a pretty but not overly bright young woman who fawned over him and thus fed his ego.

In 1822, Shelley drowned at sea, and Byron lost all interest in remaining in Pisa. He was tired of his sedentary life, of the circle of "groupies" he had attracted, and above all of Teresa Guiccioli. He had been throwing himself into the study of Greek history and culture, and now he and a trusted employee, former Venetian gondolier Tita Falcieri, became caught up in the ideals behind the Greek revolution and went to fight for the cause. However, Byron and Tita spent less time fighting than they did cavorting around the countryside, drinking and womanizing.

Byron did, however, move among the soldiers, talking to them and learning from them, writing sketchy poetry in which he tried to capture their views and their emotions. Sometime in the course of these activities Byron contracted pneumonia and died. When she heard the news of Byron's death, Mary Shelley wrote in her journal, "Albé—the dear, fascinating, capricious Albé—has left this desert world. God grant I may die young!" [29]

Byron's life, in which he alternated between amassing and disseminating facts, his preference for relationships based on intellectual rather than emotional compatibility (such as those with Percy and Mary Shelley) and his fascination with cultures beyond that of his native land illustrate the influence of his Fifth Ray soul. The passions bestowed by his Fourth Ray personality he channeled into poetry, athletics, and fighting wars whose causes appealed to him. In spite of his Fourth Ray activities, however, he remained emotionally detached, as though he were doing these things not for their own sake, but for the intellectual

---

29 Mary Shelley's Journal, Frederick L. Jones, editor. Norman, OK: University of Oklahoma Press, 1947. P. 194

satisfaction of knowing what they were like. Such an approach to life is typical of the Fifth Ray.

The Fifth Ray soul needs to curb a tendency toward narrow-mindedness, arrogance, lack of forgiveness, lack of empathy and sensitivity to the needs of others, and intellectual pride. Scholars need to cultivate feeling, devotion, sympathy, love and vision.

The role of Fifth Ray souls in the New Age is to collect and investigate the ancient wisdom, no matter how obscure such information might be, and make it available to all who want to learn. The Path to enlightenment for the Scholar is through objective, scientific research into the ancient wisdom and a thorough knowledge of the facts and philosophies contained therein.

RAY SIX: THE RAY OF DEVOTION OR IDEALISM

Role Function: Devotee

The largest percentage of souls now incarnate on this planet is vibrating to the Sixth Ray. Sixth Ray souls dedicate their lives to serving a person or institution. On the very earliest stages of development, they constitute the immense masses of slaves and servants, almost behaving like automatons and never questioning the authority of their masters. On late Stage Two and Stage Three, they make up the vast ranks of low-level workers in factories or offices, engaged in mundane, boring work, who may hate their jobs yet feel a compulsion to continue doing the work—mainly out of blind acceptance of the employment system but partly out of loyalty to their employers. Stage Two and Three Devotees also make great soldiers, for they are easily swayed by causes such as religion or patriotism.

On the latter stages of development, they can throw themselves into service occupations such as medicine, or missionary or social work. The more metaphysically inclined become devoted followers of gurus, and on the highest level of all they become Apostles. Few, if any, become actual spiritual teachers on the level of Jesus or Buddha or Yogananda, however, without some influence from the First Ray. Examples of Sixth Ray souls are the Pharaoh Akhenaton, the Apostle Peter, St. Luke the Physician, King Edward the Confessor and Queen Victoria of England, Alfred Lord Tennyson, Dr. Elizabeth Blackwell, and author Betty Friedan.

The Sixth Ray soul is almost always devout, with sincere religious impulses. Devotees are full of loyalty and sensitivity, and are generally quite intuitive. Their emotions are so intense that at times these people border on fanaticism, and on late Stage Two and Stage Three they can become full-blown zealots. Stage Three, Sixth Ray souls rarely negotiate or make compromises; everything is either black or white to them. Those who agree with them are angels; those who disagree are evil.

The Sixth Ray soul will fight valiantly and die for what she believes, but will not lift a finger to help those on the other side unless ordered to do so. Whatever Devotees believe is always the truth, for they are totally dedicated to their cause or religion. Many fundamentalist evangelists are Stage Three, Sixth Ray souls with First Ray personalities (or First Ray souls with Sixth Ray personalities).

On the latter stages of development, the fanaticism wanes a little, though total acceptance of the viewpoints of others generally does not come until late Stage Five. The evolved Sixth Ray soul devotes herself to the comfort of those around her as well as to her own spiritual growth.

The enthusiasm of Sixth Ray souls can be inspiring, but it is not to be confused with willpower. Once convinced of the truth of a particular school of thought, Sixth Ray types will allow themselves to be blindly led into abject devotion to their leader. They run into trouble when the leader becomes so magnified in their minds that they subjugate themselves totally to his interest and sacrifice what power they have. Devotees are easily convinced that "the leader is God and they are scum," as is allegedly promoted by many modern cults. Unscrupulous pseudo-gurus have a way of spotting Sixth Ray types, particularly those undergoing some kind of personal agony and therefore in deep need, exploiting this specific weakness in order to advance their own interests.

True devotion, as opposed to fanaticism, appears on the later stages of development. At this point they became aware of the inner God rather than seeing divinity as something that is "out there." They realize that the guru only enables them to bring out their own guru within—and this comprises true devotion, intelligent rather than blind.

Sixth Ray souls rarely make great businessmen, military leaders or statesmen. Whenever Sixth Ray souls are catapulted into positions of authority, such as through birth, they generally fall short of the ideal, although if they are truly devoted to the service of their country they have the potential to become the greatest of leaders. The three Sixth Ray monarchs listed above—Pharaoh Akhenaton, King Edward the Confessor, and Queen Victoria—all were distinguished in their own way, but not as great political leaders. Akhenaton was dedicated to promoting worship of the god Aton, and his dedication could only be described as fanaticism. All traces of worship of other gods were eradicated, and those who refused to accept the new religion were driven out of Egypt. Religious sources hail Akhenaton as a great leader, as a forerunner of the "one true monotheism." But as a political leader he was a failure. Fear, unrest and rebellion in Egypt marked his reign. His heir, the famed Tutankhamen, renounced the worship of Aton (his name was originally Tutankhaton), but was still marked with the stain of Akhenaton's blood, and was murdered at eighteen.

Likewise, King Edward the Confessor, the last Anglo-Saxon king of England, openly admitted that he was an ineffectual king. He was strongly religious in nature, and preferred to live his life as a monk, leaving the governing of his realm to his advisors. Throughout her life, Queen Victoria had one object of her devotion: her consort Prince Albert. The great social, economic and cultural advances that distinguished Victoria's reign were due to the influence of Albert, not Victoria. In fact, after Albert's death, Victoria often incurred the wrath of various charitable organizations who worked hard to raise money for the social causes to which Albert was so dedicated. Victoria used the money, not to benefit the people, but to erect a statue of Albert. This happened several times throughout the course of her reign.

Sixth Ray devotion, sensitivity, and idealism can cause a Devotee under the subordinate influence of the Third, Fourth, or Seventh Ray to become exalted poets or musicians. The artist vibrating to the Sixth Ray is devoted to beauty, color, and melody. Religious books or music is their forte—but they can center their devotion on anything. Remember that Tennyson's most celebrated poem was *In Memoriam,* an elegy for his best friend.

The role of Sixth Ray types in the New Age is to find an appropriate field of interest, such as holistic health or crystal awareness, and dedicate themselves to promoting that field. The best path to enlightenment for Sixth Ray types is Bhakti Yoga, or enlightenment through devotion to a Master.

RAY SEVEN: THE RAY OF CEREMONIAL MAGIC

Role Function: Artisan

This is the Ray of Creation. It is the Ray of ceremony, of systematic action, and efficiency. Seventh Ray types are as devoted in their own way as natives of the Sixth Ray, but Artisans do not seek persons or institutions to serve. They worship beauty, both in nature and in the great works of human beings. The Artisan not only worships beauty, but seeks to create it, often in a compulsive manner. Examples of Seventh Ray souls include the prophet Isaiah, Merlin, Hildegard of Bingen, Alessandro Botticelli, Michelangelo, poet/composer Guillaume de Machaut, composer Barbara Strozzi, William Blake, Franz Anton Mesmer, Sir Christopher Wren, Vincent Van Gogh, rock singer Madonna, and filmmaker George Lucas.

This is also the Ray of the Magician. Seventh Ray souls, because of their drive to create, are drawn first to sympathetic magic. On the earliest stages of development, they are the lucid dreamers, who in their waking state seek to manipulate the "real" world as they do the dream world, and formulate rituals in order to accomplish that end. In later stages, they become high priests and court magicians—on Stage Three they tend to become sectarian and ultra-conservative, on Stages Four and Five, they are drawn to sects such as Wicca, Siddha Yoga, and Krishna Consciousness which use ritualistic chanting and dancing to induce states of ecstasy.

Artisans are known for their strength, perseverance, courage, eye for detail, and self-reliance. They tend to be reclusive, but do attract a small circle of friends who admire their talent and will do anything to advance their cause. When directed toward their work, the energy of Artisans appears boundless. Often they will work for hours on end without pausing to rest or eat and stop only when so exhausted they cannot go on. Seventh Ray souls will endure poverty, cold, deprivation, antagonism from family members—anything for the sake of their work. The Artisan *must create*—and it is useless for anyone to try to convince him or her otherwise.

This drive for creation exists from the earliest stages of development, though in the uroboric substage the individual, though fascinated with beauty and vaguely aware of his own inner drive, has no concept of how to channel it. It is possible, however, that primitive music and art, perhaps in the form of singing, playing primitive instruments such as reeds, and woodcarving began to appear at this substage.

The earliest surviving evidence of the work of Artisans appears in the beautiful cave paintings and the dainty "Venus" figurines that have survived from the Upper Paleolithic and Neolithic eras. Anthropologists believe that the cave paintings (probably the work of souls on the typhonic level) were painted for magical reasons—to insure success in the hunt—and that the "Venus" statues were carved to honor the Great

Earth Mother. Hence we have the earliest evidence of both salient manifestations of the Seventh Ray—the fascination with magic and the drive to create. Some anthropologists believe that in the beginning, all art was magical in nature.

Primitive societies did not try to stop the artist from creating. To them, undoubtedly, the fact that someone could actually draw or carve an image of an animal or a human invoked awe in their simple souls. But with the dawn of civilization, it is probable that only those with some First or Fourth Ray influence had enough dedication to rise above the drive to do only what is best for the group. Our research reveals that on the membership level, many frustrated Artisans go insane or commit suicide. On the early mental substage, Seventh Ray types tend to channel their creative energies into such practical forms of art such as pottery, leatherworking, silver- and goldsmithing, armory, and architecture.

Stage Three is perhaps the most difficult stage for an Artisan. It is at this stage that the drive for worldly success rears its head, and the tendency on the part of Western society is to convince budding artists that their talents are "impractical" and that it is "impossible to make it in the world" in the creative fields. On the questor substage, many Stage Three Artisans knuckle under to this kind of pressure and go into more "practical" fields. They often end up turning to drugs or alcohol for solace, or throwing away a budding career in a "practical" field and sacrificing all for the sake of their art. The more enterprising of them learn their business thoroughly, develop a "business head" to go with their creative talent, and manage to make a success of themselves in spite of the odds against them.

This is the advisable approach for parents of Seventh Ray souls to take. Do not try to force your child away from her creative drive and into a "more practical" field; if you succeed you will only make her miserable. Rather, try to learn the business end of the creative fields yourself and inculcate this knowledge into your child at an early age.

Because of their attraction to systematic ritual, Seventh Ray souls can, in spite of the fact that their "heads are in the clouds," develop business heads as keen as those of any Wall Street executive. Witness the success of Madonna—who can truly be called a self-made woman.

In the latter stages of development, Seventh Ray souls tend to become visionaries—to "see" what isn't there, to "hear" the music of the spheres—and want to record their visions so that others can bene-fit from them as well. Abbess Hildegard of Bingen, a Stage Five, Seventh Ray soul, First Ray personality, was not only a mystic, but an artist, writer, playwright (she is credited with invention of the morality play) and a musician. Her songs in praise of Christ, the saints and the Virgin Mary are still performed today and are becoming increasingly popular in New Age circles. Vincent Van Gogh (early Stage Four) was an auditory as well as a visual mystic, and is said to have cut off his own ear to "stop the voices," though he continued to paint with an unmatched fervor.

Artist and poet William Blake (late Stage Four) produced etchings and poetry so mystical in nature that few students of art or literature ever reach a true understanding of them. Filmmaker George Lucas (also late Stage Four), known chiefly for his "Star Wars" trilogy, was a friend and student of noted mythologist Joseph Campbell and worked many mythological and spiritual themes into his films—which were noted only by other souls on the latter stages of development. The vast majority of Lucas's audience saw the "Star Wars" movies mainly as great adventure films.

The Seventh Ray soul tends to be self-absorbed, overly concerned with his own work and its value. In the earlier stages (and sometimes into the later stages) they can be bigoted and narrow-minded; in the lat-ter stages they become irresponsible about practical matters and often cause their families great pain. They need to develop their business heads so that they won't be forced to starve in a garret in order to make the most of their art. They also need to lean to look beyond their work and take the time to express their love to the people who are devoted to them.

The role of the Seventh Ray soul in the New Age is self-evident: they need to work hard on developing their potential both for magical work and for art—along with their business sense. The best Path to enlightenment for the Artisan is, of course, through ritual magic.

TREATING THE DIFFERENT RAY SOULS

For the therapist, the benefit of knowing the individual's Ray vibration is the same as knowing his or her stage of development. The First Ray soul is not going to react to a given situation in the same way as one on the Fifth or Sixth Ray. If the situation is a traumatic one, the psychological problems and their solutions will be different—and the therapist would save a great deal work and confusion by knowing the individual's Ray vibration.

Let us take a hypothetical, desperate situation—a type that arises all too often in our violent society. A thief bursts into a restaurant. At the first three tables he encounters seven people, representing each of the Rays. The outlaw holds them all hostage, threatening to kill them unless he is given a plane ride out of the country. Each of the seven people acts and reacts in accordance with the characteristics peculiar to each Ray.

The First Ray soul, fearless but not foolish, steps forward and talks calmly to the fugitive. He explains, firmly but not threateningly, that the chances of getting away with the crime are next to nil and that it would be best if he turned over the gun and gave himself up. He continues to talk, trying to turn himself into the crook's best friend. He will make it clear not only to the robber, but to everyone else in the room, that he is in charge and no one is to make a move without his approval.

The Second Ray soul, whose compassion is immediately aroused, not only for the hostages but also for the perpetrator, moves quietly among the other people in the room, talking to them, assuring them that they will be all right, allaying their fears, and providing first aid when necessary.

The Third Ray soul's mind starts working frantically, formulating plans for escape.

The King will be hard-pressed to keep the Warrior, and whatever other Warriors might be in the room, from charging forward, heedless of danger, and trying to take the thief by force. The Warrior's attitude would typically be, "He can only shoot one or two of us before we take him," without giving any thought to the innocents who might be caught in the crossfire.

The Scholar will detach herself from the situation, noting as many facts as possible—minute details of the killer's face and clothing, his position in the room, hints in his conversation as to who he is and where he's coming from, even the make and model of his gun.

The Devotee will follow in the steps of the Second Ray soul, giving succor to the people, taking no initiative of her own, but following whatever instructions the Priest chooses to give. While the Priest will feel sympathy for the thief, however, the Devotee will see him as evil and will pray for him to be overcome if not killed.

The Seventh Ray soul will appeal to his gods and retreat into his own world—possibly into a mystical state where he is only barely aware of what is going on.

Now let us imagine that the police come and storm the place, and the outlaw is taken into custody. Each of these different Ray types will develop a different trauma as a result of the above experience.

The King will be angry that he was not able to stay in control, that it was the police, and not his own actions, that resolved the situation. There is no way to assuage this anger; no amount of talk, and certainly no platitudes, will convince the King that he did everything he could and shouldn't be angry. The only way for the therapist to help the King handle his anger is to allow him to express it until it is played out.

The Priest will feel guilt that she wasn't able to comfort everyone in the room. The therapist should praise her efforts and do his best to convince her that it was have been literally impossible for her to reach everyone.

The Sage will be shaken by the violence and the horror of it—although she behaved quite coolly when it was happening—and will need a lot of time to calm down. The therapist should recommend time off from work, long walks, and lots of books and videotapes to get her mind off the experience.

The Warrior and the Scholar will probably be the least scarred of all. On the contrary, the Warrior will be exhilarated by the experience and will tell the story again and again for years afterwards. The Scholar, who was the least emotionally involved with the experience, will write up a detailed and factual account of her view of it and sell it to the newspapers.

The Devotee will be more shaken than the Sage and almost as angry as the King, and will probably spend more time with the therapist than anyone else.

The Artisan will see the event as a major turning point in his life—and he may never be the same. He will probably make sweeping new resolutions about how he handles his life, and will express his emotions and inner revelations through his work. A therapist should avoid recommending tranquilizers or trying to play down the spiritual nature of the Artisan's experience. Instead, she could encourage the person to continue in the new course of action and not slide back into his old ways.

Hopefully, an event such as this will never happen, but the point I'm making is that natives of different Rays should not all be thought of or treated as if they were the same. Each serves a different function in the world, and those differences should not be ignored, but should be understood and appreciated.

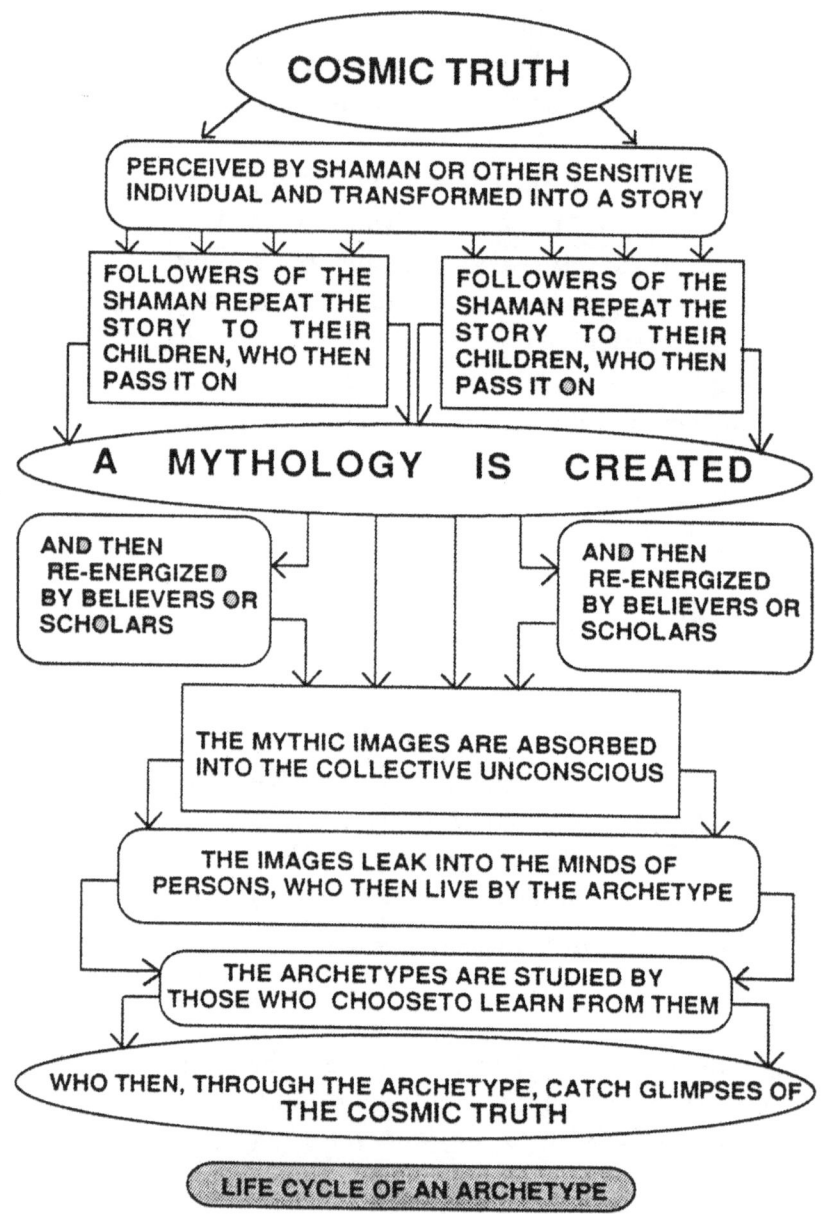

LIFE CYCLE OF AN ARCHETYPE

FOUR

Archetypal Influences

Impressions from the Akasha

In recent years the word *archetype* has been bandied around quite a bit. Its appeal, perhaps, lies in the fact that archetype, a term popularized by famed psychoanalyst Carl Gustav Jung, appears to give semi-scientific status to concepts that were previously considered fairy tales and superstitions.

Actually, the word itself goes back to classical times, to Philo Judaeus and *De optifico mundi,* and originally was a reference to the "imago Dei," or God-image, in human beings. It can also be found in *Adversus haereses,* by Irenaeus, who states: "The creator of the world did not fashion these things directly from himself, but copied them from archetypes outside himself."[30]

Jung began to make use of this ancient concept when he observed the similarity between the myths of long-dead civilizations and the dream images related to him by his patients. Why was it, he wondered, that a five-year-old child, who had never before heard of such things, reported a dream of riding on a winged horse and slaying a monster—a dream very similar to the ancient myth of Perseus and Andromeda? This type of experience occurred so often throughout the course of Jung's practice that he came to the conclusion that these hundreds of experiences could not possibly be coincidence—there had to be some source outside themselves upon which these patients were drawing. He thus formulated the concept of the *collective unconscious*.

The idea of something called the "unconscious" was not original with Jung. He himself had learned the term from Sigmund Freud, who had postulated the existence of a part of every person's mind which contained memories, impressions, and reflections the person had consciously long forgotten. Freud had drawn this conclusion after working with the dreams of his patients who drew up through their dreams forgotten memories of long-dead relatives and traumatic events of which they claimed no conscious memory.

But the appearance of ancient mythological themes in the dreams of simple, uneducated types who had never studied mythology, Jung realized, could not possibly represent the same phenomenon. Too many of his patients were working class people with little or no formal education past the elementary level, and the idea of such people ever having been exposed to Sumerian or Egyptian mythology was too remote for serious consideration. Yet the elements of those traditions were unmistakably present, in their memories, dreams, and reflections—and they had to come from somewhere. If not from their own unconscious, from where?

Jung therefore drew a distinction between the *personal unconscious* and the *collective unconscious*. The personal unconscious was restricted to

---

30 Carl Gustav Jung. "Archetypes of the Collective Unconscious," in *The Basic Writings of C. G. Jung.* (New York: Modern Library. 1959). p. 287.

memories of events and perceptions which each individual experiences and stores away in the course of a lifetime. The collective unconscious, on the other hand, represents a vast storehouse in the psychic field of the Earth in which are stored the sum total of all the memories, dreams, and impressions of everyone who has ever lived on Planet Earth.

This "storehouse" comprises all the creative concepts that ever existed, including images of all the gods, goddesses, fairy tale characters, stories, legends, even archetypes of historical figures whose personalities were "larger than life" and left a distinct imprintation on the ethers apart from their actual selves. According to Jung, these archetypes could be drawn upon at any time by anyone, appearing in that person's dreams or daydreams. Conversely, that same person could add to the myth and return the expanded version to the collective unconscious for someone else to draw upon.

Jung did not, as some more recent theorists do, equate the world of the archetypes with the same basic animal instincts that insure survival, but he did believe them to be related. What is it that drives baby birds to leave their nests and fly? Or fish to swim? Or lions to hunt antelope? Although these processes may seem complex to us, they are second nature to the animals—as it probably was for our animalistic ancestors to forage for fruit in tropical forests. These processes Jung believed were instinctual.

But what is it that drives the fox or the tiger to fear man—even when the individual fox or tiger has never before encountered this strange, vicious animal with its killing machines? What is it that allows the cow, dog, or cat to think of human beings as their friends, even though they may have encountered cruel ones? What causes newborn kittens to respond to the cry of "Kitty, kitty, kitty?" These phenomena, Jung maintained, were akin to instinct but more complex, based on the world of experience rather than the drive to survive. They are a part of the collective unconscious and therefore are archetypal.

The concept of the collective unconscious at first drew jeers from the scientific—and even the psychoanalytical—establishment. Science was then—and in many circles still is now—predicated on the assumption that everything that exists can, and at some moment in time will, be measured and explained in terms of our own three-dimensional, five-sense capabilities. And who could see, hear, feel, taste, or smell an archetype? Who could possibly measure the collective unconscious?

But Jung's somewhat metaphysical approach certainly brought results. Through his analysis, most of his patients reported vast improvement in whatever problems were plaguing them—and so the psychoanalytical establishment, at least, began to think twice about Jung's ideas. A new school of thought began to take form, which is now called "Jungian psychology."

Jung and his followers were well aware that the world is more than what it seems. The materialistic contentions of the hard-line scientists were believed to be demonstrably untrue. We now know that the Jungians were quite correct. The existence of dog whistles, which emit sound waves vibrating at so high a rare that they cannot be heard by human ears, bur are easily perceived by dogs, proves that there is at least one form of reality that humans are unable to detect with their physical senses. Bats, also, can hear high-pitched sounds that even dogs are unaware of, and there exist sound waves vibrating at so rapid a rate that even bats are unaware of them.

Our human eyes, too, perceive but a small part of the world around us. Infrared and ultraviolet light exist, but are invisible to the human eye. Experiments with the vision of frogs demonstrate surprisingly that, in spite of the infinite number of stimuli which the eyes of frogs receive from the outside world, only four different types of messages are sent from the retina to the brain, limiting the frog to awareness of only four basic types of external activities. These include the general outline of the environment, any significant movement in that environment, sudden decreases in light, and when small dark objects come into the field of vision and move close to the eye. [31] In other words, the frog's brain perceives where the frog generally is, whenever creatures approach that might be predators, and when flies or other insects come close so that the frog can catch them as food. The frog brain apparently registers *only that which the frog needs to be aware of in order to survive.* Further experiments reveal that a frog hopping happily through the forest is totally blind to the existence of such objects as a fallen log and, unless it comes quite close to the log, never even knows it is there.

Experiments like this tend to make us curious and sometimes quite uncomfortable: What is out there in our world that our brains decide we have no need to bother with, as it does not affect our survival? The work of scientists like Ralph Metzner and Stanislav Grof with psychedelic drugs such as LSD, as well as the stories told by skilled clairvoyants throughout the centuries, seem to indicate that there is a lovely world out there beyond the realm of the five senses of which most of us are totally unaware.[32]

But physical scientists—at least the older and more hard-nosed of them—still tend to hold stubbornly to their own views. They regard the collective unconscious and its archetypes, particularly the astrological ones, as ridiculous, and Jung as a harmless eccentric who managed to help some people in spite of his strange attitudes.

All the same, the physical scientists themselves live in a strange and wonderful world, far beyond the realms of the senses. The world of the molecule and atom were wonderful enough in themselves, but it was soon discovered that the atom was not, as had previously been believed, the ultimate particle. Nor was the proton, neutron or electron. A vast world of particles and rays far smaller than any of these exists. The quark, the neutrino, the positron, the antielectron, the gamma ray, and others too numerous to name here have made their existence known. And there appear to be other particles yet, even smaller and finer.

Finally the scientists came up with a "great new revelation:" The universe is composed entirely of consciousness.

Surprise, surprise. The Hindu masters have been teaching this for thousands of years.

What would a gamma ray look like if we could see it? Or a neutrino shower? Would they have form? Would they appear to be shimmering sheets of light and color that we could walk through and merge with our bodies? Would they resemble the shadowy images we call archetypes?

Although Jung postulates that the archetypes have existed since the beginning of time, he avoids the question of where the archetypes came from—though he openly admits he has no idea. "Were I a philosopher," Jung writes, "I should...say: Somewhere, in a supracelestial place, there is a prototype or primordial image of the mother [or any other archetype] that is pre-existent and supra-ordinate to all phenomena in which the 'maternal', in the broadest sense of the term, is manifest. But I am an empiricist, not a philosopher."[33]

I remember watching *The Astronomers*, a fine documentary series on astronomers, the way they work, and their discoveries. I was particularly impressed with the following story. Noted astrophysicist Margaret Geller used computer technology to project out into our galaxy and create a model of what the stars look like from a vantage point outside the Milky Way. Her first observation was that a certain cluster of stars at the heart of the galaxy, when viewed from this vantage point, resembled the body of a man.

---

31 Robert Ornstein, *The Psychology of Consciousness*. New York: Penguin, 1972.

32 For further information on these experiments, see Stanislav Grof, *Realms of the Human Unconscious*. (New York: E.P. Dutton and Company, 1976.) Also *Beyond the Brain*. (Albany. NY: State University of New York Press. 1985.)

Her curiosity piqued, Geller worked on the model further until she created a three-dimensional model, or how this sector of the galaxy would look if viewed by someone on a space ship traveling around it. Then she rotated that model—and a film of that rotation was shown in the documentary.

I was astounded. As a twenty-year student of yoga, I was well acquainted with the *naturaj,* or the figure of Shiva, God of the Universe, dancing in the middle of a ring of fire, his four arms waving, his leg kicking high. The resemblance of this cluster of stars to the *naturaj* was so striking it was unmistakable. There was the man with his four arms, his leg kicking high, in the middle of a circle of stars. So this, I thought, is the Dance of Shiva.[34] Was this what Jung was talking about? Was this the "supracelestial place" that gave rise to the myth of Shiva? Was this the world of the archetypes?

THE SIX PRIMAL ARCHETYPES

There are six primal archetypes that exist in the psyche of every human being and often appear in dreams. One is the shadow self—or our own dark side, that many of us would prefer not to acknowledge. In dreams, the shadow self often takes the form of monsters or ferocious beasts.

The second is the *animus* (in women) *or anima* (in men)—the man within every woman or the woman within every man. In dreams, the animus or anima often appears as a mythological figure—as a prince or princess, as an elusive sprite, as an unknown, sometimes faceless male or female figure. The third and fourth primal archetypes are the *juven* and *senex.* The juven is the Divine Child within each of us, whereas the senex is the wise old man or woman. Still another, related somewhat to

---

33 Jung, "Psychological Aspects of the Mother Archetype," in *Basic Writings,* p. 328.

the shadow, is the double, while the last, reminiscent of the juven, is the Trickster.

These primal archetypes have to do with the self, or parts of every individual psyche. However, there are other archetypes that clearly come from without. Those are the forces of nature, personified in the form of gods or goddesses, or other important figures such as the Divine Mother or Father. Others take the form of mystic places, such as Paradise. Still others, which Jung calls *archetypes of transformation,* represent passages in the life of every person. The most celebrated of these archetypes, at least in recent years, is the hero's journey, as celebrated mythologist Joseph Campbell defined it. Others include the battle for deliverance from the mother and the night-sea journey. The night-sea journey archetype calls to mind an ancient Druidic initiation ceremony, where an aspiring Druid was put into a boat at night and shoved offshore to survive the elements alone until morning.

Psychologist John White defines an archetype as "an energetic envelope of some new (or non-physical) energy presently unknown", or "energetic thought fields accessible through dreams, meditation and other altered states of consciousness" which lower our resistance to transpersonal influences. Archetypes, according to White, are not limited to any one person or culture but permeate the entire physical atmosphere of Planet Earth. While White has not yet resolved the conundrum of how information might be encoded in these archetypes, he believes this definition at least offers something of an explanation at least semi-acceptable to the "scientific" community.[35]

In the past twenty years, long after Jung's death, the line between empiricism and philosophy has become blurred, and so I will take Jung's postulate one step farther and say this: Archetypes arose when

---

34 One is also reminded of the vision of Hildegard of Bingen referred to on page 68.

the first life forms on this planet began to accumulate experience—to expand their consciousness beyond the instinctual drive to survive. The world of human archetypes began when the first soul-entity from the human Light Master completed the involutionary arc and began to fulfill the original desire that had caused the Monad to break away from the Divine in the first place: the desire to experience life on the physical plane.

Through dreams, this primitive human being, and all the others who followed her, gradually grew to know her animus, to experience the shadow, the double, the Trickster, the juven and the senex. Remember that to the Stage One soul on the uroboric level, there is no difference between the world of dreams and the world of the physical. Hence, to the Stage One souls evolving back in the Paleolithic era, the world was a strange place, inhabited by ghostly figures, strange monsters, sprightly beings, and wise old men and women.

The more complex archetypes—those based on cosmic truth—probably did not come into existence before the first soul evolved past the uroboric level and onto the typhonic. It was probably one of the first shamans who perceived cosmic truths that eventually became the archetypes we know so well today.

HOW ARCHETYPES ARISE

There are two main theories as to how so many religions that bear striking resemblances to each other arose in so many different places all over the world, thousands of miles removed from each other. How could it be, for example, that archaeologists researching the Indus Valley civilization in southern India excavated medallions containing the image of a horned god surrounded by oak trees—images that were

---

35 Brad Steiger. *Gods of Aquarius: UFOs and the Transformation of Man* (New York: Harcourt, Brace, Jovanovich 1976). p. 42.

highly reminiscent of carvings in France and England of the Celtic Horned God, Cernunnos, whose sacred tree was the oak?

One theory explaining so-called "coincidences" such as this is that travelers brought religious ideas from one place to the other. However, while this was certainly possible in the times of which we are speaking, this is highly unlikely. The Celts were a land-oriented society, and though it is clear that they must have traveled skillfully by boat between the continent of Europe and the British Isles, the purpose of this travel appears to have been simply to get from one place to another. They did not, it seems, possess a sea-oriented culture like the Phoenicians. Nor, according to most sources, did the people of the Indus Valley. And it is unlikely that Celtic and Indus Valley beliefs are similar because of the Aryan migrations of 3000 BC. The relics from the Indus Valley pre-date the Aryan invasion of India.

So how did it come about that the people of the Indus Valley apparently worshipped the same god as the Celts? I believe this similarity—along with many others too numerous to mention here—supports the second hypothesis: that of the primal revelation.

The primal revelation theory holds that in the beginning of human existence on Earth, the Divine Truths were revealed to all. Only the passage of millennia created the religious diversity (and conflicts) that we have today.

What I believe happened was this. Somewhere, back in the Paleolithic era when most of us were going through Stage One, shamans all over the world—possibly through out-of-body, psychedelic, or near-death experiences—began to realize that the Sun, for example, was not a mere ball of fire in the sky, but a living, pulsating entity, who sent his rays to nourish and give light and life to everyone. Other people—or perhaps the same ones—sensed that the Earth was an entity as well, Divine Mother to all. They also discovered that there once had been a realm of bliss—hence the concept of Paradise. Did a Paleolithic shaman have out-of-body experience that took him millions of light years above the earth? And did this out-of-body experience reveal to him the image of a man, arms waving, leg kicking high, in the middle of a circle of light? Did this adventure cause him to bring back to Earth the ancient Hindu concept of the Dance of Shiva and possibly to carve the original model of the *naturaj?*

Archaeological support for the existence of a primordial Mother Earth/Father Sun religion in all primitive societies continues to turn up all over the world. Only a few societies, it appears, saw the Earth as masculine and the Sun as feminine. As civilization progressed, settled societies began to favor the Mother, while nomadic tribes were more drawn toward the Father.

Historical evidence seems to indicate that the Mother societies were eventually absorbed by the Father-oriented (or patriarchal) societies, causing extreme imbalances in the statuses of men and women, but it is not our intention here to pursue this line of knowledge.

It does appear that somewhere, from Jung's "supracelestial place," the archetype of the mother attached itself to both the personal mother and to Mother Earth—or the association of Mother Earth with the personal mother gave rise to the mother archetype (the old chicken-and-egg conundrum. The Divine Mother was seen in two ways: the Nurturing Mother, meaning she who gave us life, and saw that we were fed and sheltered; and the Terrible Mother, she who punished, sent fires, storms, and earthquakes, and took us back into her body (through burial) after death.

This concept eventually took on a life of its own. According to Jung, though an archetype has energy of its own, it does not possess sufficient energy to rise from the collective unconscious and into consciousness until triggered by something in the external world. Perhaps once the existence of the Mother Earth Monad was perceived by a shaman, parallels were drawn between the behavior of the personal mother—who fed, clothed, cuddled, and yet slapped when a child misbehaved—and the Earth, who sent warmth, food, shelter, and death. Thus the mother archetype was born, and women all over the world began to live it, from the moment it was triggered by the birth of their first child.

Several years ago, when I was researching the chapter on animus and anima, "The God and Goddess Within" for *Astrology and Relationships,* I was astounded to discover that every source I consulted—including Robert Graves's classic, *The White Goddess*—traced nearly every single one of the Greek goddesses to the Earth Mother.[36] Why, I wondered, would the original Divine Mother become so diversified as to range from the concepts of loving and sensual Aphrodite to cold and distant Diana to warlike Athena—so much that the Greeks clearly thought of them as separate entities?

I found in the course of my research that it was virtually impossible to find a god and goddess in any single culture to represent every sign of the zodiac. I had wanted to concentrate on the Greek and Roman gods and goddesses because they were the ones with whom my Western readers would have been most familiar. But the Greeks, who were outrageously patriarchal, had no god that represented the nurturing and protective (or "maternal") potential in men that we associate with the sign Cancer. Nor did the Greeks have any goddesses to represent the concepts of intelligence, associated with Gemini, or freedom, a desire peculiar to Sagittarius. The Hindus, however, as heirs to the Goddess-oriented Indus Valley society, had Indra, the king of the gods, who, unlike the egotistical and vengeful Greek god Zeus, loved and protected his people. They also had Saraswati, goddess of learning and the supposed inventor of writing. And the Celts had Epona, the horse-goddess, who valued her freedom above all else. So I decided to combine Hindu deities with European ones and called it the Indo-European pantheon.

I find it interesting that each of the goddesses seems to encapsulate a feature of one of the Seven Rays. Hera, the Queen of the Gods, who loved to control those around her, appears to be First Ray; Ceres or Lakshmi represents an aspect of the Second Ray. The Celtic Brighid and the Hindu Saraswati are Third Ray, while the Hindu Durga-Kali and the Greek Athena, with their warlike natures, are perfect Fourth Ray types. Diana could be seen to personify the Fifth, as she is an observer who avoids actively participating in life. Isis, with her devotion to Osiris, could personify the Sixth Ray, while the Celtic Cerridwen, with her magical cauldron, calls the Seventh Ray to mind. Is it possible that priests or shamans vibrating to each of those Rays unconsciously perceived the Great Mother as one of their own Ray types, thus creating from one cosmic truth—the existence of the Planetary Logos—the archetypes of several different goddesses?

One myth that seems to date from deep into the realms of antiquity is the myth of the god that dies and comes back to life—most often the Sun God. The Solar Deity is usually portrayed as a beautiful youth, with long golden hair that symbolizes the rays of the Sun. He is slain by wicked plotters, who personify all that is evil in the Universe. Through certain rituals, ceremonies, and sacrifices, the young god is brought back to life—and then moves on to become the Savior of his people. This myth seems to be a constant of many mythologies, from the Native American to the South African to the Egyptian to the Norse. It even sounds familiar to Christians!

Some sources theorize that the tradition of the God who comes back to life stems from a personification of the summer-winter theme—the Sun "dies" in the winter and then returns in the summer. But this seems to me to be an oversimplification. In many places where this myth forms the basis of the religion, the summer-winter dichotomy simply does not exist, such as in Egypt and Central America, where the stories of Osiris and Quetzalcoatl are legend. Even in some places where it does—such as the Nordic countries, home of the story of Balder the Beautiful, the young Norse Sun god slain through the treachery of

---

36 Mary Devlin, *Astrology and Relationships.* West Chester, PA: Whitford Press, 1988.

Loki—the Sun does not disappear in the winter months. Only his warmth does. So it would appear that, logically, the source of this tradition must be something more than a mere personification of the summer-winter theme.

But suppose, after the primal revelation, certain wise tribal shamans wanted to tell the story of the Days and Nights of Brahm in such a way that their people—and, in fact, they themselves—would understand. So they interpreted the idea of the Big Bang and the expanding and collapsing Universe as the story of a God who dies and then comes back to life—and created and told the story to avid listeners, again and again.

The stories spread. Each teller of the tale altered it to suit his own point of view, cultural background, and Ray vibration. All over the world there sprang up religious traditions centered around the beautiful Sun God who died and came back to life. Some were crucified, including the Hindu Krishna and the Aztec Quetzalcoatl. In certain cultures—most notably the Judeo-Christian culture—there were great Masters who made use of that tradition to demonstrate the truth of their teachings.

The similarities between the ancient myths of the dead and resurrected Sun God and the story of Jesus of Nazareth do not, as some skeptics maintain, indicate that the Crucifixion and Resurrection never happened. They only mean that Jesus was *living the archetype.* The tendency of human beings to respond to the contents of the collective unconscious and live the archetypes has only recently been recognized. It has been made popular by the works of Jean Shinoda Bolen, Carol Pearson, and Dan Kiley. Innumerable books centered around ancient myths and fairy tales, with titles like *The Peter Pan Syndrome, Kiss Sleeping Beauty Goodbye* and *The Cinderella Complex,* attempt to demonstrate how people are unconsciously living their lives according to outmoded archetypes that apparently have no real bearing on today's reality.

The archetypes existing in ancient tradition that still affect people's lives are legion. Our particular Ray vibrations, along with the astrological influences in our lives and our past and present life experiences, cause us to be attracted to archetypes and subconsciously to live them. These archetypes are found in myths, legends, fairy tales, history, and religious traditions. We hear about them all the time in casual conversation, in remarks such as: "She's a Cinderella," "He's a Robin Hood," "Who does he think he is—Napoleon?"

However, just because a story is metaphoric in nature doesn't mean it isn't true. The story of Cain and Abel, for example, has been interpreted as an allegory for the triumph of agriculture (Cain) over the nomadic way of life (Abel). But that doesn't necessarily mean, as some people seem to imply, that long ago there wasn't a real pair of brothers, named Cain and Abel, one a farmer, one a herdsman, who disagreed, resulting in the murder of the herdsman by the farmer. Such a tragedy could well have marked the beginning of a legend. The same principle can be applied to archetypes. We live these archetypes all the time, so that our very lives sometimes seem metaphorical—and thus we can actually relate historical events to ancient legends.

The assassination of John F. Kennedy, for example, could well be seen to personify the ancient Old European legend of the sacrificial king, who must die so that his people may experience a new growth of knowledge and wisdom. Kennedy's death set the stage for the protests of the 1960s, which brought to public awareness the shortcomings and abuses existing in the Establishment and caused people to eschew the customs and mores of our society and explore the lifestyles and traditions of other cultures. But who is going to stand up and claim that because Kennedy's death seems to fit this ancient archetype so perfectly, there never really was a John Fitzgerald Kennedy?

I have an experiment I often do with my students. I tell them, "Quick! Think of anything in the world but the word hippopotamus!" And, of course, the first thing they think of is a hippopotamus. Then I tell them, that for that brief moment, they have created an archetype—a hippopotamus, floating around on the astral plane. Now, if they stop thinking about the hippopotamus, the archetype will fade into nothing. But if everyone in the room continues to think about the hippopotamus, it will pick up energy of its own and eventually take on its own existence on the astral plane—to be drawn upon whenever anyone feels the need to bring a hippopotamus archetype into her life.

When my children first heard the news from their school friends that there was no Santa Claus, they immediately came home to me—upset, as children usually are after this revelation—and asked if it was true. I explained it to them in this way: On the physical plane, no, there is no little old man at the North Pole, with a toy shop, who makes toys for good children and has elves and reindeer to help him deliver them every Christmas. But on the astral plane, there is.

The archetype was drawn from a historical figure, St. Nicholas, patron saint of the poor, whom legend presents as a wealthy man who saved many people from starving by anonymously dropping purses of gold through their chimneys in the night. The association between St. Nicholas and the spirit who leaves gifts at Christmas apparently came from Holland. There, St. Nicholas Day is celebrated on December 5, twenty days before Christmas. On this day, St. Nicholas, called "Sinterklaus," traditionally visits the homes of children, leaving toys, sweets, and other gifts.

In the mid-1800s, Clement C. Moore wrote his classic Christmas poem, "A Visit From St. Nicholas," in which he described the night visitor as small, round, and jolly, with a white beard, dressed in a red-and-white suit, driving eight reindeer, and bringing toys to good children on Christmas Eve. This poem was an immediate success and became a Christmas classic—and it created the image of Santa Claus that is still celebrated throughout the Western world today.

The minds of children and their parents everywhere locked into this image. Stories were told a hundred times over of Santa Claus and his annual Christmas Eve visits. All the energies of all these minds poured into the astral plane, year after year, right up until the present day, recreating again and again and energizing and re-energizing the archetype we know today as Santa Claus, which millions of parents draw upon and live at least once every year.

Years ago, when a friend of mine was performing experiments with psychedelic drugs, she reported an experience on the astral plane in which she found herself face to face with the Santa Claus archetype. And so I told my children that while there is no Santa Claus on the physical plane, on the astral plane he is alive and happy.

The way an archetype arises seems to be this: Some way, at some time, a very sensitive individual, possibly a shaman, perceived a cosmic truth. He interpreted it from his perspective and related it to other people. The stories were passed on. And the minds of the people who heard the stories created images that were impressed on the collective unconscious and reinforced throughout the ages.

ARCHETYPAL INFLUENCES IN INDIVIDUAL LIVES

According to Jung, an archetype won't manifest in anyone's psyche without some kind of triggering event, not unlike the keying incident that causes unconscious fears from past lives to surface in one's present life. Certain archetypes are associated with astrological influences; hence a woman born under the sign of Aries, which is associated with the goddess Athena, could well find herself living the Athena archetype. Something so simple as a name can sometimes trigger it. Edward Sparks named his eldest daughter Athena. When I read the section on the goddess Athena in Jean Shinoda Bolen's classic, *Goddesses in Every Woman*, I couldn't help wondering if Dr. Bolen had known my friend's daughter. Like the goddess whose name she bears, Edward's daughter is strong, both physically and mentally; she is wise beyond her years and capable of dealing with almost any situation. She is a warrior, generally peaceful until challenged—and then woe be unto anyone who crosses her!

Athena Sparks once sought a career in the military—and became the second female Green Beret to endure the rigorous training required for this elite branch of the US Army.

ASTROLOGICAL INFLUENCES

Astrology is a very important factor in the judging of human personalities, even though fundamentalist religious sects damn it as the work of the devil and empirical scientists still ridicule it. They are still unaware of any possible physical influence that can stretch from the cosmos to the individual here on Earth, and because they can't explain it they choose to assume it is totally invalid. Because they can't deduce the reason for it, they can't accept that astrology works.

However, I have been a professional astrologer for over twenty years, and every year my faith in this science is reaffirmed a thousand times over. My clients are not all nuts and quacks and impressionable morons (though admittedly there are a few); I deal with doctors, lawyers, college professors, and businessmen. (There are even a few scientists and engineers.) I haven't become a professional astrologer and made all the effort of studying, taking exams, and becoming certified in order to make a lot of money; it is only the past few years that I have actually been able to earn my living completely from astrology—and even now my income is far less than that of many of my clients.

I do believe that there is some kind of quasi-Newtonian or Einsteinian law of physics that can account for the astrological influences; our science right now is simply too young and too undeveloped to discover it. The growth of chaos theory and nonlinear dynamics certainly gives a clue as to how astrology might work. In recent years physicist/astrologer William Keepin has done considerable research and written extensively on astrology in light of the work of physicist David Bohm. Bohm explained the basic nature of reality in terms of what he called *holomovement*—defined as "a single unbroken wholeness in flowing movement." If this be the case, says Keepin, within this idea could lie the secret of why astrology works.[37]

However, for those scientists who refuse to acknowledge that there is still more to be discovered regarding the Universe and its effect on the lives and psyches of life forms on Earth, I wish to point out that the astrological influences constitute very powerful archetypes, some of which have been known to exist for as long as twenty thousand years. Therefore, it would be difficult for anyone who accepts the truth of in-depth archetypal psychology to deny that the astrological influences have some effect. The impression made on the collective unconscious for at least five thousand years has been that people born between March 20 and April 20 share certain characteristics associated with the sign we now call Aries the Ram, and so on—and since we all reverberate to the collective unconscious, it follows logically that astrology "works", at least on the archetypal level.

I must pause here to answer a question that is often posed to me at interviews and at lectures. How, I am often asked, do you really know that your clients are tuning into past lives? How do you know they aren't just repeating something they read somewhere, or drawing upon the collective unconscious?

I always reply that I agree totally with Dr. Roger Woolger author of *Other Lives, Other Selves,* who states that cryptomnesia, or the repeating of outside material under hypnosis as a source of past-life memory, is overrated. He also states that the only times he has ever encountered cryptomnesia is when people recall having been someone who was once famous.[38] I must admit my experience coincides with his.

While I have had a few cases—sixteen, to be exact—of people who appear genuinely to be the reincarnations of the great or near-great, most people who think they were once famous persons tend to take a specific experience associated with someone famous and assume this means they were that person. For example: In spite of all the millions of innocent women who were burned at the stake during the

Inquisition and the seventeenth-century witch hunts, whenever any woman I work with recalls a life in which she was burned at the stake, she almost always jumps to the conclusion that she was Joan of Arc. I have always been a hopeless history buff, and in the course of my life I have read several biographies of Joan of Arc. None of the women I have worked with related a life that was even similar to that of Joan—and yet, because they were at some time burned at the stake, they automatically assume they were Joan of Arc. (As far as I know, the real reincarnation of Joan of Arc has never turned up.) This is the only sort of instance, in the course of my work, that cryptomnesia ever has reared its head.

I have also been asked how I know that my clients aren't simply tuning into the collective unconscious. This explanation doesn't really carry any weight, either. People can, of course, tune into the collective unconscious. We do every time we tap into an archetype and start to live it. We can also tune into the collective unconscious every time we want to get a genuine feeling for a historical event and try to relive it psychically. However, my clients who are seeking insights into their own psyches simply don't appear to be doing it. There is a sense of identification that comes with past-life regression that just doesn't come when a person is tuning into the collective unconscious.

For instance, whenever Edgar Cayce gave a past-life reading, he was continually tuning into the collective unconscious (which he called the Akashic records), whether it was a past-life reading or a medical one. *But he never identified with any of the entities he tuned in to.* Although Cayce was continually coming up with a wealth of material—much of which checked out—on the past personalities of

---

37 William Keepin, Ph.D. "Astrology and the New Physics: Integrating Sacred and Secular Sciences." *The Mountain Astrologer*, August/September 1995, pp. 12ff.

38 Roger Woolger, Ph.D. *Other Lives, Other Selves.* (New York: 1990).

everyone he read for, he always spoke of "the entity," referring to his subjects in the third person. He related stories of the most tragic and heart-wrenching incidents in a flat, emotionless monotone, the way we would do when reading a news story aloud. And unless he was reading again for a prior client, he never tuned in to the same past personality twice. In fact, students of the Cayce material have pointed out the fact that even when Cayce tuned in to his own past lives, he spoke as if he were referring to someone else—which experts believe to be evidence that the information was simply being channeled through Cayce from a higher source.

However, in my work with past-life regression, clients have a way of returning to the same lifetimes again and again, continually tuning in to specific personalities who lived at specific times. They *identify* with these people, relate their feelings, their pain, their observations, and perceive them as their own. Some of them suffer horribly and have to be brought out of their experiences quickly, with the reminder that this is only a memory; there is no need to relive the experience. And they can clearly connect the experiences of the past personality to situations and problems existing in their current lifetimes. They do not, by any stretch of the imagination, relate their perceptions in the same kind of detached, impersonal manner that Cayce did—or that any past-life reader, for that matter, can do.

In one sense, everyone in the regression experience does tune in to the collective unconscious when they report lives and personalities where they were responding to specific archetypal influences. We live many different archetypes. Some—such as the archetypes of the gods and goddesses referred to earlier—seem to attach themselves to us at birth and persist throughout life. To some degree they are related to the astrological influences and may have been lived in past lives as well.

We read, for example, of young men who live the archetype of Apollo. The Greek god Apollo started out originally as a shamanic perception of the Solar Logos.[39] The beautiful golden disc of the Sun, the source of all life on this planet, when presented to the simple people of prehistoric times, was portrayed as a magnificent young man with golden curls, possessing musical and artistic talent and divine healing ability, who drove his golden chariot across the skies every day.

Our ancestors, who could only imagine their gods as human beings, saw the golden Sun God as a ladies' man who sought beautiful women to bring to his bed—and was totally flabbergasted whenever any woman turned him down. The many stories told of this god and his romantic escapades impressed themselves upon the collective unconscious—so much so that men with traits similar to those of the mythical Apollo identified with him and began to live their lives as he did.

Today we find them everywhere. These are the rock stars, the actors, the politicians, the handsome young men who charm every woman they meet as well as many who can only admire them from a distance. The John Kennedys, the Brad Pitts, the George Clooneys, and the Ricky Martins of this world are all reverberating to the ancient Apollo archetype—and they may have done so in previous lives.

The Apollo archetype brings to mind the case of a young antique dealer, also an aspiring poet, who had lived the Apollo archetype in many of his past lives and was trying desperately to do so in his current lifetime. He was limited in this capability, however, by a marked physical deformity and a seemingly irresistible inclination toward solitude. Here are some excerpts from his regression material:

[Recalling a lifetime as a young prince living at the end of the fifteenth century] I am tall, with long golden hair. I exert a power on the people around me; they seem to want to sit back and gaze in awe at me, because they know I'm the king and can't believe they ever got that close to me...

I don't think I wrote poetry in that lifetime. I wrote chants; I was more musically inclined than I am now. And I remember designing a weapon, and watching over the smith as he made one to my design.

The young prince he was remembering took his first mistress at the age of twelve and a half—a beautiful young servant girl determined to become the king's mistress.

[Recalling a later nineteenth-century personality] I can't help it; even though I know it's me I'm talking about I have to say it: That guy really looked good. He was gorgeous, and he had a powerful effect upon women. They all loved him, and followed him wherever he went, almost shamelessly. And he was such a wonderful poet; I wonder what happened to make me what I am now, when I could have continued to be like him.

My client, like his previous personalities, was quite talented, particularly as a poet, and in spite of his physical limitations he exerted a powerful effect upon women. But his prowess with women was always frustrated by his present-life need to seek solitude, to look within and study the being he had become, rather than dwelling on his Apollo-like previous personalities. He would force himself to attend social gatherings for which he had no inclination, putting up with people he found irritating and boring. He constantly whispered to his friends that he would rather be at home alone, contemplating his own inner nature. Yet he continued to feel obligated to party and flirt and chase women—in order to live up to the prowess of his previous personalities.

It never occurred to him that perhaps the Apollo archetype was an outdated one for him, that perhaps he needed to embrace a new archetype in order to learn to know himself and regenerate spiritually. The archetype he perhaps should have embraced was that of Pluto, god of

---

39 Robert Graves in *The White Goddess*, traces the cult of Apollo to a Mediterranean sect that worshipped a mouse. The *name* Apollo may stem from this cult. However, it is difficult for me to accept that any form of Sun god worship stemmed from anything other than a shamanic perception of the Solar Logos.

the Underworld, who ruled the subconscious and therefore personal transformation. (Interestingly, my client's rising sign in his astrological horoscope was Scorpio—the sign ruled by the planet Pluto.) His natural inclination was to become Pluto—yet he was constantly trying to live his life as his past personalities did, reverberating to the archetype of Apollo.

Mythology is not the only source from which we draw our archetypes. As many pop psychology books are constantly pointing out, we also unconsciously draw our life patterns from fairy tales. Perhaps the best known of these archetypes is Peter Pan, the *puer aeternus,* the boy who never grows up. Ostensibly the creation of author and playwright James M. Barrie in the late nineteenth century, its origins can be found in many ancient tales of boys who refuse to become men, including the Greek god Hermes and the Germanic fairy-tale figure Tom Thumb. Another archetype drawn from the fairy tale world is Cinderella—the quiet and unassuming, much-abused younger sister who rises from a dismal life among the ashes to be carried away by a handsome prince and become a princess. Although most of the versions of this story now existing are European, the source of this tale is said to lie in ancient China—because of the emphasis on the beauty of a very small foot.

The major effect of the Cinderella archetype seems to be that the young women who live it do little with their lives, simply waiting for a handsome young prince to notice them and carry them away on a white charger. A beautiful sixteen-year-old client of mine seemed to have just been emerging from a long series of lifetimes in which she lived the archetype of Cinderella. In her current incarnation, traces of this archetype seem to still lie deep within her psyche—limiting her ability to seek total self-actualization by pursuing a career of her own, for which she had demonstrated a marked talent since childhood.

Past-life regressions indicated that in a previous incarnation, she had been a Greek girl, a gifted musician, who committed suicide when the man in her life left her. (This, to me, shows the antiquity of the

Cinderella archetype in spite of the fairly recent origin of the versions of the tale with which we are familiar.) In a much later incarnation, in the fourteenth century, she was a young noblewoman who lived a virtually useless life until she married a powerful duke, cementing an important political alliance.

Still later, she was a young girl who actually did live as a servant in a high-strung family of artistic aspirants—and again died a suicide when the man she loved ran away with her sister. In her most recent previous life she was the perfect middle-class American girl, going to all the right schools, biding her time until she could marry the right man who could take proper care of her. Now, in the current incarnation, she apparently has outgrown that archetype, as she is driven to seek a career of her own. Yet she seems to be putting off pursuing that career, still biding her time, going from job to job, letting the months and years slip away—perhaps, on some subconscious level, hoping that the right man will come along and take her away from it all. She needs to work toward letting go of the Cinderella archetype and embracing a stronger one—perhaps Athena—so that she can gain a sense of her own identity beyond her association with a man.

A number of books on the market outline the influence of the various myriads of archetypes, so I won't go into detail about all the individual mythological and fairy-tale archetypes here. I will, however, recommend the work of Dr. Jean Shinoda Bolen, including the wonderful *Goddesses in Every Woman* and *Gods in Everyman*.

I also wish to point out that we are creating new archetypes all the time, some of them new presentations of old archetypes. A fine example is Luke Skywalker, hero of George Lucas's Star Wars series, who is actually a space-age Sir Galahad searching for a new form of Holy Grail. Other new archetypes appear to be totally new—at least on the surface. A good example of the last category of modern archetype is Mr. Spock, a personification of the ideal which began to take form in the seventeenth century, with the dawn of the Age of Reason—a being who has eschewed all emotional experience in favor of the "higher" way of thinking.

There is another class of archetype that everyone seems to live at one time or another, regardless of whatever god or goddess archetype they identify with. These relate to specific passages that everyone goes through in the course of life, and they are usually latent in nearly everyone. These archetypes include the King, the Warrior, the Magician, the Wanderer, the Orphan, the Innocent, the Siren, the Crone, the High Priestess, and the Lover. They are covered in more detail in Robert Moore and Douglas Gillette's *King, Warrior, Magician, Lover* and in Carol Pearson's *The Hero Within*.

Enlightened psychologists emphasize that these archetypes are not mutually exclusive; we can all draw upon each of them whenever we need to and can make them work for us, to create a balanced life for ourselves. Many fine meditations and other psychical exercises are recommended to enable us to draw upon them. But even though these archetypes are universal and can be used by anyone, there are people who seem to become attached to one particular archetype, and therefore the negative as well as the positive aspects of the archetype can begin to manifest in the personality.

Years ago I had an interesting case involving a lovely young woman with whom I worked for several months doing intense regression work and taking her back into a long series of many lifetimes far into the distant past (roughly 2,000 BC). This young woman apparently was one of those souls who usually prefers to take incarnation as a man. Her few female incarnations, however, including the present one, probably reflect the fantasies of her male personalities. The archetype she seems to prefer to live whenever she finds herself in a female body is that of the Siren, or, as astrologer/psychologist Liz Greene calls it, the *Hetaiera*.

The Siren, like Cinderella. is a very old archetype, and probably goes back to the early days of the patriarchies, when women were beginning to be viewed as dangerous temptresses whose aim was to distract men from their proper spiritual paths and halt their progress back to God. The Siren archetype seems to personify the ultimate in "evil" women— she who is gorgeous, erotic, highly sexual, irresistible—and unattainable. She is meant to drive men wild, to fascinate, lure, tempt—and destroy the men who love her. The downside of this archetype is that women who live it never seem to find romantic happiness—for if, like the black widow, the woman destroys all her lovers, who will keep her warm at night or be her companion in old age?

Perhaps the earliest known appearance of the Siren in Western mythology is in Homer's *Odyssey*. The Sirens are beautiful female creatures who live on an island in the Mediterranean, tempting passing seamen with their beauty and luring them to the island with their lovely singing voices. Upon their arrival at the island, however, the Sirens seize the men and devour them. In the *Odyssey*, Odysseus, upon discovering that his way home lies past the island of the Sirens, first plugs the ears of his men with wax, then directs them to bind him to the mast so that he can hear the song of the Sirens, while his men, unable to hear, can avoid falling into their trap.

Oddly enough, this particular client of mine did report a lifetime lived at the time of the Trojan War—although in that life she was a man. Later, however, in the Golden Age of Greece, she found herself as a beautiful and gifted courtesan, a sculptor whose company was constantly sought by many lonely men and for which they willingly paid dearly. In the Middle Ages, she found herself as a young English peasant girl, spurning the attentions of the young men in her village because she had fantasies of one day being the mistress of the King. However, she never attained her goal; though she did once spot the young king from a distance, she succumbed to the Black Death before she could ever meet him.

In seventeenth-century France, she found herself as a lovely young noblewoman whose attentions were sought by ambitious men from all over the world, but who failed to find happiness with one man until her mid-forties. In her youth, at least two of her lovers lost their heads—and a third seemed determined to see her dead. Like all Sirens, she outlived them all.

In the early part of the twentieth century, she was a movie star, lusted after by millions of men. Still, romantic happiness eluded her. Her first marriage was annulled; her second husband was driven to despair and eventually suicide by his own impotence; her third husband nearly bored her to death. And just as she became involved with a man who could well have made her happy, she, like the English peasant girl, died before she could find fulfillment.

Now, in the current incarnation, she has once more taken incarnation as a beautiful woman, again an actress whose attentions have been sought by dozens of men. But she never seems to be able to find that special one who can give her the love we all crave.

However, she also seems to be growing beyond the Siren archetype and moving on to the High Priestess. She is a fine amateur astrologer, skilled in the art of past-life regression, a long-time follower of Swami Muktananda, fascinated with magic, healing, and alchemy. While the archetype of the Siren will probably always be with her in this incarnation, probably even into old age, she appears to be less attached to it than she was in the past—more able to seek and find romantic fulfillment. In future incarnations, she could leave the Siren behind.

I do not mean to imply by the above statements that there is anything "wrong" with any particular archetype. Each of them serves a purpose and helps everyone to become aware of different parts of themselves and different ways of viewing the world. However, as with a favorite piece of clothing that one continues to wear even after it is virtually in rags, we do tend to become attached to the archetypes we live. This can prove karmically dangerous. Like possessions, archetypes are meant to serve their purpose and be discarded—enabling the individuals to move on to explore other parts of themselves. Clinging to one archetype after we have learned all we can from it can retard our spiritual progress, binding us beyond our time to the pain and anguish associated with the earthly plane.

The degree of attachment to a certain archetype often depends upon the individual's stage of development. The initial identification with an archetype probably begins on Stage One, on the typhonic level, when the entity is first able to grasp the significance of the stories told by the medicine men or shamans in their particular group. The attachment to it seems to emerge full blown in Stage Two, early mental substage, and can persist throughout Stage Three. On early Stage Four, however, individuals tend to experiment with living different archetypes in order to find and understand their true selves. In late Stage Four and into early Stage Five we all tend to be partial to one of the more magical archetypes—the Mystic, the Sage, the Crone, or the High Priestess—though it is not a good idea to become attached even to them.

The primary purpose of learning about archetypes is to learn about ourselves. The archetypal figures represent a part of the ancient wisdom after which we still thirst and which can provide us with valuable keys to cosmic truths. And the way we learn about them is through legend. Our favorite fairy tale, for example, can tell us a lot about the archetypal forces within ourselves that are shaping our lives.

My own father, for example, a World War II military hero, always told us that his favorite fairy tale was "The Three Billy Goats Gruff." He identified with the last and largest billy goat to cross the bridge, who challenged the troll to "Come ahead." When the troll went to trap the billy goat and eat him for dinner, the goat butted him way off into the distance. Interestingly, the purpose of my father's Marine Corps battalion, during World War II, was to knock the Japanese navy back to where it came from.

Another influence that has awakened New Age seekers to heretofore hidden aspects of themselves is the ancient "card game" called the Tarot. Most people take up the Tarot simply so they can be more effective when giving psychic readings, as the Tarot has long been known as a divinatory tool. However, the images used in designing the archetypal forms dating from antiquity—even in the newer decks that bear little resemblance to the few packs surviving from medieval times. Those who read the Tarot find themselves learning more and more about themselves, simply because their continued reading of the cards bring these ancient images before their eyes again and again, awakening cosmic truths buried in the collective unconscious. For this reason the less skilled Tarot readers who simply want to be able to tell fortunes often grow uncomfortable with the cards and leave off reading them.

The astrological archetypes are an equally powerful tool for self-awareness, and often tie in with mythology. Ancient sages saw parallels in events happening on Earth and the movements of the stars and planets in the sky, and created a mythology surrounding them. Therefore there is a reason why the planet Mars (named for the god of war, known as Ares to the Greeks) was associated with the period of time dating from about March 20 to April 20 each year, when the Sun was traveling across a group of stars known as the sign of Aries the Ram. Certain archetypal influences already existing in the collective unconscious implied that people born during that period of time possessed personality characteristics reminiscent of the god Mars: courage, enthusiasm, impulsiveness, and a pioneering instinct.

Eventually the theories and observations of these ancient sages (derided still by those who think they know everything) resulted in a rather complex science. The earliest astrological texts, based on this ancient school of thought, are found in Babylonian manuscripts dating from about 1000 BC. These texts are so complicated that they almost certainly must be based on others, long since lost.

Since then, the impression of the astrological influences upon the minds of human beings and therefore upon the collective unconscious has grown—and as a result, modern astrologers see archetypal astrology as a valuable tool for personal growth. The influences of the signs and planets are not meant to provide little boxes in which people can comfortably contain themselves, but to outline the potential of each individual. A person born under Aries, for example, can reverberate to the influences of that sign in a negative way, which is redolent of the character of the Greek war god Ares—angry, quick-tempered, childish, violent—or he can transmute those energies into their very highest manifestation, which was outlined in great detail in Dan Millman's modern masterpiece, *The Way of the Peaceful Warrior.*

Virtually all those born under the sign of Scorpio are living the archetype of the Magician—but whether the manifestation of the Magician archetype is the higher or lower is up to the individual. There appear to be no halfway measures with people born under the influence of Scorpio: they are either the greatest of sinners or the greatest of saints. They either take the lower path—associated with the Scorpion for which the sign is named, and thus with revenge, vindictiveness, and seeking power over others—or the higher path, that of the mythological bird Phoenix, which sets fire to itself and then rises from its own ashes, symbolizing transcendence of death and the limitations of the physical world.

There is another, more all-encompassing reason for studying the archetypes beyond learning about ourselves. This involves learning about cosmic truth. Our ancestors cloaked knowledge of cosmic truths in symbols, myth and fable. By studying those myths and fables, we can uncover keys to those cosmic truths. In the more sensitive, the study of ancient myths and legends can awaken some intangible element in themselves that puts them more in touch with the ancient wisdom that everyone seeks.

For example, when filmmaker George Lucas originally conceived the *Star Wars* series, his vision stretched beyond a box-office blockbuster. Lucas, as a student of famed mythologist Joseph Campbell, managed to work ancient mythological themes into a late twentieth-century context. Luke Skywalker, as we have already observed, was the Sir Galahad figure, searching for the Holy Grail; Princess Leia went from a damsel in distress to a mighty Athena figure to an Earth Mother type in the three movies respectively. Han Solo was the Trickster, while Chewbacca was reminiscent of Vishnu in Hindu mythology in his man-lion incarnation. The "Force" was simply another term for the ultimate consciousness or life force pervading the entire Universe—what the Hindus call *prana,* the Chinese call *chi* and the Japanese *ki.* Obi-Wan Kenobi—and in the later prequel, *The Phantom Menace,* Quai Gon—represented both the sacrificial king and the dying God. Anakin Skywalker/Darth Vader was Lucifer—the angel of Light who fell from heaven and embraced evil. The scenes with Yoda, the Master Teacher, and Luke represented the rather intense relationship between guru and disciple.

Most of Lucas's audience loved the *Star Wars* series for its superb story construction, the exciting action scenes, and the charm and appeal of its characters. But most of my friends and associates were strangely moved by the series in a way that went far beyond the impact of a sci-fi thriller. The films—particularly *The Empire Strikes Back,* which featured the story of Luke's study with Yoda—left them with a new inspiration and awareness, and some actually felt motivated to increase their spiritual studies after seeing the movies. This is probably true of all ancient legends (and many modern ones); the true message is there for those who wish to perceive it, and for those who don't, they still make exciting stories. Even in the latter case, however, there is most likely a subconscious impression left which the person can draw upon whenever she is ready.

Knowledge of all archetypes, whether they are related to mythology, astrology, or passages through life, can prove invaluable in a person's understanding both of himself, of others around him, and of the Universe we live in. Every archetype serves a specific purpose all its own, and enables each individual to choose his or her own path. And it is perhaps our relationship to each archetype, as well as our stage of development and Ray vibration, which determines our own individual reaction to situations—and hence our accumulation of karma.

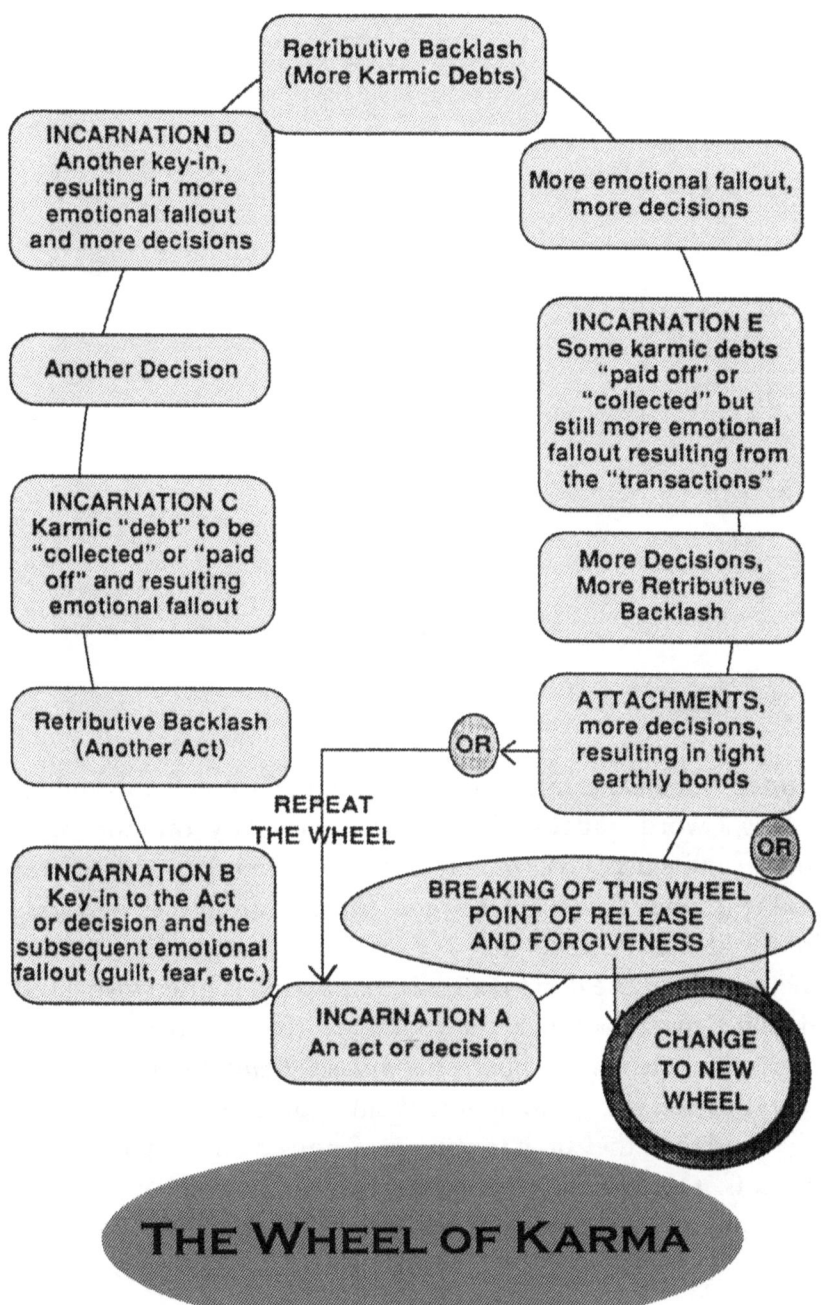

THE WHEEL OF KARMA

FIVE

Karma

As Ye Sow

As pointed out in the Introduction, karma is a much-misunderstood term. It is a word fraught with wonder, perplexity, ominousness, and humor. It can be used to comfort, particularly in times of great tragedy, because it implies that whatever goes wrong can always be righted, if not in this life, in the next one.

What many people don't realize is that karma is often visualized as a wheel. The most popular viewpoint is that expressed by Robin Williams' character in the box-office smash, *Dead Again*. "If they do it to you in this life, you get to do it to them in the next," he says somewhat bitterly. "And then they do it to you again, and so on. It's kind of an eternal tradeoff." Our research reveals that this can indeed happen—but it's hardly an attractive prospect. This vision of the wheel of karma appears to be a sort of cosmic Hatfield vs. McCoy type feud—one goes after the other continually, throughout eternity.

Another way reincarnation researchers often visualize karma is as a pendulum. In one lifetime, a person might be a religious fanatic, actively seeking martyrdom, and in the next she can be a virulent atheist, bitterly attacking any form of religious belief. The pendulum can swing back and forth for many incarnations before the entity attains balance.

Both the wheel and the pendulum are accurate metaphors, though both are incomplete. The murky congeries of factors that all work together to create the forces that we call karma is much more complex than either symbol can communicate. Karma is a difficult force to understand. Bear in mind that the Masters have been trying to reach a complete understanding of it for thousands of years and to my knowledge they have not yet succeeded; therefore, I certainly don't pretend to be able to explain it all here. But I can at least give a partial exposé—and open the minds of readers so that they can begin to discern exactly how complicated the forces we call karma actually are.

I once had a client whose mother was murdered—by the client's own daughter. I had about a half-hour conversation with her, explaining karma, emphasizing that she was unaware of the true nature of the involvement between her daughter and mother, that she did not know what both parties had to learn from the situation, and that if she did not forgive her daughter the resentment and bitterness would eat away at her like a cancer. I also emphasized that because the situation was a karmic one didn't mean that it was okay that her daughter did what she did; one can choose not to participate in the karma of another and thus save herself from being caught up in the wheel. However, it was still appropriate for the client to forgive. She left that consultation somewhat dazed, but with a new understanding.

Karma can be used as a copout. I had a very dear friend and client who was so kind and loving that people tended to take advantage of her, and she let them do it. She was, however, aware that she was being used and tended to complain about it. I often told her to stop doing it. Her continued response: "But I owe her (or him, or them as the case may be) karma!" I finally pointed out to her that perhaps karma would best be served by her backing off and not allowing them to take such blatant advantage of her; she wasn't serving them by giving in to their demands —for to allow them to use her paved the way for their doing the same to others and thus creating more "bad karma."

The word *karma,* as pointed out before, comes from the Sanskrit for "action." In modern Western metaphysics, it has come to be seen as a philosophic extension of Newton's third law of motion, which states: "For every action, there is an equal and opposite reaction." Christ himself stated, "He who kills with the sword shall perish by the sword."[40]

Basically, the connotation of the word karma is that whatever you do, for good or evil, always comes back to you sooner or later. Some believe that not only does it come back to you, it must. Some religious groups, such as the Jains and some Buddhist sects, see even good works as trapping you in the wheel of karma. Therefore even kind acts are to be avoided, they believe, and members of these cults prefer to spend all their time meditating. They wear gauze masks over their faces, so as to prevent breathing in airborne microbes. Some choose not to eat or drink, for eating even vegetarian food deprives a plant of life, and drinking kills microorganisms. Thus both activities would represent "bad karma." The upshot of this is that these people eventually starve themselves to death and (at least as I see it) probably are quite dismayed when they reach the other side. In spite of all their efforts they find themselves still trapped in the wheel of karma because of (a) suicide karma, and (b) the karma of neglect. Most modern Western Seekers,

---

40 Matthew 26:52.

and quite a few Eastern ones, now feel that seeking spiritual advancement without serving others is self-indulgent.

FREEING YOURSELF FROM THE WHEEL OF KARMA

The problem of karma is a very complex one, because the Jains and Buddhists are right: every act, whether good or evil, can trap you in the web of life on Earth. However, my colleagues and I feel that it doesn't have to trap you if you don't let it. The key, of course, is forgiveness. Let's consider again the case of my client whose mother was murdered by the client's own daughter. The bitterness and resentment my client directed toward her daughter (however understandable) could cause her to owe a karmic debt to that daughter, which would have to be paid off in a future life—complicated by the unconscious memory of the murder and the resulting pain and resentment. Here is a good example of the necessity of forgiveness.

The daughter, on the other hand, would have been much better off had she forgiven her grandmother for whatever had triggered enough anger to cause her to commit a murder. However, because she didn't do so, she is now in prison serving a life sentence and on top of that, all the karma she accrued will have to be expiated in a future life.

Another key is non-participation. At any time, we can choose not to participate in someone else's karma. While the grandmother referred to above could have done something terrible in a past life to make it her own karmic debt to be murdered, her granddaughter could have chosen not to participate in that karma, and thus saved herself from the situation in which she now finds herself. She has, in fact, created for herself an opportunity to be murdered in another incarnation—thereby trapping herself in the endless wheel referred to by Robin Williams.

Knowing that the bad things that happen to people are no more than what they have coming to them and that we can all forgive ourselves and thus avoid having to "pay off" karma, does not mean we can steal or kill or harm others with impunity. In fact, it appears that possessing such advanced knowledge and corrupting it to suit one's own selfish ends can represent the worst karma of all. For example, take the case of Adolf Hitler, who was rumored to have been versed in astrology, alchemy, and magic. To justify his atrocities, it is said, he cited the fact that everyone he murdered in the course of World War II had "bad karma." *He was right*—but his arrogance was such that he saw himself as some kind of avenging angel, choosing to participate in rather than forgive the karma of his victims. Modern Western metaphysical sources, channeled from the higher realms, indicate that everyone now on Planet Earth—from Masters like Matthew Fox and Satya Sai Baba on down to the most recently involved Stage One soul among the Himalayan Snowmen—will have long since rejoined the Infinite before the fate of Hitler is decided.

Good deeds as well as bad can bind you more closely to the wheel of karma, and consequently to life on the material plane, only if you let it happen. Yet the answer is not to sit around and do nothing, particularly when there is so much misery around that it is within our power to alleviate. Again, the key is forgiveness. If someone owes you a karmic debt and there is no chance of it being paid off in this lifetime—for example, if the person who owes you is dead—you could be forced to stick around for another incarnation in order to let him pay it off. However, if you forgive the debt there will be no need for you to wait around to collect it. The line from the Lord's Prayer, "Forgive us our debts, as we forgive our debtors," takes on an added dimension when considered in this light. The entity that owes you may still feel the urge to pay off that debt, and consequently pass on your kind deeds to someone else, perhaps to many someone elses. It is all too easy to speculate that a person like Mother Teresa was once, in a previous existence, saved from the intense pain of an illness by a particular kind act. That entity may have long since evolved beyond the material realm, and the karmic "debt" may have long since been "paid," yet until the very end of her life Mother Teresa continued to pass on that kindness that once helped her so much. She may not have intended, but she built a large store of "karmic credits," or, in the words of Jesus of Nazareth, "treasures in heaven."

Karma involves more than good acts and evil acts. It also involves unfulfilled desires, or incompletions. In an old book on reincarnation I read in the early 1970s, when I first began my studies of the subject, there was a line speculating that a woman who gave up her ambitions to be a dancer and became a housewife, but still longs to dance, should draw comfort from the fact that in a future life she will in fact be able to dance. This could be true. Still, common sense tells me now that by the time someone in the Western world realizes the reality of reincarnation, she probably longs to leave the trials of the physical world behind and join the Masters at Shambhalla. Thus, we should be capable of releasing any unfulfilled desires, such as the desire to be a dancer, and be more than willing to do so. The keyword here is release—in other words, not to resent the fact that you were never able to become a dancer, but to make it okay with yourself that you didn't. Some Seekers will succeed at doing so; others will not (depending on the level of attachment), and will come back to complete all these unfulfilled desires. Eventually, however, everyone will have evolved enough to be able to release the incompletions that still exist and move on.

Nor do we need to worry about the problem of karma in suspension. In *Many Mansions*,[41] Dr. Gina Cerminara devotes an entire chapter to the question of karma in suspension—meaning karma that exists from past lives and from the present that we may not have paid off yet and which may create disasters for us in future lives. For example, what is going to happen to the reincarnations of the Nazi soldiers who calmly escorted thousands of Jews and other innocents to the gas chambers?

---

41 Gina Cerminara. *Many Mansions*. (New York: William Morrow, 1978).

What of the new wave of serial killers that is spreading through the United States? If they suddenly become reincarnationists, should they worry about the karma they will have to suffer in their upcoming embodiments? Dr. Cerminara starts that karma in suspension may prove to be the "bugaboo" of the reincarnation age, as hell was to the Christian era. However, my position is that we really don't need to worry about karma in suspension. The key to avoiding problems from that quarter is, of course, forgiving yourself. It is far more productive to do that than to worry about any karma in suspension—for the worry in itself can create an emotional backlash that complicates the karma in question and entraps the entity on the wheel of karma.

Even the desire to attain spiritual enlightenment and God-realization can be a trap that binds us to the wheel. In *The Spectrum of Consciousness,* Ken Wilber points out that an idea circulating among many aspirants these days—the obsession with "seeking enlightenment"—tends to reinforce the idea of separateness, that God is somewhere "out there," that enlightenment is another Holy Grail still to be found and possessed.[42] Swami Muktananda often emphasized in his teachings that the Self is already attained, that you are already enlightened; you need not try to force it, but simply to relax and let it come. Though it may seem like too many are making intense dramatic efforts to "force" God-realization, most spiritual aspirants do realize this in the course of their sadhana. The early stages Ken Wilber refers to (which most of us, including myself, have gone through) can be likened to the situation outlined in the following anecdote.

Two amateur sailors were caught out in the middle of the ocean when a storm struck and their sailboat sank. Off in the distance they could see the lights of a ship. One of the sailors immediately turned to

---

42 Ken Wilber, *The Spectrum of Consciousness* (Wheaton, IL: Theosophical Publishing House, 1980, n. 130.

the other and said, "Let's swim to that ship." The second one said, "But I can't swim!" His friend returned, "Fake it!" And they both survived!

When a spiritual aspirant, exhilarated by the discovery of his new Path, makes certain that everyone knows all about his meditations, sees him smear his forehead with the sacred ash, and talks constantly about his experiences with his guru, he is probably in the "fake it till you make it," stage and will probably soon move beyond it. If he doesn't (and again this depends on the degree of attachment as well as the strength of the aspirant's self-image) it can prove just another desire that binds him to the wheel of karma—and keeps him reincarnating on Earth instead of moving on to the higher realms as he so intensely desires.

A reporter once asked Swami Muktananda if he planned to come back to Earth again in a future life. Muktananda replied that he saw no reason why he should come back—but if the Universe wanted him to return he had no problem with it. This great Master teacher, apparently, was attached neither to the material plane nor to the idea that he had to leave it.

I wish to state here that my colleagues and I are not members of the school that maintains that life in the world is either evil (as is stated in some Christian cults) or a trap (as some Hindus and Buddhists maintain). Life on this Earth can indeed be beautiful; many great Masters— among them the Apostle John, the Hindu saint Babaji, and the Comte de Saint-Germaine—are said to have chosen to remain on Earth even though they have long since evolved beyond the necessity of returning to this world. No wonder! Our regression material indicates that there are few other planets in the galaxy that can match the beauty of Planet Earth—its myriad colors, smells, natural wonders, and its vast diversity of life forms. In *The Aquarian Gospel of Jesus the Christ* Jesus is quoted

---

43 Levi, *The Aquarian Gospel of Jesus the Christ*, p. 161.

as once looking on a great palace and reflecting, "How great indeed are the works of man."[43] We are not implying that life on Earth is something undesirable, meant only to be "transcended." But we do believe that all the problems generated by psychological traumas in this life or previous lives should be transcended; for how can we truly appreciate all the beauties and wonders of this planet if we are too involved with phobias and hangups?

I once read a book about reincarnation by a well-known parapsychologist that stated: "The key to the fulfillment of karma is that we don't remember our past lives. If we remembered our past lives, that would give us an unfair advantage and we would know what we had to do."

I take issue with this statement, as do all my friends and colleagues. There are, undoubtedly, many entities that learn the secrets of karma and forgiveness in the natural course of incarnation and evolution, without the advantage of past-life regression or spiritual teachers. However, we don't see that there is any distinct spiritual advantage in aspiring to number among those, or to scorn whatever advantages come your way, whether they be past-life regression, psychotherapy or great Master teachers. We fully believe in using any tool you can find to create results. The works of all the Masters and many lesser writers on metaphysical subjects seem to bear this out. We mustn't forget the statement of America's Founding Father, Benjamin Franklin, who, some say, numbered among the highest initiates of Freemasonry: "Those who do not remember the past are condemned to repeat it."

The problem of karma is much more complex than is popularly supposed; in fact, it is more complex than I have the time and space to go into here. For the purposes of this book, I am not concerned with the specific karmic bonds each of us forges with people and places. My primary emphasis is on the psychological and emotional effects of those bonds upon the psychology of the soul as it travels along the evolutionary loop. I prefer to study how events, desires, and attitudes bind us to the earthly plane without our conscious awareness of them—for only when we have attained such awareness are we able to see our deeds, attitudes, and desires in a larger context and subsequently attempt to forgive ourselves and others, release desires, and relax and allow enlightenment to happen.

AWARENESS: "GETTING IT"

There are two kinds of higher consciousness awareness: *intellectual awareness* and *true awareness.* Intellectual awareness can be called the "fake it till you make it" stage and often precedes true awareness. Too often, however, we get trapped in intellectual awareness, lost in the "pea soup" or *maya*[44] and don't see that we really are not very enlightened at all.

Werner Erhard summed up the difference between intellectual awareness and true awareness when he formulated the est training and coined the term, "getting it." Many people out there are interested in New Age thought and in the concepts of reincarnation, spiritual awareness, and evolution. They read books, attend classes and lectures, say the right words, even teach—and still their lives do not reflect true awareness. In *Many Lives, Many Loves* Dr. Gina Cerminara tells of a woman who read books, meditated, attended lectures, and expressed a great deal of spiritual pride, maintaining that she was "probably on her last incarnation." Yet that same woman thought nothing of entering the apartment of a tenant when the tenant was not at home, taking a kitten that the tenant had adopted, and driving out into the country and abandoning it.[45] Dr. Cerminara's acquaintance was intellectually enlightened; but she had not yet "gotten it." Edward Sparks had a stock response for anyone claiming to be on their last incarnation: "Walk on water!"

---

44 A Sanskrit term used to describe the transient material world and the illusions associated with life thereon.

45 Gina Cerminara, *Many Lives, Many Loves.* New York: William Morrow, 1963. P. 193.

The difference between intellectual awareness and "getting it" is best illustrated by a hypothetical situation. Let's imagine that you are taking a vacation. All the time you are traveling to the airport, you are plagued by the nagging feeling that you have forgotten something. You think of a lot of different things you might have forgotten, some of which you actually did forget, but somehow you know that these things are not what's bugging you. Then, after you get on the plane, when the pilot has completed his takeoff and you are well on your way, you suddenly realize what it was—and you know that this is what you had forgotten, what had been bothering you all the way to the airport.

The awareness that something had been forgotten may be compared to the need within all of us to make sense of our lives; the speculations about the forgotten object represent intellectual enlightenment. The final realization of what it was that had been forgotten—the "felt shift," to use the term in Marilyn Ferguson's *The Aquarian Conspiracy*—represents "getting it," the true awareness of what is. You no longer speculate, you no longer "believe"—you *know*.

While I was speaking with the woman whose daughter had murdered her mother, I sensed that she had progressed enough into true awareness to be able to handle the idea that it was her mother's karma to be murdered and that the mother had something to learn from the experience. When I told her that, she *knew*. She was immediately able to let go of her grief for a moment and see the larger picture—and thus draw comfort from it. Hopefully, she has also reached the point in which she could stop participating on that particular wheel—and, to return to our football game analogy used in the Introduction, be the quarterback who walks off the field.

However, I wish to insert a caution here to all counselors: take care who you say these things to. No responsible counselor would ever talk about karma to just anybody. Not only would it sound crazy, but some people would find such a statement offensive—as Los Angeles District Attorney Vincent Bugliosi found it offensive (and rightly so) when

Manson family member Susan Atkins informed him that she had murdered Sharon Tate out of love, that it had been Sharon's karma to be murdered and Susan had only been the instrument of that karma. The Manson family, who firmly believed that Charlie Manson was Christ, were guilty of the same sort of arrogance as Hitler, though thankfully on a much smaller scale.

KINDS OF KARMA

If we are to learn how to release karma, perhaps it is best if we take a few moments to understand the various kinds of karma; Research done in the field of reincarnation and karma over the past hundred years or so seems to indicate that karma can fit into several different categories. The first and most widely spread notion of karma, represents what Dr. Cerminara, in *Many Mansions,* christened "boomerang karma." Briefly, this means that exactly what you have done in past lives comes back to you. If you murder someone, in the next life you will be murdered, or if you are kind to someone, in the next life someone will be kind to you— thus creating a wheel that can trap you in the maya.

Dr. Cerminara cites an Edgar Cayce reading in which a college professor who had been born totally blind had approached Cayce for a medical reading, wanting to know if there was anything that could be done about his sight. Cayce maintained that in a prior incarnation in Persia, the professor had been a member of a barbarian tribe whose custom was to blind its enemies with red-hot irons.

Cayce's reading enabled the professor to release his karma to some degree. Cayce also gave him instructions for osteopathic adjustments, electrical treatments, and a change of diet. Within three months the professor had attained 10 percent vision in his left eye.[46]

---

46 Cerminara, Many Mansions. p. 47.

Dr. Cerminara mentions boomerang karma mainly within the scope of physical karma, and indeed this situation is quite a common one. I have in my files the case of a woman who, in a prior existence, had been a king who was instrumental in causing many beheadings, often simply because he wanted the person out of the way. In the current life, my client was in a car accident that caused extensive damage to her head. She suffered from a severe concussion and her jaw was shattered, forcing her to undergo delicate surgery in order to reconstruct it. Many painful months of recovery were required before she was able to function normally again.

However, our research reveals that boomerang karma is not limited to matters of physical health; it covers all departments of life. And it is never quite so simple as "what you do in one life comes back to you in the next." I once had a client who wanted children desperately, but was never able to conceive. Her regression stretched back centuries; in lifetime after lifetime, she either never had children or they all died young. In one lifetime, as an African tribesman, she was forced to watch as her children were tortured, dismembered and finally killed by members of a hostile tribe.

The Number One incident in this case apparently is rooted in a life when, as an ancient Hebrew soldier, my client, then a man, was with the Hebrew army who stormed Jericho and murdered everyone within its walls, including the children. This man, more sensitive and compassionate than most of his fellows, was strangely moved by the fear in the eyes of the Jericho children right before he killed them. Later on in life, when his wife gave birth to a stillborn son, he saw this experience as God's judgment upon him for murdering all those innocent children. The decision was then made: "I am not worthy to have children." And the impact of that decision persisted with my client for thousands of years into her current life.

When she approached me, she was in her early thirties, and had just committed to a relationship with a man about whom she cared deeply.

The two of them desperately wanted a family, but were aware of my client's past problems. The impact of the regression session was a bit much for her to handle; I conversed for at least an hour with her fiancé and a friend of mine while she sat in the next room contemplating her new knowledge of the situation. The old guilt came up again; but because she had grown spiritually since the days of the Judean soldier, she was able to release it.

She and her fiancé left around midnight, promising to stay in touch and let us know what happened. They did. Within a year she gave birth to a healthy baby boy.

Another category could be referred to as *organismic karma,* a term also coined by Dr. Cerminara. Organismic karma relates to deliberate misuse of the physical body in one lifetime that then leads to a bodily malfunction in the next. Dr. Cerminara mentions a case where a thirty-five-year-old man approached Edgar Cayce complaining of digestive difficulties, from which he had suffered since infancy. Cayce recommended treatments, as he always did, then revealed that the man had once been a French nobleman at the court of Louis XIII, where he had spent most of his time uselessly indulging in the "sin" of gluttony, abusing his digestive system with rich, spicy, sugary foods. In the current life, Cayce related, the man's Higher Self saw to it that he couldn't abuse his body in this way again.[47]

Organismic karma turns up again and again in regression sessions. Perhaps the best known of my clients' cases involved Robert Byron, apparently the reincarnation of Lord Byron (one of the sixteen referred to in Chapter Four). His case was outlined in detail in my first book, *I Am Mary Shelley.* Robert Byron suffered from the same misshapen foot as his previous personality, Lord Byron. His doctors confirmed it

---

47 Ibid., p. 49.

through intense study of Lord Byron's medical records and by comparison to an existing cast of Byron's right foot.

What sort of karmic decision would cause someone to come back in a body with an identical deformity as in a previous life? It appears that since time immemorial almost this entity has almost always chosen to take incarnation in a body that is defective in some way, or one that meets a violent end. In the few lifetimes in which he did come back in a healthy body, he assumed a passive personality, preferring to remain in the background rather than participate in life (in true Fifth Ray style).

No matter how far back I took Robert Byron in the course of his regression work, the physical problem always popped up. I never seemed to be able to find the Number One incident that caused this problem—until one time we went all the way back to the early days of Atlantis. According to Edgar Cayce (and Cayce's theories are supported by our regression work), in the early days of Atlantis, the Light Masters who were interested in helping to develop life on this planet experimented with creating now-extinct life forms that were half-human, half-animal. Among the perfect human beings, these creatures were contemptuously referred to as Things, or *Voltars* in the Atlantean language.

In that long-ago lifetime, the entity now known as Robert Byron lived in a remote area of Atlantis where Voltars far outnumbered perfect human beings. Byron was one of the perfect human beings—yet he longed to be "one of the boys," to be accepted by his peers, most of whom were Voltars. The Voltars made fun of him, ridiculing his perfect human body and taunting him by holding up their own horns, tails and so on, which he didn't have. Eventually this young boy actually damaged his body (in what way the regression never made clear) so that he could be more like the Voltars. And the decision still remains: "A perfect body is not good."

In most cases such as this, where the decision resulting from the Number One incident lies so far back in the past, the entity would probably have long since completed this karma and let it go—even in the normal course of evolution, without the advantage of past-life regression and spiritual teachers. But in Byron's case there seemed to exist a strong attachment to his physical abnormalities. It was as if the taunts of the Voltars rang in his ears still, implying that only the imperfect are worthy and interesting. Yet though Byron drew a certain satisfaction in constantly talking about his malformity, he still balks at letting most people see it. He almost never takes off his shoes, even to go to bed. He was attached to his condition—and yet, on some level, still ashamed of it. As far as we know, Byron never released his long-ago decision nor took responsibility for resolving this conundrum.

A reconstructive surgeon once offered to straighten his foot at no charge; Byron turned him down. If the malformity were a minor one—say a misshapen ear—that didn't affect his health or well-being or his ability to work, one could understand why he wouldn't want to go through all the pain and stress of surgery simply to indulge his vanity. But Byron's foot affected the way he walked, throwing his spine constantly out of alignment, causing intense pain in his back and legs that forced him into near-addiction to painkillers. This limited the amount of time he could spend on his feet, thus curtailing his ability to work and to teach—all things he maintained he wanted to do. The case of Robert Byron represents an extreme case of organismic karma complicated by a powerful degree of attachment.

Organismic karma is also at work in some cases of suicide karma. Apparently the pattern in suicide karma—at least with the entities who approach me—is this: The entity who throws away a perfectly healthy body in one life is "condemned" to suffer negative karma in two lives. In the first, the entity dies suddenly, often violently, at a time when he or she desperately wants to live and shows great promise. In the second lifetime, the person is constantly plagued by bad health, sometimes dying of a painful disease such as cancer. The message appears to be that no matter how bad things seem, it is not up to you to take steps to end your own life through violence.

A third category of karma cited by Dr. Cerminara could be called *symbolic karma*. To illustrate, she tells the story of a young man who had suffered from anemia since the early days of childhood. The boy's father was a physician, and every medical treatment known at the time was tried in order to relieve the boy's condition, but nothing seemed to help. In desperation, the boy's family approached Edgar Cayce for a reading. "A malfunction which so stubbornly resists cure," states Dr. Cerminara, "is suggestive of a karmic cause." The reading given by Cayce traced the problem to a long-ago lifetime in Peru, where the entity had taken control of the country by force, causing many deaths. "Much blood was shed," said Cayce, "*hence anemia in the present.*"[48]

While not as common as boomerang or organismic karma, symbolic karma is certainly not rare. A prime example is that of the teacher on page 33-34, who was a priest at the time of the Spanish Inquisition and shut out the cries of the tortured; as a result he was born partially deaf in this lifetime. This latter case is a bit more complicated than the one taken from the Cayce readings, however, in that my client hadn't actually done anything wrong in his past life. It was his own helplessness and the resulting guilt over his inability to act that created the symbolic karma that limited his ability to hear.

The effects of symbolic karma, like boomerang karma, are not limited to the physical body. They appear in all different departments of life—and thus can be very complicated and among the most difficult to resolve. For instance, take the case of a handsome, intelligent young African-American in his early thirties who desperately wanted to write. He was very good at coming up with great story ideas, and started many

---

48 Ibid.

novels for which he had high hopes. However, he always seemed to lose interest and abandon his work before he came even close to finishing it.

One might think that such a problem would not actually be so difficult. This person, you might say, was simply another *author manqué*, who had youthful aspirations that in maturity he was never able to fulfill. But since he never wanted to do anything else but write he never took the time to develop another way of making a living that would satisfy him. He played around with waiting tables, selling insurance, and doing mundane work that he always abandoned for the sake of his writing, always with the conviction that this time he would finish his novel and sell it.

The problem reached mammoth proportions when, at the age of thirty-five, a friend of his pulled strings to get him an assignment to write a script for a television show about a black family living in modern-day South Africa. Even though the young man lacked writing credits, he had training in scriptwriting and also possessed an advanced degree in African-American studies, and therefore he was considered qualified to write such a script. This time he was given an advance—which he promptly spent. He then sat down to try to write his screenplay—and, as was his pattern, halfway through the script he developed a severe case of writer's block.

Now he was not free simply to abandon his work and move on. He had a contract; he had accepted money. If he didn't deliver a product, he would have to return the advance—which he had already spent. Furthermore, his rent was overdue and he had to deliver the script before the production company would pay him any more.

He came to me in desperation, referred by a mutual friend. His regression revealed a history similar to that of the young woman on page 152-153. His karma could be traced to a lifetime in ancient Carthage, in which he was a paid spy for the Romans. As is well known, the Roman army not only conquered Carthage, but destroyed it, killing every living thing in it and then salting the ground so that nothing else could grow there. As with my other client, this young man came out of his regression haunted by the frightened faces of the murdered Carthaginian children whom he had betrayed.

At first he could not make the connection. Although he certainly had been guilty of a heinous crime back in the Carthaginian lifetime, how, he asked, could being instrumental in the murder of children in a past life cause writer's block in the present?

As an astrologer, however, I had a ready answer for him. In astrology, the sign Leo and the corresponding fifth house of the horoscope rule the products of self-expression. This includes one's creative work, such as songs, poetry, paintings, and novels—and the results of the expression of love for another human being, i.e., children. Even in language, we have the expression "brain child," referring to a creative work. Often, to writers, poets, or artists, their work is almost as dear as their own flesh-and-blood children—and to damage or lose one of these products of self-expression can cause almost as much pain as if a child were to contract an illness.

And so my client, having being instrumental in taking the lives of many children in his past life in Carthage, was deprived of the pleasure of "brain children" in the present.

When I explained this to him, his first reaction was sheer astonishment. When the impact of his experience finally struck him, he sat for about half an hour, then quietly bade me goodbye and left. I wondered if the regression had done him any good.

I heard from him at about eleven o'clock the next morning. He was ecstatic. After he left me, he said, he had driven around for about an hour, still not quite grasping the impact of what the regression had revealed. Then he went to a restaurant and had dinner—and as he sat, the entire second half of his story suddenly popped into his head as if by magic. He finished his dinner, hurried home, and stayed up all night finishing the script. It was the first creative work, he stated, that he had ever finished in his life. And he thought the show was going to be a masterpiece.

Ironically, for reasons beyond my client's control, the production company canceled the project. But my client went on to participate in other projects which were quite successful. That one regression had allowed him to release the karma related to the Carthaginian experience, leaving him free to move ahead in his career as a writer.

There are other forms of karma whose effects are more subtle than the above. First of all, there is the karma of neglect. If we are to believe the Qabbalah, we come here on earth to have 613 experiences. Yet even allowing for the fact that it may take more than one incarnation to complete each experience, we remain on this planet for thousands of lifetimes, far beyond the number which logic would dictate. Our regression material demonstrates that for various reasons throughout the course of our lifetimes, we are confronted with opportunities to live these experiences—but put them off. The karmic result of this appears to be that not only is the experience put off until the next lifetime, the circumstances under which the experience is to be lived become tougher.

Take the case of a young man whom I'll call Sam. Sam came to me because of a total inability to communicate with his parents. As a child, he had been severely dominated by both mother and father, whose viewpoints regarding children were relics of the Victorian era. Sam was strictly disciplined as a child; he was not allowed to have a friend over unless his parents were friends with the parents of his playmate. He was expected to come directly home from school, not stopping off at the park or the playground. For the most part, Sam was an extremely obedient child, but on the few occasions when he disobeyed he was severely beaten. He was expected to get straight A's in school; he was put on restriction when he brought home B's. He was also expected to attend a college of his parents' choice, then go to Harvard Law School and join his father's law firm.

Usually, Sam tried to do what made his parents happy. Yet there were times when it seemed as if nothing he did was right. He would wear the suit his mother had asked him to wear, only to have her criticize him for not wearing the right shirt or tie with it. He would obligingly date a young woman who was a daughter of friends of his parents—only to have his parents object to the places he took her.

In a burst of patriotism, after his sophomore year in college, Sam decided that he would enlist in the Marine Corps and go to Vietnam. But the father (who had been a vocal critic of draft evaders) nixed that idea, saying there was no need for him to go. He was to continue at the University as dictated, then go on to law school.

Frustrated, Sam continued with his studies. By accident, in the middle of his junior year, he discovered a field that fascinated him: anthropology. He took several courses in that field, then decided he wanted to make it his life's work. His guidance counselor worked up a study plan for him, but it would necessitate an extra year at the University. However, Sam was willing to do this, for his passion for anthropology was finally making him feel like his own person with his own purpose in life.

When he returned home for the summer, Sam broke the news to his parents that he wouldn't be going to law school. He had expected that they wouldn't be pleased, but he wasn't prepared for the virulence of their reaction. They called him names; told him that he'd always been a disappointment to them and always would be. His father informed him that if Sam didn't continue with the original plan, he would cut him off completely and never speak to his son again.

Frustrated and angry, Sam packed his bag and caught a Greyhound bus back to the University. There he moved in with a friend who had an apartment near the school and got a job delivering pizzas. He went to the financial aid office and applied for various grants and loans, then found that because his grades were good he was eligible for a scholarship. He finished his final two years of school and then went on to graduate school and a position as graduate assistant—without ever having contacted his parents.

Nonetheless, through the son of friends who attended the same college, Sam's parents heard about how well their son was doing. They went to visit him, congratulated him on doing so well and ask him to come home. By that time Sam had settled into a life of his own and was living with a girlfriend he planned to marry. He was therefore faced with the unpleasant prospect of telling them he didn't want to come. But his parents ignored his protestations and insisted that he would be better off with them. When he politely but firmly told them no, they once more threatened to disown him.

By the time he came to us he was frantic. They were calling every week, using high-pressure techniques to try to get him to return to their home. Once his mother called his girlfriend and lectured her on the wrongness of living with their son and of the social unsuitability of their match. In tears, the girlfriend hung up on the mother. Furious, Sam changed his phone number.

Sam wanted a regression in order to find out why he had such a terrible relationship with his parents. The regression revealed that in several past lives he had failed to take the opportunity to make the break with his parents. In the earliest one he came up with, he was a soldier in the Roman army who had followed in his father's footsteps without a word—though his own inclination had been to be a farmer. In a later medieval incarnation, he was a younger son of a nobleman who had planned for him to go into the church. Though he did not feel the calling and resented the fact that he had been promised to the church before he was even old enough to speak, he went along with his father's wishes. Three other incarnations followed where the situation was similar—until the present one, when Sam was forced to either break with his parents or give up his passion, anthropology, for a career in law for which he had no interest.

In only one of the prior incarnations in question had he been involved with either of his present-life parents, and that was the father, in the Roman incarnation. This surprised Sam—but apparently the karmic lesson he needed to learn, and had neglected, lay not in the relationship with either of the two entities who were now his father and mother, but with himself. It is every person's job to carve out a unique niche in this world—and hence the need to break from the parents. Sam's case represents a prime example of the karma of neglect.

The outcome of this case was that in spite of continued pressure (and bribery attempts) from his parents Sam stayed with his newfound career at the University—while at the same time letting them know that he loved and appreciated them. Eventually they learned to live with his decision, although they never got over the hurt of having him reject their plans for him!

Attitudes can give rise to karmic problems as well as anything else. Rigid authoritarian attitudes, such as those embraced by Sam's parents, can cause domination in future lifetimes. The pendulum swings—any extreme in one life can lead to the opposite extreme in the next. The key is attaining balance.

ACTS AND DECISIONS

Indeed, balance sometimes appears to be the most difficult quality to achieve. Throughout the course of our incarnations, we are taught certain concepts that lead to acts and decisions to which we become powerfully attached. As we generally choose to incarnate within the same structures and racial groups in which we feel most comfortable (with occasional experimental forays into other cultures and societies) the attitudes resulting from our early education will most likely be reinforced lifetime after lifetime, with multitudes of acts or decisions, and our attachment to the results of these acts or decisions can bind us more tightly to the wheel of karma. This creates the necessity of making use of many lifetimes in order to complete our experiences. At some crisis point in our spiritual development—most commonly on mid-Stage Three—our attachments are often challenged, causing us to re-evaluate our beliefs and viewpoints. The result can be either that we experience rapid growth in our spiritual development or that we become threatened by our new knowledge and cling more tightly to the attitudes we have formed, thus further retarding our process.

Sam's parents seem to have taken the latter path, even though Sam, through his refusal to bow to their plans for him, demonstrated that it is possible to walk a fine line between rejecting parents' attitudes and rejecting the parents themselves. The karmic upshot of this situation could be that in their next incarnations, *they* will be the children whose parents try to foreordain their lives for them, and *they* will be the ones who break from their families in order to follow their own paths. And in the course of this challenge they will probably have mixed emotions—because of their new situation in which they are there to challenge their parents, and also because of subconscious memories of their past-life attachment to the belief that children should do whatever their parents want.

As you can imagine, this can result in a disastrous mess. A Number One incident results in an act or decision, which then creates an emotional fallout—anger, grief, fear, and so on. The next lifetime in which the decision is keyed in can bring about a retributive backlash, or boomerang karma, and other decisions and emotional fallout can result from these acts. These matters can then lead to karmic debts that need either to be paid or collected, or both, which result in emotional fallout of their own—for example, resentment at having to spend ten years of one's life taking care of an elderly parent, even though the entity either owes a karmic debt to that parent, or needs to accumulate the experience of devoting oneself totally to another, or both.

My mentor, Marcia Moore, a well-known reincarnational researcher, once speculated on the karmic reasons for the behavior of some of the more unbalanced of black militants in the late 1960s and early 1970s.[49] According to Marcia's theory, these entities incarnated when they did because they had a role to play in the long, painful, drawn-out battle to eradicate racism from society on Earth. But they also had their own karmic axes to grind. Many, Marcia theorized, were the reincarnations of cruel Southern slaveholders who had abused their black slaves, creating a karmic debt to learn what it was like to be black.

Because of their current ethnic orientation, and because of the racial tension they were born into, these entities hated whites—but because of their subconscious memories of their Southern slaveholder attitudes, they also distrusted blacks. When we consider these three factors—their karmic debt to help wipe out the racism which they in their previous lifetimes had helped perpetuate, their own anger at the treatment their people were receiving, and the conflicting antagonism they felt toward their own race—we can easily see why their behavior sometimes verged on extremism. This behavior, in turn, created more negative karma and more violent emotions, which will undoubtedly have to be resolved in some way in future lives.

Another example: In the early 1970s I was acquainted with a woman who throughout the course of her life had been constantly mistreated by men. Her father was a hopeless misogynist, who continually abused his wife and two daughters both physically and emotionally. Helga married at seventeen to get away from the father who had hurt her so mercilessly, only to find that her husband just as abusive as her father. She divorced her husband at thirty-two, then became involved with a man who was not physically abusive, but nonetheless treated her shamefully. He used her, took unfair advantage of her love for him, stood her up for dates she had long looked forward to, and eventually dumped her for a younger, more beautiful woman.

---

49 Marcia Moore, at a lecture given at Venture Centre, Ventura, California, in November 1976. See Marcia Moore and Mark Douglas, *Reincarnation: Key to Immortality*. (York Beach. Maine: Arcane. 1972).

Throughout the course of my acquaintance with her, Helga was continually expressing bitterness over the fact that she had been born a woman. She was a champion of feminist issues such as abortion and equal employment opportunities, and was instrumental in forcing her labor union to specify equal pay for equal work in their employment contracts. In spite of these positive accomplishments, however, Helga was constantly torn between resentment of the obligations involved with motherhood (she had three children) and her love for her children; between her desire for independence and self-sufficiency and her need for a nurturing relationship with a man; between her need to rebel against the patriarchy by throwing all vanity to the winds and her desire to look beautiful for the men in her life.

The overall feeling most people drew from conversations with Helga, however, was that she basically hated being a woman. Eventually she developed breast cancer, necessitating a total mastectomy of both breasts. The cancer spread to her reproductive organs, which also had to be removed. It appears as if, psychologically, she was determined to destroy that female body—which she eventually did. The cancer spread to her brain, and she died at the premature age of forty-four.

I never worked with Helga; she died before I began an active practice in past-life regression. However, I did do extensive regression work with her daughter, whom I'll call Linda. Linda had shared many lifetimes with the entity who had been her mother, and there were powerful karmic bonds between them. Using Linda's regression material, she and I managed to piece together a sketchy past-life history for Helga. Helga, it appeared, was basically a yang entity who in most of her prior existences had been a man. At some point, probably in the early days of the patriarchy, the entity had apparently undergone a Number One incident which reinforced the views taught at the time—that women were less than human, mere chattel, to be used and discarded at the pleasure of men. In several subsequent incarnations, this entity had been, to use Linda's words, a "real bastard," thus necessitating her return to Earth as a woman who suffered at the hands of men. And the suffering undoubt-edly created new resentments.

Hence, we can easily see the parallels between Helga's situation and the speculative case of the hypothetical black militants outlined previ-ously. Helga was torn by inner emotional conflicts generated by her karmic need to experience the same abuse she had inflicted in prior existences, the cosmic need for the liberation of women on this planet, her own anger at the treatment of women by men, her unfamiliar expe-rience of the feminine instincts, and her unconscious attachment to the patriarchal system and attitudes.

Therefore, it appears that negative attitudes embraced in previous embodiments can lead to a jumbled psychic morass of inner conflicts, emotional confusion, and complexes which can only nap the entity in further destructive attitudes and behavior, reinforcing the old karmic debts and at the same time creating new karma.

Even positive karma can create its own problems, particularly in soul-entities on the earlier stages of development. I once worked with a young woman who recalled being a nun in the Middle Ages who spent most of her life caring for the sick. Many people were healed and went on to live rewarding lives because of this nun's untiring efforts and her dedication to bettering the human condition.

However, secretly the nun despised most of the people she cared for. She came from an upper class family and was trained to look down on the peasantry, regarding them as creatures of little more value than ani-mals. She cared for them because she believed she had been sent to do "God's work," that it was "her duty" to help these people. Though she always wore a mask of kindness and compassion whenever she dealt with them, deep down she resented having to spend her life nursing the "rabble."

In a later incarnation, she found herself an orphan, a small girl, aban-doned to fend for herself in the slums of nineteenth-century London. Like Oliver Twist, she was rescued by a kindly old man and taken into his home. The old man proved to be the reincarnation of one of the peasants cared for so diligently by the nun, and so he felt he owed her a karmic debt. But while the child was all too willing to take advantage of her benefactor's good nature, secretly she despised him as a weakling—an opinion composed partly of the dimly-remembered prejudice of the nun compounded by the overwhelming opinion of the London slum-dwellers that kindness was synonymous with weakness.

The old gentleman's household consisted of the re-embodiments of others whom the nun had once helped, who "did their karmic duty" by serving the child now—but, in accordance with the snobbery typical of the late Stage Two servant class, they resented the intrusion of the slum-dweller into their well-ordered world. The child knew this; the servants made no secrets of how they felt. When the old man died, leaving every-thing he owned to the orphan, she returned to the slums—using her inheritance to become a brothelkeeper and a slum landlady.

In the current incarnation, she found herself romantically involved with the entity who had once been the nun's patient and the orphan's benefactor. He was nearly twenty years older than she, and sometimes tended to play the same fatherly role as he had in the nineteenth cen-tury. Once more he was determined to make a good life for her—though he did it in rather unconventional ways: acting, dubbing voices for foreign films, cleaning houses, working backstage for a magician, selling fashion accessories. He had little real ambition and even less commitment to any one kind of work; his foremost ambition was to spend his life traveling around the world. She, on the other hand, came from an upper class family to whom career success was all-important, and though she herself aspired to a career in the entertainment world, she was much more committed to it than he. They began to have mari-tal problems. Her regression work, however, allowed her to see things in a clearer light: she became more aware of both her motivations and his, and between them they worked things out. They relocated in Europe and he worked hard on developing a career in the field of fashion.

KARMIC CONDITIONS AND COMPLICATIONS

Several human conditions are karmic in nature, relating to an initial decision made when the entity was in the early stages of development. The entity continues to incarnate within these conditions throughout the course of many lifetimes and does not feel comfortable without them. The conditions, however, though basically harmless in themselves, are not without complications.

The most common of these conditions is intelligence. At least, it seems to be the most common. Admittedly, most of the people with whom my colleagues and I work are intelligent, sometimes exceptionally so, and therefore we probably are not totally unbiased in this area. However, the pattern with intelligence appears to run thus: When these entities are on Stage One, something happens which piques their curiosity, and they seek to satisfy that curiosity. Such individuals eventually realize that seeking answers to questions and accumulating knowledge gives them pleasure, and so they find themselves, between embodiments, seeking out future parents with a high degree of intelligence so that they may inherit the appropriate genes. But, as with all types of karma, superior intellect brings its own problems. For one, it sets the individual apart from the crowd, and therefore the entity may feel like a freak, an outcast—particularly in early Stage Two when conformity with the norms of the group is most vital. It also causes the individual to challenge ideas and mores everyone else takes for granted, thereby threatening those in positions of authority—which can prove dangerous at any stage of development. The consequences can, of course, cause deeply buried complexes in future incarnations.

The method in which complications manifest varies, of course, with Ray vibration. Third, Fourth, and Fifth Ray souls tend to be incapable of hiding their intelligence, and speak their piece no matter what the result may be, while natives of other Rays are more adept at hiding it. First and Seventh Ray souls are more subtle and insidious about their use of it, while Second and Sixth Ray souls simply pretend it doesn't exist. The emotional backlash of each of these complications can therefore be vastly divergent—as are the karmic consequences in future lives. So we can see that even a highly valued trait such as intelligence can be at the root of many psychological traumas.

Another karmic condition that can cause extreme alienation is artistic talent. According to our research, most people who show exalted artistic talent belong to that small elite group of souls who have never totally passed through the Fountain of Oblivion and forgotten their divine origin—and therefore are constantly trying to express their subconscious awareness of our divinity through their work. But anyone with artistic talent can identify with the problems such talents pose. While most people love to enjoy the fruits of the artists' labor, they seem to distrust the artists themselves. They tend either to ridicule and condemn the artists or to set them up on pedestals as if they were gods. One need only study the lives of Van Gogh, Beethoven and Mozart to realize the pain such attitudes can cause the artist—and to imagine the possible emotional backlash in the artists' future lifetimes.

Still another karmic condition that appears positive but can cause extreme psychic trauma is beauty. As with intelligence, most entities who prefer to incarnate in bodies of unusual beauty seem to have chosen that condition in the early days of their path along the evolutionary loop. Our research indicates that the advantages of physical beauty were discerned around the time that the human animal adopted the face-to-face position for sexual intercourse. Faces rather than buttocks became the primary source of sexual excitement—and so the seeds for the growth of the legends of the Sirens, the songs of the troubadours, and the Miss Universe pageants were sown. Many entities made a decision that "beauty brings security" and began a pattern of incarnating, whenever possible, in bodies of rare beauty.

Many people may wonder why, if it is a matter of choice, everyone would not choose to be physically beautiful. But recall that we are not speaking of freshness, youthful attractiveness, or pleasant-featured good looks. We are speaking here of the beauty of which legends are born. Consider the lives of some of the great beauties of our own century, both male and female—Montgomery Clift, Marilyn Monroe, Elvis Presley, Elizabeth Taylor, Rock Hudson, and the ill-fated Dorothy Stratten. Would you willingly live your life *exactly* the way they lived theirs?

First of all, godlike good looks set a standard for behavior that few human beings can ever reach. Secondly, such an appearance sets one apart from the crowd and attracts attention; such individuals can never go unnoticed. Thirdly, it can actually cause heartbreaking loneliness, because so few people are breathtaking beauties. Surveys demonstrate that in spite of their admiration for gorgeous movie stars, when it comes to forming long-term personal relationships, most people feel more comfortable with partners whose looks more closely match their own. Fewer entities choose the beauty condition than one would first tend to believe. Our research with past-life regression bears this out—particularly the few cases we have that offer access to portraits of past-life personalities.

First, Fourth, and Seventh Ray souls generally choose an appearance suggesting strength and personal power rather than beauty; Second and Third Ray entities tend to want their wisdom to shine through. Fifth—— and Sixth Ray souls, particularly because of their desire to blend into the crowd and retain a certain amount of anonymity, tend to choose bodies that are average-looking to attractive—but almost never seem to incarnate in bodies that resemble either the Venus de Milo or Praxiteles' Charioteer.

In fact, one of my case histories involves a young woman who deliberately shifted from the path of rare beauty to the path of near-homeliness. One man described her as "unattractive, working hard on being ugly." She was basically an average-looking person who seemed to prefer ragged army fatigues and cheap thong sandals to attractive clothing, and who had a way of chopping her hair off in an unbecoming Prince Valiant style. Whenever anyone tactfully suggested that she fix her hair and buy some new clothes—one friend even offered to treat her to some—she would lash out with, "This is me, and you're going to have to accept me the way I am!"

No one had any problem with accepting her the way she was. She was a kind and generous soul, always helping and giving. Yet her friends couldn't help wondering if she'd feel better about herself if she dressed more attractively. Then she began intense past-life regression work. Sessions revealed that in many prior incarnations she had, in fact, been considered a great beauty, but had felt extremely unappreciated. Her lives had all been sources of constant frustration because men would fall in love with her beauty and never bother to get to know the person behind the mask. However, in the early nineteenth century, the pendulum began to swing the other way. When she passed through the Second Initiation and went from Stage Three to early Stage Four, she made a shift—and began to choose bodies that were no more than average looking, simply so that she could be appreciated for what she was inside. She realized that she had to learn that it was all right to be attractive, all right to wear nice clothes and makeup, and to fix her hair in a becoming fashion. Again, the keyword is balance.

Even in the light of this knowledge, however, she still seems most comfortable in old, worn-out clothes, even for semi-formal occasions. She has an abundance of friends who love and esteem her, but has yet to find romantic happiness.

The most complex of these karmic conditions is homosexuality. There are many factors that may lead to homosexuality, but in a significant number of cases it seems to be rooted in an innate androgyny on the part of the soul. Strictly speaking, all souls are androgynous, possessing no gender in the strictest sense of the word, but there are souls who lean towards being primarily either yin or yang. The former generally prefer to be born as women, though they occasionally take incarnation as men, and the latter do just the opposite. But there are some souls who seem neutral, neither yin nor yang. These individuals appear to be most comfortable taking earthly incarnation as homosexuals, feeling most comfortable in sexual situations with members of their own sex. They may assume bodies that are either male or female, but still prefer the homosexual lifestyle. An entity that was a lesbian in one embodiment may reincarnate as a gay man, or vice versa, and the pattern could continue for hundreds or even thousands of years, with only occasional forays into the "straight" way of life.

For some of us, this may seem strange. As we all know, in most cultures homosexuality has often represented a one-way ticket to ridicule and social ostracism of the individual by one's peers. Subsequently, the individual experiences rejection and bitterness, which can lead to karmic backlash. Hopefully, homophobia will soon become history, along with racism, sexism, and other forms of bigotry, and thus our androgynous spiritual descendants won't have to suffer this way.

As with gender and race, sexual preference is something all souls experiment with from time to time. As we have all been black in one life or another, we probably have all been gay in at least one existence. But when a soul continually takes incarnation as a homosexual, it appears that this is an innate condition, like intelligence. It does *not* necessarily indicate that the entity has been a member of the opposite sex in many lifetimes past. The latter condition does not incline a soul-entity to homosexuality. A yang soul in a female body generally takes the aggressor role in relationships with men, while a yin soul in a male body often assumes the passive role and waits for women to approach him—but in most cases they still retain their heterosexuality.

In extreme cases, where the entity has incarnated for hundreds or even thousands of years as only one sex, and then suddenly moves to the other, we have the transsexuals—those who feel like women trapped in men's bodies and vice versa. We need not emphasize the dire results of this condition. Modern medical technology has given relief to many transsexuals through sex-change operations, but the number of recipients of this kind of surgery who return to their doctors asking to be put back the way they were is rapidly increasing. I feel that such individuals, when they sought a sex change, were responding to their past unconscious identification with the opposite gender—*but that they still could nor escape the karmic necessity of experiencing life as a member of the sex into which they were born.* It is my recommendation that those who think they want a sex change should undergo extensive past-life therapy before actually taking such a drastic step so that they can better understand the cosmic reasons for their situation.

When we consider the masses of psychic garbage that are generated life after life, and all the traumas and complexes they can cause, some may wonder how we ever manage to emerge from the "pea soup" and become fully functional human beings. Thankfully, in the course of evolution, eventually these problems take care of themselves. The Second Initiation, for example, marking the end of Stage Three and the beginning of Stage Four, represents a milestone where the soul begins to relax a little and to release old attachments, incompletions, unfulfilled desires and "karmic debts." Also, fewer new problems are created, and a spiritual school of thought is often embraced which gives the individual the strength and conviction to forgive, release, and move on. However, the early centaur substage, immediately following the Second Initiation, can also be marked by a great deal of trauma as the need to move on battles with the desire to hang on.

Modern metaphysics has developed many processes that can help the entity to let go of the pain and confusion that stems from the past and learn to release and forgive. The overall term for these processes is clearing. "Clearing" your psyche of all the dead weight it has been carrying for so many centuries can help you cross over the fine line that exists between intellectual awareness and "getting it." The most effective tools for enabling people to clear themselves and "get it" are past-life regression (including rebirthing), meditation and learning at the feet of an enlightened Master. These processes can be helped along by enlightened, drug-free psychotherapy, psychotechnologies such as The Forum, Omega Vector and Making Love Work, and intense study of scripture, philosophy, and other spiritual texts.

Clearing, "getting it" and actually learning to release and forgive— not to mention actually doing the latter—can give the individual a sudden boost in spiritual growth. As pointed out in Chapter Two, a soul-entity can, and many in these changing times will, go from the Second to the Fourth Initiation in the course of one lifetime, releasing old karma, forgiving old "debts," performing good works and generally serving all forms of life on Earth without any conception of reward, or "payoff."

At the same time, the entities who do this can use their advanced knowledge to look back on what they went through in the course of their own evolution and thereby understand what's going on with the rest of the world. Such understanding leads to further forgiveness— without condoning or excusing undesirable behavior. This latter attitude is one to which all of us should aspire.

If peace, serenity and enlightenment are what we all want, at least one of the secrets of the final earthly initiation is the release of all karma. For in the long run, what does it matter? From Brahman we all came, and to Brahman we will all return. It may take some longer than others, but all time is but a blink of an eye to the Lord of the Universe. This, according to the Masters, is the ultimate truth that underlies all being.

SIX

Practical Application

The Psychology of Spirit and Psychotherapy

Most of the people who come to me for astrological consultations or past-life therapy are amazingly mentally healthy. They come to me not out of a dire need to regain their sanity, but to iron out whatever traces of neuroses or hangups remain in order to free themselves for future growth. On the few occasions when I have been asked by frantic relatives to work with individuals who have severe mental and emotional problems, I must confess I have not had much luck. As the goddess Saraswati told Queen Lila, for a person to progress, he or she must be willing to make the effort themselves. The majority of people with genuine difficulties—severe neuroses or character disorders—ironically, see no reason to make such effort. They have no concept that they have a problem; they sincerely believe that the problem is with everyone else.

For the most part, I am thankful that so far I have been faced with few genuine psychoses. I am not a psychiatrist, nor do I have any specialized training in abnormal psychology, and would prefer to recommend such cases to people who had the proper training. However, a few years ago, in an article in *Discover* magazine, I read of a case of a full-blown psychosis that I would love to have gotten my hands on. To mainstream psychiatrists, the problem was acute schizophrenia; to me, it seemed a clear case of a bleedthrough from a previous incarnation.

The article told the story of a young girl in her mid-teens who believed she was living a lifetime back in the days of the American Revolution. Every noise brought her running to the windows to see if the British were coming; she spoke of Paul Revere and Patrick Henry as if they were about to walk through the door at any minute. This was not a case of an occasional lapse, or of possible role playing. The girl actually lived her life as though the Revolutionary War were being fought outside her home at that very moment, even though everything around her screamed of the late twentieth century. No amount of counseling, confrontations with newspapers, TV, etc., shook her from her conviction that she was living in the American colonies of the 1780's.

As the article concerned the nature of schizophrenia rather than the treatment of it, there was no mention of how the girl was treated. However, if her psychiatrists were of the unenlightened type (which an ominously high percentage of them are), I shudder to think of what might have been done to her. She was probably dosed with every drug possible—Prozac, Ritalin, Valium, you name it—to make her docile and tractable and more accepting of the pronouncements of authority figures. She may have also been subjected to electric shock therapy, followed by heavy-handed, threatening, wrong-making brainwashing techniques.

If, under these circumstances, she appeared to be "cured"—if she eventually appeared to accept that she had been living in a fantasy world—my guess is that it resulted less from "abandoning her delusion" and more from fear of parents, doctors, etc.—even from the fear for survival. In her heart, she was probably still living in the eighteenth century, fearing that at any minute the British would come to her door. In addition, she was scared to death that if she spoke honestly of what she was feeling, her parents would take her back to the hospital, where she would once more have to face the psychiatrists.

I hasten to assure you that I do not know what happened in this particular case; I am only guessing. I am not an M.D., nor a licensed psychiatrist, and so I know nothing of what should be done medically in cases of severe psychosis. I am certainly not stating that all psychiatrists are bad and wrong and should never be consulted, though I do emphasize that caution should be exercised in choosing a psychiatrist. If such a doctor seems too rigid in his or her viewpoints, too attached to a particular type of therapy, or too self-important and authoritarian, then say "no thanks" and look for a more enlightened one. They are out there.

THE NEED FOR ENLIGHTENED PSYCHOTHERAPY

Many prominent psychologists and psychotherapists have expressed the need for changes in modern psychotherapy. Noted Jungian analyst James Hillman is the author of several books and articles on the subject of revolutionizing the field of psychotherapy, including *Re-visioning Psychology* (San Francisco: HarperCollins, 1990). Perhaps his most interesting work is *We've Had a Hundred Years of Psychotherapy and the World's Getting Worse* (San Francisco: HarperCollins, 1990), written in a rather acerbic and somewhat humorous vein with journalist Michael Ventura.

Hillman and Ventura are all for psychotherapy. However, they argue, present attitudes and methods associated with therapy need to be radically altered if the process is to be meaningful. The problem with psychotherapy, state Hillman and Ventura, is that the state of our society is left out of the formula. In the days of Freud and Jung, much attention was paid to the sickness of civilization, but today all psychopathologies are reduced to the individual, who is supposed to ignore the world around him, anesthetize and devaluate his passions and discontent, and learn to cope. In this way, the patient becomes assimilated into a system that is itself pathological and dysfunctional. It is important, Hillman and Ventura contend, to do therapy on the soul of the world itself.

Religious and family therapist David E. Roy, Ph.D., associated with the Center for the Healing Journey and the Interdisciplinary Psychotherapy Institute is the author of a number of books and articles on the subject of a psychology for the soul, including *Psychotherapy for the Soul* and *Spirituality for Growth and Healing*. He is not only a licensed and highly accredited psychotherapist; he holds a Master's degree in theology as well. Roy emphasizes the need for the integration of clinical psychotherapy and spirituality in such a way that does not invalidate either school of thought. "There are a growing number of clinicians who feel called to this kind of awareness and practice," writes Roy, "yet there is also a deep uneasiness in many of these same professionals about the apparent necessity of collapsing the boundaries that have kept [the scientific and the religious] realms so separate…Yet…there is something deep in our being that persists in bringing us back to the awareness of…our connectedness to the whole of creation."[50]

Noted British psychoanalyst John Heron, M.D., is founder and director of the Human Potential Research Project at the University of Surrey, at this time the oldest established center for humanistic and transpersonal psychology and education in Europe. He, like Hillman and Roy, is the author of a significant number of books and articles on the subject, including *The Complete Facilitator's Handbook*, London:

---

50 David E. Roy, Ph.D., "Psychotherapy for the Soul." Online essay available at http://www.soulfulpsy.com/psyc4soul.html.

Kogan Page, 1999, and *Sacred Science: Person-centred Inquiry into the Spiritual and the Subtle,* Ross-on-Wye: PCCS Books, 1998. Heron agrees with theologist Karl Rahner in believing that the boundaries of the human experience "are sent in the context of unlimited horizons. In this sense, the human being is transcendent, a spirit, open to infinite being, the fullness of…infinite reality."[51] Heron goes on to state that human beings are both world-dependent and world-independent; individuals both need to deal with the world they live in and transcend it, directing their consciousness and actions where they will.

In *Towards a Science of Consciousness* Kenneth R. Pelletier, Ph.D., points out that since all science uses intuition and speculation, psychology should not be condemned because it does the same. Pelletier questions seriously the tendency of modern psychology (indeed, of all sciences) to stick to a rigid dogma that adheres to similar rules adopted by the physical sciences. "The paradigm," writes Pelletier, "dictates the questions to be raised and the means by which they are to be resolved. The paradigm itself is never questioned."[52] Such a limited outlook, Pelletier believes, limits the efficacy of the science.

Dean Radin, Ph.D., director of the Consciousness Laboratory at the University of Nevada at Las Vegas, actually devotes an entire book, *The Conscious Universe* (New York: HarperCollins, 1997), to disproving the idea that there is no scientific evidence at all of psychic phenomena such as clairvoyance, telepathy, etc. He cites thousands of successful experiments which have taken place which, at best, prove that these experiments demonstrate that at the very worst, the results rule out chance at a rate of twenty to one, and at best, at no less than *one billion*

---

51 John Heron, M.D., "Space and Consciousness." Online essay available at http://www.lpiper.demon.co.uk/spaconsc.htm.

52 Kenneth R. Pelletier, Ph.D., *Towards a Science of Consciousness.* Berkeley, CA: Celestial Arts, 1985. P. 37.

to one. Studies with near-death experiences conducted by the British Heart Foundation in London demonstrate that consciousness actually does continue to exist after the brain has ceased to function. And Dr. Radin maintains that there actually is scientific indication of the probability of reincarnation—because of the work of Dr. Ian Stevenson and other researchers like him.

It is nice to know that these highly learned, thoroughly educated, and infinitely qualified psychologists share the viewpoints of most New Age thinkers. A new paradigm with regard to psychotherapy is definitely needed at this significant moment in history. The world is changing; people are changing; and therefore the attitudes of those to whom we trust the health of our minds and bodies must change as well.

PSYCHOPATHOLOGIES

To clarify what will be said in the following paragraphs, it is necessary to know what I mean by certain terms. For me, a neurosis represents some kind of trauma or phobia that colors our feelings and perceptions. A person can be plagued by one or more neuroses, yet still function perfectly normally and be totally capable at all times not only of taking care of oneself, but of performing such intricate or monumental tasks as running a business, performing scientific research or creating great works of art. Some people are more neurotic than others, but, in my opinion, only the saints have managed to overcome all their neuroses (and some people express doubts even about them).

A psychosis is far more severe, inhibiting the individual's perception of reality and thus inhibiting his ability to function. A psychosis rarely appears full-blown, out of the blue, but does appear to grow. I once had a client who was frantic over her daughter's growing psychosis. As a child, the girl, whom I will call Susie, probably a Fourth Ray soul, had occasionally indulged in uncontrollable temper tantrums, alternating with periods of extreme shyness and withdrawal. Adulthood had not alleviated Susie's symptoms in any way; in fact, she appeared to be worsening. On a few occasions I witnessed what my client still referred to as "Susie's temper tantrums," but which to me appeared to be more like sudden outbreaks of hostility and paranoia which bordered on the psychopathic, all triggered by insignificant occurrences. Most of these were directed at her mother, whom I will call Reba.

When I began working with Susie, she was still able to function. She held down a prestigious job and was involved in what appeared to be a happy romantic relationship. She had a good driving record, never drank or used recreational drugs, and was popular with her friends. Yet my client, Reba, was concerned that if Susie continued as she was, the life Susie had built would come tumbling all around her.

For several years, Susie had seen a psychiatrist, who had done little good other than to prescribe medications which calmed her down and helped her to control her tantrums. I confess to being very leery of using drugs in cases of mental illness; in my opinion, they merely suppress the symptoms while forcing the actual condition deeper into the psyche, where it can continue to worsen. However, there are cases when responsibly prescribed medications can represent the lesser of two evils. In Susie's case, the prescription enabled her to stay in control while she and I tried to ferret out the cause of her tantrums.

Past-life regressions revealed that Susie had been one of the girls who made the accusations at the Salem witch trials. Contrary to what many historians have concluded, according to Susie's regression material the girls did not make the whole thing up. There actually was some kind of evil force in the air that did take possession of the girls. To this day, Salem is still associated with strange forces, and many psychic researchers are drawn there to learn more about what happened there, both in the past and in the present.

According to Susie, whatever force it was that took over the girls was not totally responsible for the deaths of the so-called witches. The girls were terrified, not only of the forces that plagued them, but of the stern, self-righteous and judgmental Puritan elders around them. They knew:

If they did not accuse someone of afflicting them, they themselves would be condemned as witches.

And so, petrified with fear, they accused everyone they knew who was different in any way. One of them, in the current lifetime, was Reba.

I trust I will not be violating my clients' confidentiality when I reveal that these regressions took place in Ojai, California, a place similar to Salem that has since the days of the Indians been associated with the same sort of otherworldliness. Ojai seems to be traditionally on a bit of a higher level than Salem (and I make this judgment guardedly). This colorful little town has attracted the Theosophical Society, Krishnamurti, and the Rosicrucians, not to mention my own mentor, Marcia Moore. What I believe happened was that Susie's previous personality, who appears to have been either late Stage Two or early Stage Three, never fully recovered from the trauma of the experience. In addition, because she was still several incarnations away from the Second Initiation and not yet aware of the astral light, she never quite understood what had happened to her, and the fear, however deeply buried in her psyche, stayed with her.

In the current incarnation, Susie, now an early Stage Four with an early Stage Four mother, was capable of being in better touch with the forces around her—and growing up in Ojai brought her into constant contact with them. It is my opinion that the presence of the forces in Ojai, to which this soul-entity is apparently vulnerable, brought the old trauma to the surface once more. Subconsciously Susie recognized her mother as her previous "victim", and began to repeat the same experience that she had gone through before.

It was difficult for Susie to handle. "I can't have been one of those girls!" she said after her regression session. But the knowledge seemed to help her. While the psychotic episodes did not totally vanish, they decreased, and, because Susie was aware of their source, her control over them increased. Gradually, their household became more relaxed.

I wish I could claim Susie as one of my total successes. However, less than a year after I completed my work with her, she moved out of her mother's home and into an apartment with her boyfriend in a different town. I lost touch both with her and with Reba, and so I have no way of knowing if Susie's problem was eventually "cured" or not. I do feel, however, that even if it still reared its ugly head from time to time, her regression experience caused her to recognize the cause and enabled her to control it better, especially since, as an early Stage Four, she possessed enough innate awareness to understand at least in part what had happened. With this awareness, and with the knowledge revealed through the regressions, Susie had the power to overcome her condition—if she actually desired to do so. Remember the importance of self-effort.

If cases like Susie's are not treated in some way, it is likely that the psychosis will eventually absorb the individual's entire life, which may result in what I call total insanity: complete dissociation from the environment and from reality, and total inability to function as a human being.

In Britain, people diagnosed as schizophrenic are rebelling against the drug and shock therapy which is usually the domain of mainstream psychiatrists treating their condition. An organization has been formed by people who hear voices who have undergone the usual treatment for schizophrenia and have chosen to discontinue it, though they do check in with their doctors periodically. Against all the psychiatrists' expectations, these people actually seem to function quite well after they discontinue their treatment. They declare that there is nothing wrong with them; they are perfectly normal human beings. They merely hear voices speaking to them. Their chosen self-effort is basically to ignore them. "Sometimes they tell me stuff that I find quite helpful," said one former mental patient. "When they don't, I just tell them to fuck off."

A psychosis as pronounced as that of the young girl trapped in the American Revolution, however, does need intense treatment of some kind. The key is ability to function—and while people who hear voices can just tell them to "fuck off," a person who expects horse carts and dirt roads when the reality is automobiles and freeways can be in actual physical danger. So how would I treat so challenging a case?

Unlike the case of Susie, the first step would not involve past-life regression. First of all, I would talk to the patient, gain her trust, induce her to talk to me about her entire eighteenth-century life. I would learn who her parents are, who her friends are, brothers, sisters, lovers. I would want to know what school she went to, what church, what she and those around her did for a living. In this way I would try to learn exactly what it was that kept her trapped in a lifetime that was two hundred years gone. Then—and only then—would past-life regression be appropriate, and only if the patient understood the concept well enough to agree to it. If she didn't, I would probably use karmic astrology, such as that outlined in *Astrology and Past Lives,* to try to seek the cause of her psychosis in her karmic past.

What incompletions were there that she was literally staying behind to complete? What attachments were keeping her consciousness two hundred years behind the time? And finally, why was the karma that had brought her to that long-ago era so strong that she was desperate to complete it centuries later? I would have attempted to attain the astrological chart of that long-dead personality. I would have counseled her in light of that chart as well as her present one. I would have made an honest effort to find the truth about why she was trapped—and done the best I could to point her in the direction of whatever was possible to alleviate the problem. This would have involved finding the incompletions and completing them, and also unearthing the attachments and breaking them.

Maybe I would have succeeded. Maybe I would have failed. The important difference between the approach of mainstream psychiatry and the approach of a past-life therapist would be the acceptance of the reality of the situation—for the patient if no one else. A past-life therapist would behave as if the girl really were back in the 1780's and counseled her thus. The therapist would not have tried to beat it out of her with drugs, shock, brainwashing or whatever The important difference is that the past-life therapist would not have invaded her space or denied her reality.

THE RELATIVE NATURE OF REALITY

The difference between a hard-nosed, conservative mainstream psychiatrist, a more moderate one, and an enlightened one such as those mentioned above lies mainly in their concept of reality. Like everything else in this Universe, reality—like time, space, distance, and so on—is not an absolute, but relative. However, a mainstream psychiatrist, usually a Stage Three, defines reality as that which *he personally* can hear, see, touch, and explain, and nothing more. If the reality of the patient includes a six-foot rabbit named Harvey, then, in the mind of the psychiatrist, since he himself cannot see or hear Harvey, the patient must be mentally unbalanced and needs to be balanced. In short, the patient needs to be forced to accept the psychiatrist's view of reality at all costs, even if it takes "treatments" that resemble very closely the tortures of the Inquisition.

A moderate attitude is that of the psychiatrist or therapist who accepts that Harvey is very real *to the patient.* This type of therapist acknowledges that the patient is not deluded, that in his mind, Harvey exists. Still, the moderate therapist does not accept that Harvey has any reality outside the patient's mind and tailors his treatment of the patient so as to cause the patient eventually to abandon his delusion. This attitude is, of course, highly superior to the first. Nonetheless the moderate therapist, no matter how understanding and kind she tries to be, is always in danger of appearing to be patronizing, of treating the patient as though she were a child. A patient with any intelligence at all will sense this, eventually if not immediately, and will resent it, which will, of course, limit the effectiveness of the therapy.

The enlightened psychotherapist accepts that reality is relative, and that on some level, perhaps on the astral plane, there really is a six-foot rabbit who calls himself Harvey that could well be sitting in the chair right next to the patient. The patient obviously is able to hear and see Harvey, and is being visited by him, for a reason. The therapist's job is not to convince the patient that he is deluded, that Harvey doesn't exist, *but to uncover why Harvey is there.*

I recall, years ago, a TV movie about a little girl named Hannah, who was accompanied everywhere she went by the ghost of a favorite teacher, whom she called "Mister George." Hannah was an orphaned heiress hounded by greedy relatives who were trying everything they could to get their hands on her inheritance.

Mister George was her guide during this rough time, telling her exactly what she needed to do to thwart those who wished her ill. He was there telling her what to do when she needed to destroy papers, intercept phone calls, hide valuables, listen in on conspiratorial conversations and report them to her lawyer. Every time Hannah's position was threatened, Mister George told her exactly how to protect herself. So her greedy relatives, frustrated at being constantly beaten by a little girl, finally decided to do away with her, and locked her in her room so that she wouldn't disappear while they were getting ready.

Mister George told Hannah of a secret passage under a loose board that led out of her room. In that passage her father had hidden a small cache of emergency money, which Mister George told Hannah to take with her. He then guided her out of the house, used his powers to stop a taxi for her, and told her to tell the driver to take her to the train station. She caught a train to a small town where she then took another cab to the home of a favorite aunt, who, while Mister George was still living, had been his sweetheart.

When they reached the house, Mister George told Hannah goodbye at the door. Hannah was shocked. "But Mister George, you can't be leaving me!" she cried.

"Yes, Hannah," said Mister George. "I have to go. Your Aunt Laura will take care of you now."

Like Mister George, the Harveys of this world have a reason for being here, and once that purpose is accomplished they leave. A good example is the common phenomenon known as the "imaginary playmate," when lonely children are said to "make up" a playmate, give it a name, and spend most of their time with it, often setting a place for it at the dinner table. Generally, when the children are in a better position to make friends, the imaginary playmates disappear. Mainstream psychology assumes that since the child no longer has any need for the person whom they made up, they stop making it up. Esoteric philosophers speculate that "imaginary playmates" are actually ghosts, thought forms, another form of poltergeist, astral visitors, and so on. Or perhaps all of the above.

If there is a Harvey in the life of anyone you know, what was going on in that person's life at the time Harvey appeared? Did the person suffer a crushing loss, such as a divorce or death in the family? Did he suffer an illness that zapped his energy? Did he lose a job, or suffer another deadly blow to his self-esteem? Did some tragedy appear emblazoned over the headlines of all the newspapers, which could possibly have awakened a long-buried memory of a similar tragedy in his own life?

Good therapists are less concerned with whether Harvey is "real" or not, and more concerned with why he is there. In most cases, once Harvey's reason for being around has been resolved, he returns from whence he came, whether that is the patient's mind, the astral plane, or Heaven. Always remember Mister George! And if Harvey decides to stick around after all, if the patient is finally happy and healthy, and if he can function well in the world and make a good life for himself, so what if he believes his best friend is a six-foot rabbit from the astral plane?

There are enlightened psychiatrists out there who actively practice past-life therapy. Many of them still doubt reincarnation, yet nonetheless they acknowledge the basic validity of anything that comes out of the psyche and avoid taking any kind of judgmental, heavy-handed position that puts the patient on the defensive and damages what is most likely already a very shaky self-image. These psychiatrists are less concerned with whether or not past-life memories fit into their own personal concept of "reality" and more concern with the benefit to the patient.

Yet too many psychiatric professionals see it as their mission to stamp out "delusion." And, to them, the idea of past lives and past-life therapists is among the most ridiculous of delusions. It would be greatly to their benefit—as well as to the benefit of a too-significant number of New Age therapists—to consider their own delusion that their point of view is always right and everyone else's is always wrong.

SCHIZOPHRENIA

The case of people who hear voices (or see things) is a bit different. What would have been important to the therapist of the young girl trapped in the Revolution would have been the discovery of the attachments and incompletions that needed to be handled. However, hearing voices or seeing things is a slightly different phenomenon. In order to counsel someone with this condition, it is important primarily to know the stage of development, and, to a lesser degree, the Ray vibration.

The cases of Hildegard of Bingen, who had powerful visions and heard celestial music, of Joan of Arc, who heard the voices of saints telling her to lead the French Army, and of the psychotic killer who supposedly heard the voice of God telling him to murder his wife and children because they were evil, in essence represent the same phenomenon. Put simply, these are cases of individuals with powerful psychic abilities, in close communication with the higher planes, who can actually hear or see messages coming from the collective unconscious—and who may or may not have the wisdom and understanding to deal with them in a positive or effective manner.

Even some mainstream psychiatrists acknowledge that the line between mysticism and schizophrenia is very thin. Famed psychoanalytical pioneer William James wrote extensively on the subject. James wrote that mystical experiences were characterized by (1) a strong sense of significance, as if profound knowledge were both purpose and result of the experience; (2) time/space distortion; (3) experience of unity; (4) ineffability, and (5) a sense of holiness or sacredness. Unfortunately, many schizophrenic episodes also are marked by these characteristics.

The difference, it is believed, is that the mystic knows how to handle his voices and visions, while the schizophrenic does not. The mystic can separate the wheat from the chaff, and knows which voices are the voices of Light Masters and which are mischievous or even evil lower astral entities. The former he can listen to; the latter he ignores. Eventually the latter get tired of being ignored and go find someone else to bother.

The schizophrenic, on the other hand, is frightened by the voices he hears. He confuses the messages of the lower astral entities with those of God or the angels, and often fears that they will destroy him. The entities sense his fear, derive pleasure from it, and feed on it. And the more he dreads them, the more they plague him. Schizophrenia, if not treated, can result in complete retreat from the world into total insanity, characterized by loss of contact with the environment and disintegration of the personality. If the individual does not get help, eventually he will either give in to the demands of the voices plaguing him—like the man who murdered his wife and children—or withdraw into unqualified madness or catatonia. In my humble opinion, once more, *the focus should be not on the voices or visions themselves, but on the person's response to them.* Hildegard of Bingen heard music and saw visions for most of her life—and yet she had enough presence of mind and control to run an abbey full of nuns (who must have been a trial at times), to deal with bishops, cardinals and popes, and to write several books. David Berkowitz, the Son of Sam, heard God or the Devil (my sources differ) telling him to kill people and so he did. Berkowitz was crazy; Hildegard was not.

It is easy to see what role the stage of development plays here. For a Stage Two individual—one who has not yet undergone the First Initiation—contact with the other planes can indeed be terrifying. Unless the individual is one of the elite group who never totally passed through the Fountain of Oblivion, the Stage Two individual is far more likely to develop schizophrenia than to become a mystic. The individual will probably react in a manner consistent with his Ray vibration. A First or Fourth Ray individual could become violent. A Second, Sixth or Seventh Ray individual is likely to associate the voices with those of God or the Devil indiscriminately, while the mystic would know how to tell the difference between them. Third Ray or Fifth Ray individuals would probably write down or otherwise record what is said to them and become obsessed with keeping those records. The reaction of any Stage Two would primarily be paralyzing fear—fear of the unknown, fear of the otherworldly, fear for his survival. However, for a Stage Two, the self-image is rarely affected in an adverse way. The Stage Two's primary self-image would still be that of the toddler: "I'm great!"

A Stage Three individual would probably react in much the same way as a Stage Two individual, but with an additional complication. The growth in awareness that came with the First Initiation would enable the individual to realize that this is not a common occurrence, that it sets him apart from the society that means so much to him. Thus he begins to feel that there is something wrong with him, that he is abnormal, that he is "crazy." His self-image nose-dives and self-doubt sets in. The therapist's problem is therefore compounded in that she has to help the client deal not only with the voices and/or visions, but with the plummeting self-esteem as well.

In the case of those who see visions, the effect is even more startling than that of hearing voices. And too many mainstream psychotherapists dismiss all visions as hallucinations.

We all have hallucinations; they are a part of our daily life. Everyone occasionally sees things that aren't there. Light tricks us; our eyes trick us; our brains do numbers on our vision. How many times have you been engrossed in a movie which you are watching on TV, then turned away for a moment and seen what appears to be a negative image of the hero's face on the wall beside the set? We are all familiar with the dark stranger who turns out to be a shadow, or with stories of travelers in the desert, near to death from thirst, who see an oasis ahead only to learn that it was a mirage, a trick of the light. We all are well acquainted with the little stars and snowflakes that dance before our eyes when we open them after having kept them shut for awhile. These are true hallucinations.

But a significant number of visions are actually not hallucinations at all. As with the voices, they are actually impressions from the collective unconscious, or the higher planes, that people with extremely high levels of psychic sensitivity perceive through their eyes. Consider, for a moment, the vast numbers of sightings of the Virgin Mary that have occurred in the past ten or twelve years. Those who are not present at such a sighting tend to think that the visionaries imagined the whole thing. However, too many people who were totally independent of each other shared the same vision, identical even to the color of her cloak— and even those present who did not actually see the Virgin Mary still perceived an intense atmosphere of peace and love. I doubt very much if even the most hardened and skeptical of mainstream psychiatrists would dare to try to convince all those who saw Mary at Medjugorje that they had been hallucinating.

They might, however, if they could, try to drug or shock the person who was visited by Mary in her own living room into believing that she had been seeing things. Even more unbelievable to the hard-line school of therapist would be the type of vision perceived by Hildegard of Bingen—vast, intricate tableaux of symbolic images meant to convey a specific message, which Hildegard preserved for posterity in beautiful illuminations. Yet throughout the transition from the second to the third millennium, more and more people have been reporting sightings of Mary or Jesus, of angelic beings, and even of non-Christian figures such as the Celtic horned god Herne and the Olympian gods. A few brave visionaries have reported visions such as those immortalized by Hildegard. Some of these are personal, others universal. Some are demonic. Some are so apocalyptic in their message that the psychics who receive them are hesitant to tell anyone about them.

Both visions and auditory phenomena (voices) are often said to be drug-induced, and thus are automatically condemned as illusory. Drugs can and do produce auditory and visual aberrations. However, it is my experience that true hallucinations really don't last all that long. A voice that is not there, or a vision redolent of the phantom image of a TV screen vanishes as suddenly as it appears; the lifespan of a true hallucination is no more than a second or two at most. This includes drug-induced hallucinations. Even if an individual has abused drugs, if the visions or voices persist, chances are what they are seeing is, on some level, real.

FACING AND HANDLING SCHIZOPHRENIA

Being plagued by evil visions can be frightening. I once had a client who had, for a period of two days, been plagued by visions of horrific, demonic creatures. She was not insane; she was quite intelligent, and other than being twenty years old and still vulnerable to the hormone fluctuations of youth, there was nothing physically wrong with her. She was, however, a gifted psychic, whose accuracy with her readings had often proven uncanny.

She told me that only a few days before, she had ended a relationship with a man who was rather wealthy and used to getting his own way. He had not taken the breakup well, first cajoling, then threatening—and my client was astute enough to know that both the entreaties and threats were motivated less by genuine love for her and more from a bruised ego and an affront to his power. The visions, she related, were accompanied by overwhelming feelings of longing and desire for this man. After telephoning him to make arrangements for returning some of his belongings, she learned from one of his associates that he had flown to New Orleans to consult with some "witch-lady."

Immediately I knew the source of the demonic visions. The rejected lover had joined forces with a shamaness of some kind to try to use psychic projection to coerce my client into resuming her relationship with him. Whether the visions were actual lower astral beings taking advantage of the situation, or whether they were images from the mind of the rejected lover sent telepathically, I don't know. I do know, however, that a quick guided meditation in which I suggested that my client first summon the demons, then send them away, took care of the "hallucinations" forever. My client was also a friend, with whom I actually lived for over a year, and I know for a fact that she was never plagued by evil visions again. She also never resumed contact with her ex-lover!

Again, a caution: My client was early to late Stage Four, a devout meditator, and possessed an innate understanding of such matters. Therefore she was well equipped to deal with actually summoning the "demons" so that she could send them away. Stage Twos and Threes might not be able to do that; in fact, for a Stage Two the fear resulting from an actual confrontation with "demons" might prove dangerous. However, as with the voices, a guided fantasy or psychodrama in which the therapist plays the role of the demons could probably accomplish the same goal.

Early Stage Four individuals have passed through the Second Initiation and thus are aware, subconsciously at least, of the astral light, of the reality of psychic abilities and the existence of other entities in worlds beyond our own. Therefore, they are probably more conscious of exactly what is happening and thus less likely to react with fear. Still, they are not always too certain as to how to deal with it. I have had a number of early Stage Four clients who heard voices or had visions and wished to know exactly that: how to deal with their experience. Late Stage Fours and above, in my experience, basically know what they are going through and how to handle it, and thus are the easiest to assist.

Once the initial problem has been dealt with, it is perhaps a good idea for the individual to consider, with or without assistance from the therapist, his own Ray vibration and whatever archetypes he seems to be living. In this way, the client can get a handle on what his own innate inclinations are towards making use of the psychic abilities that gave rise to his experiences. Any form of therapy should be followed up by psychic development classes, meditation, and shamanic journeying techniques in order to enable the individual to appreciate the abilities that once seemed so much of a problem and turn them around so as to contribute to her development rather than impede it.

By Stage Five, the borderline schizophrenic has given way totally to the mystic. I have never had a Stage Five client consult me for anything resembling schizophrenia. They seek astrological counseling or past-life regression simply to obtain more self-knowledge. Their stories of their own mystical revelations are actually quite therapeutic for me! As pointed out in Chapter Two, depression is about the only severe neurosis to which Stage Fives are still vulnerable. Usually this is the result of feeling strange, of feeling out of sync with other human beings, and out of touch with the people one loves. There is no relief for this other than putting them in touch, through guided meditation, with the higher selves of those around them. On that level, the sense of love, unity and ultimate communication come much more easily.

One client, a young man who had been through the entire course of drugs, shock therapy, institutionalization, and so on, and yet still heard voices, seemed amazingly in control of himself. He appeared to be the typical early Stage Four, highly educated, eager to learn all he could about New Age thought, and, in spite of everything, pursuing a successful career in the restaurant business. But he still could make no sense of the voices. "I'm kind of used to them now," he said, "but I still would like for them to shut up."

"Have you ever tried asking them what they want?" I queried.

He was thunderstruck. "Ask them what they want!" he exclaimed.

"Yes," I said. "Ask them what they want. If it's within your power to do so, and if it isn't illegal or immoral, give it to them."

Another client who heard voices was a young Native American, ironically, a psychology major who seemed calm and in control, but whose studies of schizophrenia made him uneasy. He was afraid that he would have to undergo the usual treatment, and he knew that the "cure" was often more traumatic than the condition. So, as a last resort, before seeking help from a mainstream psychiatrist, he came to me. I gave him the same advice I had given my other client: Ask them what they want.

He heaved a deep sigh. "You know, my mother told me the same thing."

"Your mother is a very wise woman," I informed him.

He shook his head. "I never thought it could be that simple," he finally said.

The results in both the above cases were the same. When the voices were confronted, the higher beings made their desires known—which mostly concerned my clients' spiritual progress, advising meditation and recommending books to read. (Yes, the saints and angels are aware of books that exist on this plane!) The lower astral entities—assuming that they had been among the ranks of the choruses who plagued my clients—apparently vanished. The reason for this is that my clients, instead of being a victim of the voices, suddenly came from a position of power, turning the tables on their tormentors. My experience is that mischievous astral beings are as incapable of handling this as schizophrenics are incapable of handling the voices. In the face of this newfound power, they flee.

I hasten to add here, again, that these two clients were both Stage Fours, who had passed through the Second Initiation and were aware of the existence of the higher planes. Simply "asking them what they want" probably wouldn't work with anyone on Stage Two or Three, because they have not yet been awakened to the reality of the astral light and probably don't believe in it. However, a skilled therapist can still make use of the same principle, through guided fantasy and psychodrama, where the client actually fantasizes a conversation with the voices, or where the therapist plays the role of the etheric voice.

Again, I am not a psychiatrist, and for all I know new techniques akin to "asking them what they want" may be in common use. Some enlightened psychiatrists, even those skeptical of the idea of the existence of otherworldly entities, recall the teachings of Carl Jung and view the voices as emanations from the collective unconscious However, I have had a number of clients contact me who have undergone the standard drug and shock therapy regimen and have suffered tremendously from it—only to find that the voices still tortured them. (In my experience, voices are more common than visions.)

PARANOIA

There are many other types of schizophrenia, some more subtle in their effects than the actual seeing of visions or hearing of voices. Paranoid schizophrenia, for example, is characterized by the client's seeing enemies around every corner, often imagining that the CIA, or the KGB, or even agents of the Devil are following him. In cases where the person is addicted to tobacco, alcohol, cocaine, etc., or when he is inclined towards such practices as gluttony or womanizing, this condition may partially be the result of being plagued by a "hitchhiker": a lower astral being, sometimes literally riding on the person's back, who misses the pleasures of the flesh and enjoys them vicariously through psychically encouraging the weaknesses of its "host". The "host" usually senses the presence of a malevolent being. Since "hosts" of this kind are generally Stage Threes who have not yet been initiated into knowledge of the astral light, they project their awareness of a follower onto known *human* entities usually viewed as malevolent—e.g., agents of the CIA, FBI or IRS.

In some cases, however, paranoid schizophrenia represents an incompletion from a past life in which the person was a spy, a criminal, a refugee, or perhaps a woman afraid she would be accused of witch-craft. Past-life regression can prove invaluable in such cases. What was the situation? Who was following him, and why? Why is the matter still so unresolved that the person must relive it in this lifetime? Early Stage Fours and above are somewhat, at least on an intellectual level, aware of exactly what is going on, but the situation still needs to be resolved.

I had one client who experienced a mild form of paranoid schizo-phrenia every time she saw a man in uniform. When this happened, she was convinced that he was after her and thus, no matter where she was, who she was with or what she was doing, she would always quickly remove herself to another place out of sight of the uniformed man. Past-life regressions revealed that in her last life she had been a Jewish woman who had been on one of the trains in which the Nazis trans-ported the Jews to the concentration camps. The soldier guarding them had dozed off, and she had seized the opportunity to throw herself from the train. Relatively unhurt, she picked herself up and ran into the woods. She tried to make her way to Denmark, petrified with fear every step of the way, for she knew the Nazis were everywhere.

Unfortunately, she died before she could reach safety, not at the hands of the Nazis, but in a freak accident: she tumbled into a river and drowned. For this reason, the fear was never expunged and she carried it with her into the present incarnation. Needless to say, because the trauma was a fairly recent one, the regression totally erased the para-noia, and thus there was no need for any kind of conventional therapy. Her husband, however, was a sixties war protester who had refused to go to Vietnam!

MULTIPLE PERSONALITY

No discussion of psychotherapy would be complete without the mention of the amazing phenomenon called *multiple personality*. While schizophrenia has been defined as "split personality," it is not the same as multiple personality. The "split personality" of schizophrenia is the total disintegration of the personality that results if phenomena such as those discussed previously are not treated. Multiple personality is a term used to define a rare condition in which more than one personality exists within the same body—all totally independent of each other. This condition appears to result from fragmentation of the personality—which appears to be a survival mechanism resulting from physical or emotional abuse which the individual suffers in early childhood. Fragments of the individual's essence dissociate from the personality and develop personalities of their own in order to forget the abuse. Often one personality exists as a sort of control, to protect the others from whatever pain may come their way. The most famous cases of multiple personality are perhaps Chris Costner Sizemore ("Eve"), Sybil Isabel Dorset, and Billy Milligan.

Fragmentation of the personality is nothing new. Native peoples have been aware of this phenomenon since ancient times. According to some shamanic traditions, every time a person is traumatized in any manner, he loses a fragment of his soul, which retreats into the deeper levels of the astral plane. Modern shamanic practitioners have developed a technique known as soul retrieval, in which the client is placed in a meditative state and the shaman goes on a shamanic journey on the astral plane to retrieve fragmented parts of the client's personality and re-integrate them. This technique is brilliantly outlined in Sandra Ingerman's *Soul Retrieval*.

This ancient shamanic tradition sheds new light on the phenomenon of multiple personality. If everyone loses fragments of his being whenever he is abused, and those fragments flee to the astral plane, then the personalities in a multiple are *not* totally fragmented. They are still connected psychically with the body and with the core personality—and thus the pathology appears to be that these semi-fragmented beings lose sight of the fact that they are partially fragmented and still try to function through the body. At the same time, because they are still connected to the core personality, they should be easier to re-integrate than such segments of the personalities of most ordinary human beings, whose fragments are hidden somewhere on the inner planes. But it appears that not all the personalities inhabiting the body of a multiple represent fragmentation. Marcia Moore, a psychology major who was Phi Beta Kappa, when studying the case of Sybil Dorset, expressed the opinion that Sybil was a trance medium with different entities speaking through her. Not having Marcia's experience working with trance mediums, and never having actually worked with Sybil, I do not feel myself qualified to judge[53]. However, one of Sybil's personalities, who called herself Mary, appeared to bear a powerful resemblance to Sybil's grandmother—whose name was Mary. Perhaps Sybil's grandmother did attempt to protect her abused granddaughter by taking possession of her body whenever it appeared necessary.

Also, consider the case of Billy Milligan, who was tried for rape and used as his defense the statement that the rape was not committed by

---

53 The most recent research regarding the case of Sybil questions whether or not she was a true multiple. Apparently Sybil (which is, by the way, a pseudonym), when dealing with friends and relatives, never gave any indication whatsoever that she ever manifested any personality except her own. Some psychologists now believe that her "multiple personality" symptoms may have been induced by her psychiatrist and the author of the book *Sybil* in order to create their own blockbuster like *The Three Faces of Eve*. If so, this adds credence to Marcia's theory, for Sybil definitely experienced missing time, sometimes feel as if she were someone else, and occasionally speak in different voices. However, since Sybil, her psychiatrist and the author of the book are now all dead, there is no way to verify this idea for certain.

him—meaning Billy, the core personality—but by one of his frag-mented personalities. One of Billy's personalities (not the one accused of rape), who called himself Regan, maintained that he was from Yugoslavia. This statement was supported by the fact that Regan spoke fluent Serbo-Croatian—a language that Billy Milligan had never even heard, much less studied.

Could Regan, rather than being a fragment of the modern Billy Milligan, represent a bleedthrough from a past personality, possibly one who had lived in Yugoslavia? If this is the case, then the phenomenon of multiple personality is more complex than we think.

I have only worked with one multiple personality, and this was a mild case. This was a young man with three personalities who were only par-tially fragmented, meaning that they were all aware of each other and knew when another was taking control. (The separate personalities of multiples—at least the more famous ones—seem to black out when another takes control of the body.) None of my client's personalities appeared to be either a separate entity or a bleedthrough from a previ-ous incarnation. So I do not consider myself a hands-on expert with regard to the treatment of multiple personalities. However, in view of my studies on the subject, I consider that past-life therapy, as well as analysis of Ray vibration and archetypal influences, could well prove invaluable. Is the abuse that caused the fragmentation a pattern from a number of previous lives? What karmic factors exist that should be con-sidered in light of the relationship between the client and the abuser? Was the client in the past an abuser herself, and what could be done to expiate the guilt? Again, the stage of development and Ray vibration could aid the therapist in both deducing the receptiveness of the client to different therapeutic methods—and in gauging the person's reaction to reintegration. Perhaps shamanic techniques, such as those described by Sandra Ingerman, could be of help. Thankfully, the therapists who treat multiple personalities appear to be among the more enlightened.

They make extensive use of hypnosis, counseling, and the boosting of self-image, and only use drugs when no other course seems available.

An interesting side note is that some therapists have observed that multiple personalities report being plagued by premonitions and precognitive dreams. My client mentioned above was quite psychic, and said that he had been so since he was three years old. Chris Costner Sizemore reported a vision of Jesus that occurred when she was a child. The Master informed her that her dangerously ill sister did not have pneumonia, but diphtheria. The vision (only one of hundreds that Sizemore experienced for many years) saved her sister's life. Again, thank Heaven the psychotherapists who treat multiples appear to be among the more enlightened ones!

TREATMENT FOR MENTAL ILLNESS

So: Am I totally against drug therapy and hospitalization for schizophrenia? No, I am not. I am totally against shock therapy, and, I am happy to say, so are an increasing number of mainstream psychiatrists. Drugs should only be used as a last resort, to calm a patient down and help him regain control—but it is my experience that this is all drugs can do. They cannot stop visions, voices or paranoia. Hospitalization, too, should only be treated as a last resort, when the patient is incapable of functioning and needs to be in a controlled environment.

Am I against psychiatrists? Certainly not. The purpose of this chapter is not to promote the idea that all people suffering from mental and emotional problems, ranging from mild neurosis to severe mental illness, should fire their psychiatrists and start looking for a New Age shamanic healer or past-life therapist like myself. I must emphasize: Most of the people who consult me, and who benefit from what I have to give them, are early to late Stage Fours who are amazingly mentally healthy, but who acknowledge that they are still plagued by certain neuroses, ranging from mild to severe phobias to early or mild cases of schizophrenia which limit their growth and keep them from living the type of life they want to live. I have no training in abnormal psychology or license to treat advanced and dangerous mental conditions and have no desire to assume the responsibility of doing so. I admit this, and any other ethical psychic counselor and past-life regression therapist would admit the same.

What I am thoroughly against is any kind of "therapy" that involves telling the patient that he is "abnormal" and needs to be made "normal," or that makes use of "make-wrong" pronouncements and heavy-handed imposition of specific belief systems. I have confronted this myself on several occasions, by licensed psychologists who informed me that, since I remembered my past lives and had reported a few mystical experiences, I needed intense psychiatric treatment and possibly hospitalization for schizophrenia! And this was from two men who taught in a university that offered degrees in higher consciousness! (Even after all my years in yoga, meditation and psychic studies, I still can count my mystical experiences on one hand. I am no Hildegard.)

Like the two young men mentioned previously, I have had clients come to me in desperation when mainstream treatment was not only not helping their problem, but hurting them and exhausting their family finances as well. Others have turned to me when they were tired of being treated as idiots or automatons, of having their doctors regard them as pathetically insane and talking about their conditions to their families as if they weren't there. Colleagues have informed me that therapists who take these attitudes are now in the minority, and that most therapists out there are at least moderate in their attitudes. I hope to God that this is true.

Of course, I believe that the best possible therapist one could find would be one who is a fully-trained psychologist or psychiatrist and has years of hands-on experience with all kinds of mental and emotional problems—and is also a New Age counselor and therapist who uses past-life therapy and/or soul retrieval (not to mention nutrition) as a matter of course. They are not all that hard to find. Authors Roger

Woolger, Ph.D., Brian Weiss, M.D., Larry Dossey, M.D., Raymond Moody, M.D., and Bernard Goldman, M.D., are only a few examples. If you know of no one in your area who can direct you to one, you could write to the American Holistic Medical Association, 6932 Little River Turnpike, Annandale, Virginia 22003, or The Huxley Institute, 210 East 31st Street, New York, New York 10016.

The most successful therapists are those who are able to fire the client with enthusiasm for whatever future developments may occur as a result of releasing neuroses, transforming schizophrenic tendencies or overcoming depression. The therapist needs to place herself in the place of the Goddess Saraswati, as in the story at the start of this book. By sparking the client's passion for advanced knowledge, the therapist creates the drive towards recovery. Remember that the most important tool towards any kind of psychospiritual regeneration is self-effort.

Even for the more mainstream types of therapists who doubt such concepts as reincarnation or the existence of angels or astral beings, the psychology of spirit can prove useful. The concept of the stages of development, if not viewed as indicative of the progress of the soul, can be considered in light of traditional developmental psychology. The existence of the Rays can be viewed in light of personality "types", as can archetypal influences. And karma? Well, if the therapist doesn't accept it, she should at least acknowledge that for the patient, anyway, it probably has some reality.

Conclusion

One of the most annoying irritations we researchers confront in the course of our business is being challenged by skeptics. If people don't want to accept otherworldly beings, reincarnation, archetypes, or soul fragmentation, we have no problem with that. Again, we feel that reality is relative and that their reality simply does not include these concepts. All paths lead to God and everyone has to choose the one that is best for them.

We don't seek to convert those who feel that ideas such as those mentioned above do not serve them; we only seek to present the fruits of our years of research to anyone who is interested in learning about it.

Yet skeptics feel they must challenge us—though why, we have no idea. Most of the time we avoid such discussions, since the theme running through most of them is, "Prove it!"

"Proof" is actually a legal concept more than anything else. While it can be "proven" in a court of law that a certain person was in a certain place at a certain time and performed a certain act, it is virtually impossible to "prove" anything in any other field. We cannot actually "prove" that Newton's Laws of Motion always work, that under all circumstances hydrogen will combine with oxygen to form water, that George Washington did or did not chop down the cherry tree. We certainly cannot "scientifically prove" the existence of otherworldly beings, though some people have tried using heat-sensitive equipment. However, experienced ghost hunters who are firm believers in the existence of spirits hesitate to accept evidence produced by this equipment. "It's interesting that these people have found unaccounted-for heat sources in haunted houses," said one expert in a television interview. "But I don't think their equipment really proves anything about ghosts, because we don't really know exactly what ghosts are!"

Nonetheless, it would be interesting, if nothing else, to turn such heat-sensitive equipment on a person suffering from schizophrenia who claims to hear voices. Would such equipment show the same perplexing sources of heat as there appears to be in some haunted houses?

It is our contention that people have died in the execution chamber on the strength of much less convincing evidence than there is supporting reincarnation. This evidence includes our work with past-life regression, noting how the patterns from prior existences appear to explain hangups and phobias in the present, along with our historical research in which we have documented the existence of many of the personalities uncovered. In a few rare cases we have managed to obtain portraits and/or handwriting samples of the past personalities—which bear striking resemblances to the appearances and handwriting of the present personalities. In our minds, that evidence is pretty convincing. But if others do not want to accept such evidence, that, of course, is their right.

Many researchers feel that "proving" the reality of reincarnation is irrelevant anyway. On many occasions, when a client discovers the source of a problem rooted in a past life, and releases it, never to have to confront that problem again, the therapist is often asked, "But what if she's just making it up?"

The answer to this is usually: "So what?" The bottom line is the trauma has been discovered and the resulting problem released. Because of past-life therapy, for example, I have said good-bye to chronic low back pain, a crippling phobia about fire, an intense fear of going downstairs, a fear of strange men with big noses that caused me to scream out as a child, and the petrifying terror that I would lose one of my children. If I was making up the experiences that caused me to release them, so be it. I am hardly going to take them back just so that I can conform to someone else's idea of "reality."

Yet even though "proof" of the concepts outlined in this book at present still eludes us, we still feel that the gap between science and spiritual studies is slowly but surely closing. We have already mentioned the realization of the quantum physicists that the entire Universe is composed of consciousness. In the spring of 1992, when I was first putting together my material for this book, an article was released by the Associated Press describing the similarity between the "Big Bang" theory of the origin of the Universe and the mythology of Creation.

The momentous findings supporting the "Big Bang" theory of creation provide a common ground for two old antagonists—religion and science—in the eternal debate over whether the universe is the work of a majestic guiding hand.

The discovery, indicating that an explosive birth billions of years ago led to today's expanding cosmos of stars and galaxies reinforces religious themes that order was created out of chaos by divine intervention, some scientists and theologians say

"I think one could argue that these results firm up one's view of the presence of some deity whose purpose is being worked out," said Arnold Wolfendale, Britain's Astronomer Royale. (David Briggs, Associated Press. "Will 'Big Bang' discovery finally unite religion, science?" *Houston Post*, Saturday, April 25, 1992.)

Couple this with the discoveries of quantum physics and you get an entirely new picture of the cosmos, straight from the mouths of the empirical scientists. The universe could well be the creation of a purposeful God who has filled its depths with consciousness.

And how does this statement affect the idea of otherworldly beings, or the doctrine of reincarnation? In the light of modern discoveries, let us paraphrase the Law of Conservation of Energy: "Energy can be changed, but it cannot be created or destroyed." Consider this: "Consciousness can be changed, but it cannot be created or destroyed." In other words, eventually the physicists may draw the conclusion which animates an atom, plant, animal, or human being does not cease to exist simply because the body ceases to function, but must move on and continue in some other form.

When they do, it will undoubtedly be touted in all the scientific magazines as a "great new discovery" on the part of the scientists. Dr. Dean Radin believes that that day is closer than you'd think.

There are even a few brave and enlightened scientists who are sticking their neck out to use the new discoveries in cosmology and quantum physics to make sense of concepts long known to the great Masters. Fritjof Capra's 1974 watershed work *The Tao of Physics* was the first to draw parallels between physics and spirituality. In recent years, more and more scientists are following in his footsteps. As pointed out previously, a number of physicians are finding past-life therapy to be invaluable in treating both physical and psychological dysfunctions. Now scientists are actually sticking their necks out and holding out for the actual reality of the human soul. Award-winning San Francisco physicist Fred Alan Wolf has written several best-selling books on the subject of consciousness and the universe, among them *Star Wave: Mind, Consciousness and Quantum Physics; The Eagle's Quest: A Physicist's Search for Truth in the Heart of the Shamanic World; The Dreaming Universe,* and my favorite, *The Spiritual Universe: How Quantum Physics Proves the Existence of the Soul.* Dr. Wolf is in great demand both as a consulting physicist and as a lecturer both on scientific and spiritual subjects. *In The Spiritual Universe,* Dr. Wolf digs deeply into the subject of reincarnation, at one point comparing karma to the motion of electrons in the universe.[54] He likens the nature of the Universe to the Buddhist concept of one soul and one soul only—the Absolute.

> **One** (the personal sense of being and that sense you feel inside of you) is always present in all life-forms. That **one** has been, will always be, the *one and*

---

54 Fred Alan Wolf, *The Spiritual Universe: How Quantum Physics Proves the Existence of the Soul.* New York: Simon & Schuster, 1996. P. 206. Also pp. 234ff.

only. Stand up and take a bow. The **one** might wonder: Will I reincarnate? The answer **one** gives is: Most definitely, for I have never died nor was I ever born.[55]

"Do you have a soul? Yes," Dr. Wolf said at a lecture I attended at the San Francisco Whole Life Expo. "Can you lose your soul? Yes. Does it come back? Yes."

David Darling, author of *Soul Search* and *Zen Physics: The Science of Death, The Logic of Reincarnation* is another author/physicist who has studied reincarnation within the concepts of modern physics. He maintains that reincarnation is not only possible, but inevitable. Dr. Darling points out that, as our bodies are constantly rebuilding and recreating themselves, we are actually reincarnating all the time, even in the same lifetime. He also brings up his own conception of the Law of Conservation of Consciousness, and adds to this the inevitability that a brain vastly similar if not identical to one which had previously existed would eventually come into being and thus could house a previously-existing consciousness.

> New selves emerge as new brains emerge, because what a brain does is to act as a funnel, a filter, a limiter of consciousness, and therefore a shaper of self—a separator of subject and object. The brain effectively pinches off a little bubble of introverted awareness and stores and manipulates information relevant exclusively to the survival needs of the individual so created. Using its archived memories, the brain builds and subtends the myth of personality and self, its onboard programming working ceaselessly to substantiate and immortalize this phantasmic inner being. And such a fine job does it do that the projected self not only feels itself, to be tangible, but it fails to appreciate, or even suspect, that it is never the same from one moment to the next.[56]

---

55 Ibid., p. 261.
56 David Darling, *Zen Physics: The Science of Death, the Logic of Reincarnation.* New York: HarperCollins, 1996. P. 170.

In view of all the new scientific theories which finally seem to be bringing science and religion together, the pressing need for a psychology of spirit may become more obvious, giving more credence to the ideas outlined in this book. For this, we can thank all other pioneers in this field, such as Carl Jung, Ken Wilber, Raymond Moody, Brian Weiss, Larry Dossey, Dean Radin, Carol Pearson, Marcia Moore, Bernard Goldman, Roger Woolger and Liz Greene—not to mention all the great Masters who have ever lived. Those interested in helping themselves and others who learn the basic principles now will have a head start when this happens. And the day is not that far away.

In the meantime, we must all do whatever we can to make our lives better, more peaceful, and more fulfilled. Remember the pronouncement of the Goddess Saraswati: Self-effort is of primary importance, if we are to live the highest of lives and return to our God with heads held high and proud. For what good is life on this beautiful planet if we are all too psychically messed up to enjoy it?

The psychology of spirit can help to clear away the maya, release the Divine Self within and put us more in touch with the higher forces of the Universe. It will also help to render us happier and more loving throughout our sojourn in this world. The knowledge outlined in this book represents only a small part of the overall picture, but it does represent a start.

I wish you all the blessings of greater awareness.

About the Author

Author/singer MARY DEVLIN is quite well known in the fields of astrology, New Age thought and medieval music and history. Her many published works include books such as I AM MARY SHELLEY, ASTROLOGY AND PAST LIVES and ASTROLOGY AND RELATION-SHIPS, and YOUR FUTURE LIVES, as well as two novels—MURDER ON THE CANTERBURY PILGRIMAGE and PORTRAIT OF VIC-TORINE, and a significant number of magazine articles on a number of subjects. She studied under Marcia Moore, a pioneer in the fields of reincarnation and karmic astrology, and then went on to pursue a career and research of her own in those fields. An accomplished vocal-ist, she directs the Sherwood Consort, a mixed vocal ensemble dedi-cated to medieval and Renaissance music of the British Isles. Ms. Devlin's work, as well as that of the Consort, has been featured on both radio and television.

Glossary

ANIMA:
: In Jungian psychology, a term applied to the secret side of the psyche of every man that is feminine in nature.

ANIMUS:
: A term applied to the secret side of the psyche of every woman that is masculine in nature.

ARCHETYPE:
: An image stamped upon the collective unconscious that has taken a life of its own and with which other life forms subconsciously identify.. Also defined as an "energetic envelope of some new (or non-physical) energy presently unknown", or "energetic thought field accessible through dreams, meditation and other altered states of consciousness."

ASTRAL PLANE:
: Another world, slightly higher in vibration than that of Planet Earth, which occupies the same space as Earth. It is on this plane that dreams, ghosts, psychic insights, and visions begin, though they may descend to the slightly denser etheric plane and in rare cases to the earthly, where they are visible to especially sensitive beings. Out-of-body experiences can also take place here. Beings on the astral plane can see those on the earthly plane, but only the very psychic on the earthly plane can see beings on the astral.

ATLANTIS:
: An ancient continent in the mid-Atlantic, said to have flourished between roughly 60,000 and 15,000

B.C., which according to tradition, and to the ancient philosopher Plato, sank beneath the sea when massive geologic upheavals tore it asunder.

ATMAN:
The Supreme Universal Self; the part of each individual that eventually unites with Brahman; the innermost spiritual essence of every individual life form.

ATMIC PLANE:
The highest plane of all existing in our solar system, whereon souls start on the involutionary arc which brings them into physical incarnation on Planet Earth. Souls who have completed the evolutionary loop and have attained full solar consciousness exist on this plane. This plane of existence vibrates at a very high level and thus is inaccessible to anyone in physical incarnation, except perhaps to God-realized masters.

ATTACHMENT:
An intense psychic need to hang on to something at all costs, be it a soul-entity, a place, a station in life, a philosophy, a profession, an attitude, a religion, etc. This need can and very often does transcend the boundaries between different physical incarnations.

BEHAVIORISM:
A school of psychology founded by B. F. Skinner in the mid-twentieth century which maintains that abstract concepts such as love or honor have no reality and that the only proper concern of psychology is the objective evidence provided by observable behavior.

BODDHISATTVA:
A highly advanced soul who compassionately refrains from entering the state of unity with the Absolute until all beings evolving on Planet Earth

have evolved to that point and can enter that Unity along with him.

BUDDHIC PLANE: The "plane of enlightenment," the next plane down from the atmic plane, slightly more dense. All knowledge of the realms beyond the capacities of the ordinary human mind, such as the concept of God-realization, are drawn from this plane. The more enlightened of mystics can sometimes travel on the buddhic plane.

CENTAUR: In Greek mythology, a creature that was half horse and half god. Some believe this was a survival of ancient memories of the Voltars which existed in Atlantis. In this book it is used to describe a particular stage of development, marking the fourth stage when the soul has virtually completed learning about existence on the material plane and starts to work its way back to God.

COLLECTIVE UNCONSCIOUS: Also known in metaphysics as the Akashic records, the accumulated memories, dreams and reflections of every life form that has ever lived on this planet.

DEVELOPMENTAL PSYCHOLOGY: A school of psychology which studies the development of the individual as he progresses through the different stages of life—from infancy through toddlerhood, childhood, adolescence, young adulthood, adulthood, maturity, and old age. Differences between the mindsets associated with each stage are considered very important.

EARLY EGOIC: The stage of development of the soul that marks the beginning of the development of the individualized human ego.

EARLY MENTAL: The latter substage of the early egoic stage, which marks the beginning of advanced use of the intellect.

ELECTROMAGNETISM: A cosmic force that involves magnetic attraction between electrically-charged subatomic particles such as the electron.

ELECTROWEAK FORCE: A cosmic force supposedly composed originally of the weak nuclear force and electromagnetism. This represents a rough parallel to the Second Ray of Love-Wisdom, as love can either cling or let go, depending on the individual.

ELEMENTAL: A lower astral being possessing a primitive form of consciousness, which exists on the astral plane and is generated by the forces and elements on earth such as sunshine, rain, bodies of water, wind, plant growth, soil, fire, electricity, and mineral radiation. Oftentimes elementals are newly-involved souls waiting to take human incarnation and start their way up the evolutionary loop. Fire elementals are called *salamanders*, earth elementals *gnomes*, air elementals *sylphs*, and water elementals *undines*.

ENGRAM BANK: The storehouse in your unconscious mind of accidents, traumas, betrayals, violent or painful deaths, and other painful experiences which has left scars on your psyche that affect your progress from lifetime to lifetime.

ENGRAM: The impression left on your psyche by a major traumatic event, as well as its effect—such as (a) being trapped in a fire, which leads to (b) a crippling phobia concerning fire.

ETHERIC PLANE: The higher dimension closest to the Earth in speed of vibration, between the astral and the earthly plane, and accessible to everyone on Earth. Sometimes ghosts or other unearthly beings manifest on this plane, so that even those with minimal psychic talents can see them. The etheric plane is sometimes associated with the darker side of psychic or visionary experiences.

EVOLUTIONARY
LOOP: The path the involved soul takes from the initial point of earthly incarnation on up to the ultimate attainment of full solar consciousness.

FOUNTAIN
OF OBLIVION: A term borrowed from L. Frank Baum's Oz series of children's books. Outside the Emerald City in the Land of Oz, a fountain existed which could totally wipe out the memory of anyone who drank from it. I use it to mean the point in the involutionary process at which the entity loses all memory of its divine origin.

GOD-REALIZATION: The attainment (or re-attainment) of total innate awareness of an entity's divine origin and Oneness with God.

GRAVITY: The weakest force of attraction in the Universe, manifested by acceleration toward each other of two free particles of matter or bodies or radiant-energy quanta.

GURU:　　　　From the Sanskrit meaning "bringer of light." Often used to describe a God-realized spiritual teacher with a Hindu orientation. In this book, used to describe the fifth stage of soul evolution, when the entity has let go of much of his baggage from previous stages and acquired a vast amount of spiritual wisdom. The Guru stage is the last stage in which an entity is "required" to take incarnation on the earthly plane.

HIGH EGOIC:　　The third stage of soul development on the earthly plane, where the ego is fully developed and definitely hard at work.

INCOMPLETION:Something desired and yet not attained, such as an object, a profession, a love, a dream or goal. A psychic "loose end" that was never "tied up." Often incompletions carry over from incarnation to incarnation.

INDIVIDUALIZATION: The process of becoming aware of one's uniqueness, of one's separateness from other physical beings on the earthly plane, and the differences between everyone.

INTELLECTUAL
AWARENESS:　　Intellectual acceptance of a concept, but not necessarily accepted on the higher levels of awareness. Example: Someone who knows that smoking is bad for him, but isn't so strongly aware of the concept that he actually can put it to work and quit.

INVOLUTIONARY ARC: The path that a fragment of the Absolute takes when descending through increasingly dense planes of existence on the way to taking human incarnation.

JUVEN: A personal archetype—that part of a person's psyche that always remains young, the Inner Child.

KEYING
INCIDENT: An incident that takes place in the current incarnation that is reminiscent of a past-life trauma, and thus awakens the engram bank and creates a phobia or hangup concerning that incident. Example: A person falls off a horse in the current lifetime, which stirs unconscious memories of a past life in which he fell off a horse and was trampled to death—and results in a crippling fear of horses. The fall from the horse in the current lifetime is the keying incident.

KUNDALINI
YOGA: A yogic discipline in which one seeks to perfect his or her being by awakening the Kundalini, or life force, which rests at the base of the spine.

LEMURIA: An ancient continent that is believed to have existed in the Pacific and flourished from between 250,000 and 50,000 years ago. Australia, the islands of the South Pacific, and that part of California which lies west of the San Andreas Fault are supposed to be the remnants of Lemuria.

LIGHT MASTER: Fragments of the Absolute that exist on a galactic, solar, or planetary level. Other Light Masters also rule over different biological groups such as phylums, classes, orders, families, and species. In the human kingdom, there are Light Masters who rule over racial and ethnic groups, cultural groups, and groups of soul groups.

MAYA: Generally translated as "illusion," but more aptly defined as the creative activity of the gods. Existence on the lower planes of existence is generally considered illusory because it is nothing more than a game, and because it has no existence outside of Brahman. This is supported in modern physics, as everything that seems solid to us is actually nothing more than empty space. The solidity of objects is the result of the illusion created by the electromagnetic activity of the subatomic particles making up the form of the object.

MEMBERSHIP: A state of mind wherein the individual feels less like a unique human being and more like a cog in the wheel of a particular group—a family, tribe, nation, culture. Also used to describe the first substage of Stage Two, the early egoic stage. Though individualized, soul-entities at this level have not yet come to terms with their own personal individuality and identify themselves only as a member of a particular tribe or culture.

MENTAL PLANE: The plane of existence below the buddhic plane and above the astral plane, where all exalted intellectual concepts are believed to be born.

MONAD: See LIGHT MASTER.

NUMBER
ONE INCIDENT: A severely traumatizing experience which is so hor-
rifying that it creates an engram that if reinforced
by similar future experiences, can lead to the forma-
tion of an engram bank. The effect of a Number
One Incident can be felt for thousands of years,
throughout many lifetimes.

PARALLEL
SELVES: A rare phenomenon in which one soul-entity can
take incarnation in two places at once. Sometimes
the two selves know each other, but more often than
not, they incarnate in different places and different
groups, for the sake of cleaning up in a hurry more
attachments and incompletions that could be
accomplished in one earthly incarnation.

PLANETARY
LOGOS: The yin, Third Ray entity that is the Light Master,
Monad or soul of Planet Earth. The Great Mother.

PLEROMA: The final stage of involution, between the Fountain
of Oblivion and birth onto Stage One, in which an
entity has a vague sense of awareness. This awareness is apparently a womblike consciousness in
which the entity feels undifferentiated with the rest
of Creation. This is a pre-personal unity (see below)
and is not to be confused with transpersonal unity,
which is the level reached after the long cycle of soul
evolution.

PRE-EGOIC: Stage One, the level of soul development that exists
prior to individualization and realization of one's
own uniqueness as an individual.

PRE-PERSONAL: The state of awareness that exists prior to earthly incarnation, before any sense of personal existence exists.

SADHANA: A course of spiritual studies designed to lead to enlightenment or God-realization.

SAMADHI: A state of consciousness where one transcends the limitations of the earthly mind. My own experience is that there are no thoughts and no images on this level, only a powerful sense of bliss.

SAT-CHIT -ANANDA: Literally, "being, consciousness, bliss." The first manifestations of Brahman after the Big Bang; the three primary rays; the initial Trinity; the strong nuclear force, the electroweak force and gravity.

SELF-REALIZATION: See GOD-REALIZATION.

SENEX: A personal archetype. The part of us that is ourselves as we are or will be as a wise old man or woman.

SHADOW SELF: A personal archetype. The dark or evil side of ourselves.

SHAKTI: The ultimate receptive, life-giving force in the Universe. The same word applies to the Hindu name for the Great Cosmic Mother, or the Great Goddess. In Hindu mythology, the primary consort of the god Shiva. The parallel in modern physics would be the force of gravity.

SHAMAN: A person with highly developed psychic gifts who can both communicate and identify with beings on the other worlds. Shamans are also able to travel at will throughout the etheric, astral, and sometimes the mental planes.

SHIVA: In classic Hindu mythology, the third member of the Hindu trinity of Brahma, the Creator; Vishnu, the Preserver, and Shiva, the Destroyer. Also seen as the primary aggressive force in the Universe, a parallel to the Chinese concept of *yang*. In Kashmir Shaivism, identified with the Absolute. The parallel in modern physics would be the initial combination of the strong nuclear force and the electroweak force.

SIDDHA YOGA: A yogic practice taught in the twentieth century by Bhagawan Nityananda, Swami Muktananda and Gurumayi Chidvilasananda. It involves reaching enlightenment or God-realization through meditation and by accepting the grace of an already-enlightened Siddha guru.

SOLAR
CONSCIOUSNESS: The state of awareness reached when one completes the earthly cycle of soul evolution. The level of consciousness of the Light Masters who become the souls of suns.

SOLAR LOGOS: The yang, Second Ray Light Master that is the soul of our Sun. The being worshiped as Apollo, Mabon, Vishnu, Surya, Amon-Re, etc. Some identify the Solar Logos with the Christ who has taken incarnation in the past as Krishna and Jesus of Nazareth—and others whose names are lost in the veils of antiquity.

SOUL GROUP: A group of souls of the same Ray vibration that stem from the same Monad. Members of the soul group whom one encounters on the path through earthly incarnations are popularly referred to as "soul mates."

STRONG NUCLEAR
FORCE: A cosmic force that binds subatomic particles together in the atomic nucleus. A rough parallel to the First Ray of Will or Power, as this is the most powerful of all the primordial forces.

SUBSTAGE: A stage of development within a Stage of Development. There are likely to be many, but for the purposes of this book I have kept the number down to two major substages per Stage.

TABULA RASA: The theory that the mind of every newborn child represents a blank slate on which all life experiences are written, causing the development of a unique personality. Now mostly abandoned, this theory was discredited when studies of identical twins with identical genetic patterns and near-identical childhood experiences showed that they tended to turn out quite differently from each other.

THEOSOPHY: A philosophy developed by Mme. Helena Petrovna Blavatsky in the nineteenth century developed from Egyptian Hermeticism, Hindu philosophy, and information channeled from Ascended Masters. Probably the first major influence in the development of the modern New Age movement.

TRANSPERSONAL: Extending beyond the realm of the personal and into the solar or cosmic level of awareness.

TRUE
AWARENESS: Knowledge or awareness that has become a part of one's very being instead of being simply an intellectual concept learned from sources outside oneself.

TYPHONIC: The substage of Stage One in which self and body are not yet clearly differentiated, and when the verbal and conceptual mind aren't fully developed, but the ability to visualize and to create images and symbols, as well as the ability to focus and to some degree calculate, is just starting to blossom.

UROBORIC: The first substage of development which the incarnating soul enters. At this point, the entity sees little if any difference between himself and others, has no self-awareness, possesses few if any conceptual or communicative abilities, has no sense of time, and lives in a constant state of fear.

VOLTARS: Half-animal, half-human beings that existed in the early days of Atlantis. It is said that our concepts of harpies, centaurs, satyrs, and the animal-headed gods of Ancient Egypt and India represent ancient genetic memories of these creatures. In most metaphysical literature they are referred to as Things. The term "Voltar" was first used by a client of mine who was an excellent regression subject and who had obviously spent a number of incarnations in Atlantis. We have no way of knowing for sure if this was the genuine term used in ancient Atlantis, though it would be interesting to study similar roots in Nahuatl (the language of the Aztecs), Mayan, Pictish, Basque, and ancient Egyptian—all of which are said to be survivals of the Atlantean tongue—and see if there is anything that might possibly verify it. However, since, to my mind anyway, it's a more interesting word than Things, I like using it.

WEAK NUCLEAR
FORCE: A cosmic nuclear interaction that releases sub-atomic particles from atomic nuclei and thus causes radioactivity.

YANG: In Chinese philosophy, the primary aggressive force in the Universe, parallel to the Hindu Shiva. See SHIVA.

YIN: In Chinese philosophy, the primary receptive force in the Universe, parallel to the Hindu Shakti. See SHAKTI.

Bibliography

Bailey, Alice A. *A Treatise on Cosmic Fire.* New York: Lucis, 1925.

Bailey, Alice A. *Esoteric Psychology I.* New York: Lucis, 1940.

Bailey, Alice A. *Esoteric Psychology II.* New York: Lucis, 1942.

Bailey, Alice A. *Initiation, Human and Solar..* New York: Lucis, 1922.

Bailey, Alice A. *The Seven Rays of Life.* New York: Lucis, 1995.

Baker, Dr. Douglas. *Anthropogeny: The Esoteric History of Man's Man's Origin.* Hert, England: Little Elephant, c. 1975.

Baker, Dr. Douglas. *Esoteric Psychology—The Seven Rays.* Hert, England: Little Elephant, 1976.

Blavatsky, Helena Petrovna. *The Secret Doctrine.* Wheaten, IL: Theosophical Publishing House, 1974.

Bolen, Jean Shinoda. *Goddesses in Everywoman: A New Psychology of Women.* New York: Harper & Row, 1985.

Bolen, Jean Shinoda. *Gods in Everyman: A New Psychology of Men's Lives and Loves.* New York: Harper & Row, 1989

Boslough, John. *Masters of Time: How Wormholes, Snakewood and Assaults on the Big Bang Have Brought Mystery Back to the Cosmos.* London: Dent, 1992.

Capra, Fritjof. *The Tao of Physics.* Boulder, CO: Shambhalla, 1975.

Capra, Fritjof. *The Turning Point: Science, Society and the Rising Culture.* New York: Simon & Schuster, 1982.

Cerminara, Gina. *Many Lives, Many Loves.* New York: William Morrow, 1963

Cerminara, Gina. *Many Mansions.* New York: William Morrow, 1978.

Cookson, Bernard Wesfield. *Rudolf Steiner's Vision of Love: Spiritual Science and the Knowledge of the Heart.* London: Aquarian Press, 1976.

Danielou, Alain. *The Gods of India.* New York: Inner Traditions, 1985.

Darling, David. *Soul Search.* New York: Random House, 1995.

Darling, David. *Zen Physics: The Science of Death, the Logic of Reincarnation.* New York: HarperCollins, 1996.

Devlin, Mary, *Astrology and Past Lives.* West Chester, PA: Whitford Press, 1987.

Devlin, Mary, *Astrology and Relationships.* West Chester, PA: Whitford Press, 1988.

Grof, Stanislav. *Beyond the Brain.* Albany. NY: State University of New York Press. 1985.

Grof, Stanislav. *Realms of the Human Unconscious.* New York: E.P. Dutton and Company, 1976.

Heron, John, M.D., "Space and Consciousness." Online essay available at http://www.lpiper.demon.co.uk/spaconsc.htm.

Hildegard of Bingen, *Book of Divine Works. With Letters and Songs.* Matthew Fox, ed. Santa Fe, NM: Bear & Company. 1987. Pp. 25ff.

Hillman, James. *Re-visioning Psychology.* San Francisco: HarperCollins, 1990.

Hillman, James. *We've Had a Hundred Years of Psychotherapy and the World's Getting Worse.* San Francisco: HarperCollins, 1990.

Jung, Carl Gustav. *The Basic Writings of C. G. Jung.* New York: Modern Library. 1959.

Keepin, William, Ph.D. "Astrology and the New Physics: Integrating Sacred and Secular Sciences." *The Mountain Astrologer,* August/September 1995, pp. 12ff.

Levi, *The Aquarian Gospel of Jesus the Christ.* Santa Monica, CA: DeVorss, 1972.

Moore, Marcia, and Douglas, Mark. *Reincarnation: Key to Immortality.* (York Beach. Maine: Arcane. 1972).

Moore, Marcia. *Hypersentience.* New York: Crown, 1976.

Moore, Robert, and Gillette, Douglas. *King, Warrior, Magician, Lover.* New York: HarperCollins, 1990.

Muktananda, Swami. *Play of Consciousness.* New York: Harper & Row, 1978.

Ornstein, Robert. *The Psychology of Consciousness.* New York: Penguin, 1972

Pearson, Carol. *The Hero Within: Six Archetypes We Live By.* New York: Harper & Row, 1985..

Pelletier, Kenneth R., Ph.D., *Towards a Science of Consciousness.* Berkeley, CA: Celestial Arts, 1985.

Radin, Dean, Ph.D. *The Conscious Universe.* New York: HarperCollins, 1997.

Roy, David E. Ph.D. "Psychotherapy for the Soul." Online essay available at http://www.soulfulpsy.com/psyc4soul.html.

Shelley, Mary. *Mary Shelley's Journal,* Frederick L. Jones, editor. Norman, OK: University of Oklahoma Press, 1947.

Sparks, Edward, "Forgive Yourself." *Your Future Lives,* Skye Alexander, ed. West Chester, PA: Whitford Press, 1988.

Starhawk, *The Spiral Dance.* 10th Anniversary Edition. New York: Harper Collins, 1991.

Steiger, Brad. *Gods of Aquarius: UFOs and the Transformation of Man.* New York: Harcourt, Brace, Jovanovich, 1976.

Stevens, Dr. Anthony. *Archetypes: A Natural History of the Self.* London: Routledge, 1982.

Venkatesananda, Swami. *Vasistha's Yoga.* Albany, NY: State University of New York, 1993.

Wilber, Ken. *The Atman Project.* Wheaton, IL: The Theosophical Publishing House. 1980).

Wilber, Ken. *The Spectrum of Consciousness* (Wheaton, IL: Theosophical Publishing House, 1980.

Wilber, Ken. *Up From Eden.* (New York: Harper & Row. 1985).

Wolf, Fred Alan. *The Dreaming Universe.* New York: Simon & Schuster, 1993.

Wolf, Fred Alan. *The Spiritual Universe: How Quantum Physics Proves the Existence of the Soul.* New York: Simon & Schuster, 1996

Wood, Ernest. *The Seven Rays: A Theosophical Handbook.* Wheaton, IL: The Theosophical Publishing House, 1972.

Woolger, Roger, Ph.D. *Other Lives, Other Selves.* (New York: 1990).

Yarbro, Chelsea Quinn. *Messages from Michael.* New York: Berkley. 1980.

Yarbro, Chelsea Quinn. *More Messages from Michael.* New York: Berkley. 1986.

Index

A

Absolute, 2-3, 22, 66, 185, 208, 214, 219, 223
Actualization, 54
Agreement, xxv, xxvi.
AIDS, 37
Akhenaton, 95-97
Albert, Prince, 141
Alta major center, 20
American Revolution, 176, 183
Amon-Ra, 32
Andromeda, 107
Anima, 112, 117, 213
Animus, 112, 114, 117, 213
Anubis, 8
Aphrodite, 117
Apollo, 126-129, 223
Aquarian Age, 76
archetypes, 106
Archetypes, 106, 108, 110-114, 118-120, 122, 124, 126, 129-131, 133-137, 194, 205
Archetypes of transformation, 113
Ares, 135-136
Arieti, Silvano, 20
Artisans, 32-33, 98-99
Aryan migrations, 115

D

T

U

V

www.ingramcontent.com/pod-product-compliance
Lightning Source LLC
Chambersburg PA
CBHW061338280526
45784CB00001B/61